NOTES ON THE DEVELOPMENT OF

THE LINGUISTIC SOCIETY OF AMERICA

1924 TO 1950

MARTIN JOOS

for
JENNIE MAE JOOS

FOREWORD

It is important for the reader of this document to know how it came to be written and what function it is intended to serve.

In the early 1970s, when the Executive Committee and the Committee on Publications of the Linguistic Society of America were planning for the observance of its Golden Anniversary, they decided to sponsor the preparation of a history of the Society's first fifty years, to be published as part of the celebration. The task was entrusted to the three living Secretaries, J M. Cowan (who had served from 1940 to 1950), Archibald A. Hill (1951-1969), and Thomas A. Sebeok (1970-1973). Each was asked to survey the period of his tenure; in addition, Cowan, who had learned the craft of the office from the Society's first Secretary, Roland G. Kent (deceased 1952), was to cover Kent's period of service.

At the time, Cowan was just embarking on a new career. He therefore asked his close friend Martin Joos to take on his share of the task, and to that end gave Joos all his files. Joos then did the bulk of the research and writing, but the two conferred repeatedly, Cowan supplying information to which Joos would not otherwise have had access.

Joos and Hill completed their assignments in time for the planned publication, but Sebeok, burdened with other responsibilities, was unable to do so. Since the Society did not wish to bring out an incomplete history, the project was suspended.

Joos continued to rework his segment of the report up to the time of his death on 6 May 1978, making refinements and producing an Index. The latter, as Joos left it, covered also Hill's part of the report, which he had been attempting to dovetail with his own. The form reproduced herewith is the ribbon copy of Joos's last version, except only that, upon Hill's request, the dovetailing has been eliminated and references in the Index to material from Hill's pen have been deleted.

This document is *not* a history of the Linguistic Society of America and should not be read as one. It is a set of notes and observations on the early career of the Society, made from Martin Joos's always very special and sometimes highly personal stance. Several informed readers of the unpublished document have spotted what they consider to be serious factual errors. But this is not a history; it is only source-materials for one. As the historiographer and historian R. G. Collingwood tells us, when we find an assertion in such material the proper question is not "Is it true?" but rather "What does it mean? Why was it said?" Taken that way, Joos's treatment sheds interesting light both on the early Linguistic Society and on himself; and both the Society and the man deserve to have that light in the record for posterity.

Ithaca NY   J M. Cowan
August 1986   C. F. Hockett

Preface

Accounting for the Linguistic Society of America, nearing half a century of life as a group-entity still functioning upon the same basic principles, was the charge accepted early in 1973 by two narrators, Archibald A. Hill and Martin Joos, who both sign this Preface. We write from our separate points of view, but start from the same premises, a pair of premises: that our Society began, and continues, as an autonomous entity and at the same time as a self-sustaining group of persons. Here we must speak from the point of view of the Society in pointing out that our publications or other costly undertakings have always been at the risk of the Society's own funds; and we have functioned from the start under one Constitution whose wordings guarantee that we do all such things at our own risk.

These points merit explicit statement here, particularly because the contrary is true of the other noteworthy scholarly associations and of their journals everywhere. Some of them were created by publishers, some by governments, some by clusters of persons who associated themselves with pre-existent publishers, or by publishers who assembled the requisite group of scholars, and so on through a myriad variations. Language, the quarterly journal of our Society, is published at the Waverley Press as it has been from the 1925 beginning, but by the Society. Our three successive Editors, George Melville Bolling first, Bernard Bloch then for the central quarter-century, and finally William Bright, are thus central to this History.

The Constitution adopted on 28th December 1924, stable in this regard through all the years that we narrate, established a Publications Committee and assumed each of its members would naturally be a competent Editor, so that there could hardly be any serious problem in making up quarterly issues: it foresaw having a distinct, presumably new, responsible Editor for each publishing year, namely the senior member (or some otherwise automatically identifiable person) within that Committee, the Editor for one year only rarely and exceptionally continuing for a second year but hardly for a third or later year in succession. And yet the 1924 Constitution prescribed the electing, after formal nomination by a Nominating Committee whose membership could not include any officer or member of the Executive Committee, of the next year's Editor during the year-end Annual Meeting scheduled between Christmas and New Year's Day.

Details of just how that recognizably Athenian plan collapsed are not known to us—not one word of print or writing has turned up during diligent search—but the oral tradition is compelling. Learning in the 1925 Annual Meeting that Bolling had the first 1926 issue in press already and was editing the next one, nobody was willing to accept nomination to be Editor as if competing with George Melville Bolling. That made the Editor the first of our so-called 'continuing officers' re-elected year by year without competition. The other was Roland Grubb Kent, the Secretary and Treasurer, whose functions constitutionally included the duty and authority of Comptroller, although that word was nowhere printed; the incumbent was to make sure that nothing printed could be issued in the name of the Linguistic Society of America unless there was money to pay for it; in other words it was his function to keep the Society out of debt, for the Founders knew, from experience beginning in the 19th century, precisely how earlier scholarly societies had been wrecked on those rocks. Now although no Article of the Constitution has ever employed the term 'continuing officer' or any synonym, that term or a synonym was spoken in conclaves from around 1928 and onward, so that it eventually became Unwritten Law and continued in force, all the more firm for remaining unwritten, throughout the years which we undertake to cover with this History, namely through 1968.

Editor and Secretary-Treasurer are, then, the two key persons upon whom the Society's scholarly health and economic survival depend; neither can reasonably be called 'more important' than the other; each is indispensable, and that's all. Luckily, the Society has never been forced to replace them both within the same year. Each Editor's years in office will appear in the Table of Contents next below and will serve as a natural time-scale; likewise, each Secretary–Treasurer's for parallel reasons. Presidents and Vice-Presidents, however, have [through 1968!] held quite another sort of relation to the course of events; details will emerge in suitable context man for man for the first two decades. No LSA President has so far died in office, and that fact is so curious as to be nothing short of astonishing. It is noteworthy especially because custom has provided us with Presidents of far greater age than is likely to be the rule henceforth; and secondarily it has meant that the duty of substituting for the President in periods of his absence was at first the only stable duty of a Vice-President, so that he was typically a younger man.

Motives for selecting the first three dozen nominees to the Presidency are so transparent that we are disconcerted at finding nothing in print or writing on that; the actual sequence of incumbencies, however, is compelling. Each Signer of the Call—see the reprinted Call on page 244—was to be made President in turn, in any sequence that seemed natural at the moment; and the eldest of them was Hermann Collitz, 1925 President, and so on. Equivalently, the President was to be a senior scholar that was to be alive to enjoy it. Distinguished work by certain Presidents—wise guidance, and decisions given force by the respect due to a white-haired scholar—were welcome sequels, while the ineffectiveness that could be an unwelcome sequel had usually been foreseen in contrary cases and was an only temporary inconvenience: no permanent harm could develop in a twelve-month, during which continuity was safeguarded by a Secretary's watchful eye.

For 1946, E[mma] Adelaide Hahn was chosen President during the 1945 Summer Meeting (during the first 'atom bomb' period) amid total uncertainty as to whether the ban on travel to national conventions would prevent the normal Annual Meeting vote (which it did!) and moreover a fresh memory of the Louise Pound drop-out determined the result: of course she must be made President, and high time, too.

Austin and Madison, 1976/1977, A. A. Hill
Martin Joos

TABLE OF CONTENTS

I: FOUNDATION: 1924—1928

The Organization Meeting designed to create our Society had been entrusted, by the three-man Organizing Committee, to Roland Grubb Kent. In Philadelphia, he had recruited two Latin Seminar students to staff its Registration Desk, one or another (and most of the time both together) to serve throughout the announced hours, from 10:00 o'clock to 1:00 p.m., and from 2:00 to 5:00. After that hour, long past sunset, The Lecture Hall and its ancillary rooms must be vacated without delay. That Hall was spacious. It could accommodate more than 200 persons in the amphitheatre-type seating sloping down to a stage-level podium; there now a pulpit-like reading-stand, with reading-lamps, awaited speakers, all planned by P. E. Goddard.

Franz Boas, another Signer of the Call, had simply requested all these things; President and Trustees of the Museum, political and other public personalities all, routinely granted him even more costly favors; the huge Museum building had to be heated in any case, because of professional staff needing access; Custodial Staff patrolled the grounds as usual, though not so very many on this Holidays Sunday.

The Call had named the Museum without stating its location in New York City. Visitors 'from out of Town' would certainly come by railway; and in or very near a Station of arrival there were 'stations' of the Subway—the underground electrified railway system—fare 5¢ within Manhattan, 10¢ to and from the rest of Greater New York—plus a swarm of taxicabs. Each visitor had home-town acquaintances who told him, at home in Columbus or Chicago or Madison, how to get oriented in New York; thus addresses by street-name and house-number were otiose, as still today.

The printed Call, with its 15th November 1924 dating already in the typescript, from Leonard Bloomfield's personal typewriter, that the printer had before him, came (in an unguessable number of single copies printed on one side of a single sheet of paper) from a campus-area print-shop at Columbus, Ohio, where both the local Signers—George Melville Bolling and Leonard Bloomfield—were Professors in 1924; but Bloomfield was sole author. That is to say, evidence of every possible sort converges to that conclusion, and there is no evidence that any other person contributed more than single words or short phrases to the semi-final versions which Signers saw during the twelvemonth of letter-writing and of colloquies at the meetings of at least four antecedent learned societies (the MLA and the others) when consenting to figure as Signers.

Bloomfield even sent his last galley-proof, approved, to the printer without two names which the Proceedings added to the approved list of 27 to make it up to 29—and one of those two was author of one of the four 'scientific addresses' reported there on page 13. Definitely earlier than the printed Call's self-dating, 15th November, 1924, dissemination had begun by shipping parcels to the Signers, each at his own University or home. There clearly was no intention of withholding the fliers from any sort of person, no matter how vague or frivolous his interest might be. The distribution, finally, in the immediately preceding MLA meeting in downtown Manhattan was massive, and on the Sunday a good many persons turned up who had no interest, personally, in the Organizing Meeting, but instead accompanied others for lack of anything better to do that Sunday: their names are fairly easy to spot, except that some few refused to let the Registration Desk staff hear any name.

Launching such an enterprise in the 1920's was daring, or even foolhardy, as any expert would surely be aware. Both Roland Kent and Edgar Sturtevant were experts, to name only two. Kent had long managed the business affairs of the American Oriental Society; Sturtevant was an investment and banking insider. The out-of-pocket costs had to be personally guaranteed by some minor fraction of those Signers, or by other non-signing persons—a minor fraction (a dozen or fewer) because most were relatively impecunious; details are unknown, for the history of such a fiasco as an LSA that had vanished before 1929 would never even have been researched, much less published, a half-century later as a weighty book. Presently we mean to present snippets of information on the first three precarious years; first we set the stage for the events of Sunday 28th December 1924. By chance we have barely sufficient information to enable reconstructing the day in outline, plus letters from the sole survivor received by Martin Joos during 1974. Franklin Brunell Krauss was born in 1901; in 1924 he and his fellow postgraduate student of slightly greater age, James Roland Ware, had agreed to serve R. G. Kent in the Organization Meeting by maintaining the Registration Desk. He had charged them to get names and institutional addresses from each person who came for the Meeting; but no provision had been made to record times of day or even which half-day each person was present. LSA Emeritus Member Krauss in his letters to Joos is our sole witness for the dramatic details which follow, here displayed on a frame of certified fact and beginning with the names of three key persons: Boas, Kroeber, Goddard.

Franz Boas participated in the initial stocking of the Museum even before 1900 and was its first Curator of Anthropology; in 1924, long previously replaced as a Curator by younger men, he still needed to bring students in from Columbia for advanced seminars; thus he routinely had to shuttle to and fro (a good quarter-hour each way by the best scheduling, varying by time of day, on the two-mile street-car connections) when lecturing either in Columbia University to young men or else to young women in Barnard College across the street and likewise up at 116th Street and Broadway: we cannot guess just when or how he got to the Museum at 77th Street and Columbus Avenue, but we believe he was on hand betimes to welcome old friends.

In 1924 the Museum's Curator of Ethnology (an office that had been split off from the original Boas office meanwhile) was Boas's protégé Dr. Pliny Earle Goddard, trained in—and sent into the field from— the University of California at Berkeley by an early Boas protégé, Alfred Louis Kroeber, who was a Signer of the Call as both Goddard and Boas were. Kroeber was not on hand this time: he would have had no other errand on the East Coast in late December 1924, and no good excuse for the long and somewhat uncertain and surely rather wearying transcontinental train. Kroeber's personal copy of the printed Call has been photographed as copy for our Appendix page where it is printed as a reduced-size replica: hence the two-line legend in its upper-right corner reads 'Museum of Anthropology Files' and then 'University [of California] Archives' with the same stamping as our reprinted circular of January 25, 1925, sent out by the Society's first Secretary, Roland G. Kent. That circular now has Kroeber's mark in its margin flagging the notice of how much the 1925 dues were to be, in agreement with his permanent listing as a Foundation Member and also as a Signer of the Call.

Pliny Goddard had first joined the professional staff of the American Museum of Natural History in 1909, when Boas had retreated from being 'the' Anthropology Curator to become a full-time Professor in Columbia University, retaining status at the Museum but escaping the administrative burdens of a Curator. Now Goddard kept an apartment in the Museum's space provided for that in a back-yard annex at the northern end of a short covered passage, and when in New York he regularly made his own breakfast and frequently other meals, and even entertained a visiting researcher or two on occasion. In December of 1924 he was experiencing the coldest month of his lifetime, though not the coldest in the lifetime of Franz Boas, who retained painful memories of the Frozen 1880's, and on the 28th he was in charge of the two or three custodial-staff men who had been promised overtime pay for Sunday service. To the nascent Linguistic Society of America, all that was free of charge; the Museum maintained an Entertainment Fund for just such purposes, and in due course its President and Trustees were the addressees of the 'bread and butter letter' which our then newly created Executive Committee directed our Secretary Roland Kent to send. We can only guess what sorts of wires were pulled to relieve the Treasury of the Linguistic Society of America of that group of costs, perhaps even the cost of the noon-hour meal in a near-by hotel, said to have stood on Columbus Ave., which has since been demolished and forgotten, even its name lost to us now. Franz Boas as he was known to students at that epoch is brilliantly sketched by Margaret Mead in Blackberry Winter, New York: Morrow, 1972, 121-122:

Boas was a surprising and somewhat frightening teacher. He had a bad side and a good side to his face. On one side there was a long dueling scar from his student days in Germany — an unusual pursuit for a Jewish student — on which his eyelid drooped and teared from a recent stroke. But seen from the other side, his face showed him to be as handsome as he had been as a young man. His lectures were polished and clear. Occasionally he would look around and ask a rhetorical question which no one would venture to answer. I got into the habit of writing down an answer and nodding when it turned out to be right. At the end of the semester I and another girl whom I did not know but whose name rhymed with mine were excused from taking the examination for 'helpful participation in class discussion.'

The rest of the same chapter (to her page 124) interests us for its treatments of Franz Boas, Edward Sapir, Ruth Benedict, and Leonard Bloomfield — whose sister Marie's room in the Residence Hall was close to Margaret Mead's; Marie's death, as reported in the New York Times in detail, occurred two days earlier than we see reported in Blackberry Winter; therefore Miss Mead was not yet back in town! In her book she blames herself for not preventing the mishap; she must have now revised her half-century-old memories subconsciously without documentation; contrary to all other contemporaneous episodes, there is not one photograph for this episode. Within a handful of years after our 1924 Foundation, Miss Mead began to occupy the attic levels within the Museum's western terminal tower, the one next to Columbus Avenue, of the American Museum of Natural History. Her collectanea, we understand, are still partly there; but that seems rather unlikely.

When Pliny Goddard came from breakfast on Sunday 28th December 1924 into the designated Lecture Hall — occupancy legally limited, they say, to 240 persons, but that is today no longer verifiable because of intervening structural changes — he either came ready to serve as the day's factotum or was persuaded by Boas and Kent together. Greetings among successive dozens of arrivals kept most people on their feet and milling about, until at 10:15 George Bolling began his agreed part. He came to the platform beside the reading-stand, called a great many persons by name with appropriate witticisms, and so procured silence; that done, he called a Temporary Chairman forward, moving his election himself; 'Second the motion!' came from uncountable voices; Bolling declared R. G. Kent elected and swiftly went down to an aisle seat where the active confederates were ranged alongside others who felt anough interest in the announced purposes to desist from retiring too far back. We cannot reconstruct the placement of the Registration Desk; Krauss says he can't either; but that does no real harm. Truman Michelson somehow became the day's Recording Secretary, the obvious choice for his competencies. At that point there were perhaps four dozen persons in the room, and we continue by lifting blocks of text from Krauss letters and filling interstices with known facts.

The two students staffing the Registration Desk had come separately to New York City from the Philadelphia area. Starting late Saturday evening, Krauss and Kent came up on the same overnight train and breakfasted together on board; but James Roland Ware had been somewhere in New York, visiting friends, since about a week before Christmas Day. ⟦Three decades later, Ware resigned his membership just as the Annual Dues increased, from $5.00 to $8.00 for full membership while simultaneously the new class of Student Member at $4.00 was created. His career meanwhile was puzzling to these historiographers, and still is. From the 1924 Meeting he went to Paris for advanced studies on Sanskrit and on Chinese; he returned to America then, and eventually climbed the academic ladder to a Harvard appointment which eventually reached the rank of Professor. He never, as far as our records disclose, participated in our Society's War Effort; and we have found, in our sources at least, nothing about Professor J. R. Ware.⟧

Reconstruction of the 1924 scene in our imaginations is severely handicapped. Lighting is an essential part of any comparable scene; the chronology of lighting or 'illumination' by the year, witnessed by competent encyclopedias, informs us that in 1924 Manhattan Island (at least, probably much more of Greater New York) had direct current as its only electricity, as it still did in Joos's 1931 Summer there. That means that even if the present-day auditorium lighting with brilliant-white fluorescent tubes overhead had already been invented (instead of in the 1930's) this room would still have had a dim religious atmosphere with simple incandescents.

The '69' eventually printed as the number of persons present in the initiating meeting inevitably came to be doubted by a good many skeptics, notably because it coïncided with the current age of Hermann Collitz, the Society's President in its first year, and such doubts can arise even today because a great many of us can mention numerous **false datings** and false statistics as parallels. That leads us to state the adequate reason for believing in the literal accuracy of '69' this time: it is simply the fact that E. Adelaide Hahn was there, and eventually ready to challenge the number if she knew it to be false, which she did not do. Nobody has ever found her out in an arithmetical error, and that's that. Unaccountably, that item is missing in the sketch of Miss Hahn's personal traits in the Obituary in Language 43.960. What's the letter-count in this question, Adelaide? — 33!

Sixty of those 69 appear in later Lists of Members, where academic affiliations normally appear, or at least a professional label of equivalent value as a classifier. The remarkable exception is Morris Berg, ultimately the subject of the posthumous biography by a trio of baseball enthusiasts, under the title that they chose with the publishing firm's agreement, Moe Berg: Athlete, Scholar, Spy, Boston: Little, Brown and Company, 1974. There his polyglot achievements are emphasized, and there is no hint of real understanding why he came to the Linguistic Society's organizing meeting from the immediately preceding MLA where he heard of it; that book calls him 'a charter member of the American Linguistic Society' as if polyglots would be the characterizing membership. In the midwinter season of our Annual Meetings, he came and registered, always as 'M. Berg' but never presented a paper nor figured as a discussant—the old custom of printing all such facts in Bulletins is the solid basis for most of our historiography: beyond 1967, our historical research will perforce suffer for lack of such contemporary registering—so that we can only testify that Morris Berg was a soft-voiced giant in elegantly tailored charcoal gray whom we listened to with interest: his sotto-voce technical comments were memorable.

The nine persons whom we know by name as non-joiners allowing themselves to be recorded were: Mrs. J. L. Gerig, wife of a conspicuous Signer of the Call, plus E. W. Berlingame, A. Busse, Susan Fowler (who took courses in the 1930 Linguistic Institute, the first of the two New York City Institutes), P. Kaufman, Alma Leduc, E. S. Quimby, H. V. Robbins, and V. Sharenkoff.

Among the sixty pioneers, the most striking figure was Franklin Edgerton. His imposing stature, burly torso, and red-blond beard combined to reinforce the controlled power and restrained impatience in his manner and especially in his sonorous operatic barytone, clear and crisp, which needed no amplification for addressing an audience of many hundreds. Even when urbanely modulated, that voice was usually audible in corridors outside meeting rooms when papers were being presented and then discussed—for the most part inaudibly from the corridor if we were out there, so that we understood little of the paper and less of the discussions, until an Edgerton intervention came along: then we got it all. At the last visit of George Melville Bolling to an Annual Meeting, or anyhow a late one some time in the 1950's, the present historiographer once sat with him in such a corridor—we used to take turns as companion to Bolling during such sessions when he was effectively blind and nearly but not quite deaf—because he could no longer profit from being inside but was eager to keep in touch through our mediation, and this time I pressed him to account for the swift adoption of the fateful Article in the 1924 Constitution, inserted early in that afternoon, even though its wording contained enough dynamite to produce hours of wrangling and then defeat on the spot, after a forenoon session in which 'publication' seemed to be a matter of occasional or annual issuance of symposium volumes plus or instead of guest-space in established journals such as PMLA. After fully half a minute of silence, our first Editor said, 'Franklin was just the man to do it: one Stentor was enough.' Instantly it was all crystal-clear, our word stentor, and our Stentor and the original Greek with its omega, just then hearing Edgerton.

Roland Kent at the 5:00 o'clock adjourning assembled a group—the whole Executive Committee plus a considerable number of others—who dined together as they planned the next steps; then he took an overnight train to Philadelphia and immediately composed his circular of January 25, 1925: See p. 245 here!

Kent printed a typically Kentish date. He had promised to mail it to key persons
early; then from a total press-run of about a thousand he supplied requests from
other persons until his stock was exhausted early in 1927.

Meanwhile Truman Michelson had converted his notes into typescript—like
any field ethnologist he was skilled in the art of noting significant details of social
interaction swiftly, including a private phonetic shorthand version of language not
fully understood, such as Old French—and combined that with Registration Desk
papers to construct his manuscript for the Proceedings. As already planned, he
promptly sent that to our newly elected Editor, Bolling, in Columbus, Ohio.

From the letter to C. F. Hockett, dated 25th May 1967, by E. A. Esper, we
quote a 42-year-old memory of how the 1925 issues of Language were set up:
. . . in the psychology department shop we had a sawbuck table at which our
[= Psychology's] staff, together with friends from other departments, had a
sort of smörgåsbord lunch every day. Bolling and Bloomfield were members
of this group; . . . At that sawbuck table, much of the planning for the first
issues of Language took place. It was there that I heard Bolling say something
that has cheered me through the years: "We can surely get a paper from
[Maurice] Bloomfield; that old man must have many things in his drawers!"
Hockett had queried Esper by letter in the course of collecting data for his book
A Leonard Bloomfield Anthology, Bloomington: Indiana University Press, 1970.
The Index to Language Volumes 1—50 lists a total of five items by Erwin Allen
Esper, including a 6-page article in 1966 whose first footnote thanks Leonard
Bloomfield for having invented material used in Esper's 1925 Monograph.

Returning to the Linguistic Society's self-creation, Sunday 28th December,
1924, we next consider more of its background, its social and physical context.
The handful of years since the Great War of 1914—1918 had experienced rapid
developments in communication, largely derived from wartime inventions. Both
domestic airmail and transcontinental telephone service began before 1920, adding
warmth to the favorite mode for urgent technical messages, the telegraph. Bulky
items perforce went by swift and certain ordinary mail at 3¢ per ounce [= 28 g.]
and crossed the continent in 5 days at most, including doorstep delivery after a
ride, of 3000 miles [5000 km], in the mail-&-express sections of passenger trains
for which the Post Office paid subsidy rentals and why not? It was a matter of no
comment but simply the way the world went on its way, now that The War had gone
where good wars go. The dozens of undersea cables that had been destroyed early
in the fighting had been either abandoned as obsolete anyhow or repaired; mostly
they had been superseded by fewer and vastly improved cables such as the perm-
alloy-tape-wound copper conductor cables or by radio telegraph channels; the ITT
company contracted to transmit transatlantic messages but never said whether a
particular telegram had been received by cable or by radio; hence telegram was
no longer a usual word, and cable did duty for both—which harmlessly prevents
literal accuracy in some of our historical statements. Also, our sources often say
things which confuse transcontinental with transoceanic communication: telephone
communication was invariably by wires (perhaps dozens of them enclosed within a
single leaden sheath to form a 'telephone cable' strung from pole to pole across
the whole breadth of a continent, and 'repeaters' to strengthen the voice-currents
every so many kilometers were taken for granted) and the 'long-distance telephone
call' cost as little as $5.00 for three minutes between Chicago and New York City.
Still, the telegram was the channel of choice for urgent messages, and very cheap.

December of 1924 was extraordinarily cold and dry, with no night without frost
in New York, and on the 28th the maximum for the day was 22° Fahrenheit [-6° C]
after an overnight low of 12° F. [-11° C]. Gas heating lay far in the future; dusty
grit was underfoot everywhere, and every puff of wind brought cinders in smoke.
Philadelphia conditions were identical; F. B. Krauss makes no comment on them.
'When Professor Roland G. Kent and I emerged from the Pennsylvania Railroad
Station (33rd Street and Seventh Avenue, New York City), we both commented on
what a bracing day it was, sunny and rather cold. Professor Kent suggested that
we walk to the American Museum of Natural History [2.3 miles or 3.7 km],' [about
40 minutes, or at most 45, for Roland Kent, always a brisk walker], says Krauss,

'and thereby clear our heads for the work of the day ahead, and I readily acceded, for even then hiking was one of my major hobbies.'

Twelve of the 29 Signers of the Call were absent all that day, each for a known or easily reconstructed reason. (1) Leroy C. Barrett of Trinity College, Hartford, Connecticut, was a low-paid Professor of Sanskrit and Latin in an institution where nobody had spare cash [he became Emeritus with 1953 and died in July of 1960.] (2) Harold Herman Bender of Princeton University was in Chicago at the Annual Meeting of the American Philological Association. (3) Maurice Bloomfield was also at that APA meeting; he became the 1926 LSA President. (4) Carl Darling Buck of the University of Chicago naturally belonged at the APA meeting too. He was President in 1927 — and was once more elected President for 1937. That was unprecedented; nor has it ever been appealed to as a precedent for again having the same person as our President a second time. The unique second electing of Buck took place in late 1936 of course, and resulted from the sudden demise of the man originally chosen amid confusions caused by Bolling's incapacity with cataract operation and slow recovery during the 1936 Linguistic Institute, the first Institute at Ann Arbor after the hiatus of four summers, and the conspicuous activities at that one of Professor Buck as seen by Executive Committee and Nominating Committee members at the end of July 1936: we cannot guess on what day the decision was arrived at, or how.

(5) Carlos Everett Conant (27 November 1870 — 27 January 1925) was living in Boston with his wife and personal library — see later — too depressed to travel to New York or to face other scholars, apparently because that was the one and only December since their 1908 marriage in which he was not employed full time; after one more month of brooding, he eluded his wife's vigilance and ascended to the snowy roof from the edge of which he fell fifty feet (15 m) to a paved courtyard and was killed instantly.

(6) Louis Herbert Gray, our 1938 President, had been Professor of Comparative Philology at the University of Nebraska, at Lincoln, since long before the Great War of 1914-1918; this time he was at the Chicago APA meeting where he belonged. (7) Hans Carl Günter von Jagemann was too frail for winter travel at age 65; he died 22 January 1926. (8) Alfred Louis Kroeber stayed wisely in Sunny California. (9) John Matthews Manly's Obituary Note, signed by R. G. Kent, in Language 16.263, will best explain why he could not leave Chicago. (10) Dr. Walter Petersen, who had come from Germany before 1914, was saving money towards moving with books and papers to the University of Florida from his post as a teacher of Classics at the University of Redlands in the orange groves 50 miles (80 km) due East of Los Angeles. (11) John R. Swanton, Ethnologist in the Smithsonian Institution, had some commitment or other, today beyond discovery, in Washington.

(12) Benjamin Ide Wheeler (*1854) was already President Emeritus of the University of California when he signed the Call. In 1887 — the year Leonard Bloomfield was born — Wheeler had recently joined the Comparative Philology staff of Cornell University in Ithaca, New York, and William Gardner Hale had just joined its Classics Department. Hale's exhaustively elaborated treatise on the history and functions of the Latin constructions with cum was No. 1 of the Cornell University Studies in Classical Philology, 1887. Issued simultaneously as No. 2 of the Studies was a neat little job, Analogy and the Scope of its Application in Language, by Professor Benjamin Ide Wheeler. A decade later, when the Library of the University of Wisconsin purchased the Cornell Studies in toto, the two earliest of them were bound together. When Leonard Bloomfield spent two years there as a graduate student in Germanics he read the whole volume as a matter of course during the first year, 1906-1907, so that we find it peculiarly significant that Wheeler's treatise became a principal source underlying both (a) Bloomfield's 1933 Language and (b) Erwin Allen Esper's 1973 Analogy and Association in Linguistics and Psychology. Now on Sunday 28th December, 1924, Hale was in Manhattan and registered as an LSA Foundation Member, appearing in the earliest List of Members as Prof. Emer. Wm. Gardner Hale, Van Rensselaer Av., Stamford, Conn. (Latin, Univ. of Chicago). Kent's Obituary Note on Hale is in Language 4.217-218, 1928, just one year later than his Note at 3.208, reporting Wheeler's career in outline: born 15 July 1854, Wheeler had died May 2nd, 1927, at Vienna. Austria.

Seven Signers were so inconspicuous as to leave no impress in the Krauss memory a half-century later, especially as he had his nooning apparently remote from the place, a hotel, where the principals foregathered. We list those seven next:

(1) Aurelio M[anuel?] Espinosa of Stanford University, there chosen as member of the crucial Publications Committee for the three-year term 1925–1927, was one of the elders, for his spinster daughter was born in 1906 at Albuquerque; in Who's Who (for 1954/1955) we find that she was prominent as a secondary-school teacher of Spanish and of language pedagogy; her father is lost to our view after his 1937 resignation. (2) George Tobias Flom was our 1936 President. (3) John Lawrence Gerig lost the 'SC' from his listing through neglect to pay annual dues and then defective procedure when asked to pay arrears; he was an ordinary member in the 1930's. (4) Pliny Earle Goddard slipped in and out without any fuss.(5) Mark Harvey Liddell (Purdue University, English), and similarly (6) Claude Meek Lotspeich (Cincinnati, English and Comparative Philology) were by preference silent in large meetings. (7) Truman Michelson (Ethnology, George Washington University, and Smithsonian Institution ethnologist) silently recorded everything as Temporary Secretary.

Prospective signers of a call, after some uncertain date in the academic year 1922/1923, are believed to have originally numbered close to fifty in the list that was building up in Leonard Bloomfield's hands in Columbus, Ohio. The tragic loss by suicide of his young sister Marie, brilliant student in Barnard College, on Wednesday 7 February 1923—Margaret Mead's dating is late by two days—halted everything for roughly a year. Then in 1924 a shrunken list of thirty-odd persons were approached, some of them through unidentified intermediaries, and certain of them refused to let themselves be listed as Signers of the Call. Refusals are of course generally undocumentable; but when Tobias Diekhoff long afterward was asked about a rumor that he was one of them—after all, his favorable view of Bloomfield's An Introduction to the Study of Language, Henry Holt: New York, 1914, was widely known, especially at the University of Wisconsin where the questioner was a member of the German Department staff—he promptly confirmed it and said there were plenty of Signers without him, so that he had no 'need to regret it.'

Finally, from the Krauss letter to Joos dated February 25, 1974, we quote:

> Since all the Signers of the Call are now deceased, I cannot give offense by naming those who, in my opinion, participated most prominently and effectively in the discussion at the Organization Meeting for the creation of the LINGUISTIC SOCIETY OF AMERICA, namely, Leonard Bloomfield, Franz Boas, George M. Bolling, Hermann Collitz, Franklin Edgerton, Paul Haupt, Roland G. Kent, Edward Prokosch, Edward Sapir, Edgar H. Sturtevant. It must have been obvious to others, as it was to me at my then tender age, that they were masters of the situation, as they adroitly dribbled and passed the ball from one to another before making a score from under the basket. I doubt that any other society anywhere in the world owes its creation and subsequent success to a similarly outstanding group of professional giants.

Each of the 29 Signers of the Call emerges from our research as a person whose publications Leonard Bloomfield had profited from. For family reasons, there were no women; otherwise (as Joos was told in 1931 by one of them) at least Louise Pound and Cornelia Catlin Coulter would have been included. The contemporary gossip identified Miss Pound's outrage at the routine ignoring of all female scholars as the decisive impulse toward the prompt founding of her (as she thought of it) quarterly American Speech—soon dominated by men in turn, and by the educationists bent on improving oral performance by teaching what was called Euphonenglish: see Bloch's review of Phonetic Transcriptions from 'American Speech' (New York: Columbia University Press, 1939) which assembled 75 transcribed passages of English prose from that journal, from its years 1933 to 1939, for his report on the mildest of the aberrations perpetrated in our schools. [Eduard Prokosch's name appears above as 'Edward'; he regularly printed 'E.']

The Signers of the Call were not rebels. They were continuity men. Their research, teaching, and publication continued unbroken the patterns of linguistic thinking defined in the neogrammarian [translated from German Junggrammatiker] movement long before Leonard's birth on April 1, 1887; but now after 1918 that was (at least in the thought of schoolmen generally) viewed as the least promising of many competing treatments of languages in public education, ranked below the art of punctuating by rule and memorizing spellings and pronunciations of English for essay-writing, off to one side (along with Esperanto) of the ladder of personal improvement, and obviously not worth serious consideration for students of literature. The neogrammarian tradition itself was being carried on by relatively few persons, for instance by far too few young students of those 29 fully mature scholars whose average age was above 50: Leonard Bloomfield at 37 was the youngest of them, the youngest of the other 28 was above 40. The 1914-1918 Great War had suspended normal participation of Americans in European culture, apart from what just such senior citizens made themselves responsible for, while the mass of Americans in their communal behavior lacked a good deal in qualities worthy of emulation. East of the Atlantic, scholarship was all but paralytic: Scotland, England, and Scandinavia were still there (Scandinavia was the area of the most vigorous linguistics) but the heartland of scholarship had for half a century been obsessed, or beclouded, in a crescendo of military and of cultural adventurism and its seemingly natural concomitant, a commercial view of the nature and the values of science.

Academic generations are not 25 or 30 years long, but more like five or at most seven years. Since 1914 there had not been a normal succession of academic generations in any language field: young men had been killed or disabled; their mentors were exposed to the cold winds of economic uncertainties quite usually made over into academic uncertainties by the workings of public and campus politics. An extreme case is reported in the Obituary, Language 28.417-28, by E. A. Hahn on E. H. Sturtevant: 'The post-war period was one of uncertainty and enforced economy; and the Columbia University Department of Classics came to a decision from which it apparently never since has departed—namely, that a specialist in classical linguistics was a luxury (or a frill? or an irrelevancy? [this editorial listing of alternatives offered by Bernard Bloch was converted into text by some private interaction with Miss Hahn]) that it could no longer afford. Edgar Sturtevant was dismissed from Columbia in 1920, just as his eldest child was entering college. For three bleak years he served as clerk to the Irving National Bank. Strangely enough, this was a job for which the scholar was by no means unfit. All his life he was an assiduous follower of the stock market, turning eagerly to the financial pages of the newspaper, and both preaching and practicing an unorthodox audacity of investment which, in his case at least, yielded considerable success. But of course his real interest lay in a career of scholarship. Tenaciously and courageously he clung to his research; but it was a sad period. ... In 1923 he was called to Yale as Assistant Professor of Greek and Latin'—his rank when he put his name down as a Signer of the Call and one of the three-man organizing committee (L. Bloomfield, G. M. Bolling, E. H. Sturtevant) awaiting the responses.

The 29 Signers already held no less than 75 memberships, more likely closer to 100 of them, in those four antecedent language-concerned learned societies which had earned greatest renown in North America. Each of the four published a quarterly, and typically also various unscheduled publications, monographs and the like. Their dates of founding are normally treated as a prestige ranking:

1842 The American Oriental Society, the AOS for short;
1869 The American Philological Association, the APA;
1883 The Modern Language Association of America, the MLA;
1902 The American Anthropological Association, the AAA;

—and yet the youngest of them could (by an oddity of history) claim seniority.

That was an appeal to a sort of apostolic succession from Benjamin Franklin's activities, his assembling of indigenous-language books and manuscripts, both locally and by purchase from England and France, by which a collection was initiated that eventually was augmented by the works and collectanea of Major John Wesley Powell (1834-1902) and emerged as a society and a museum: Today's AAA plus the University of Pennsylvania Museum's 'American Section' (Curator: John Alden Mason, 1926 member of the LSA) where by 1928 a young student named Zellig Sabbettai Harris definitely had commenced seriously researching the boxes of uncatalogued items aloft in the dust under leaky skylights.

We briefly shift to scenes of a twelvemonth later, from 28 December 1924 to 28 December 1925, quoting first from the Report to our Annual Meeting signed by R. G. Kent in his capacity as Chairman of the special Committee on Coöperation with Other Societies (other members: Franklin Edgerton, Leonard Bloomfield, Truman Michelson apparently representing the AAA, and, apparently because the significance of that word 'Other' called for it, one permanent outsider to the LSA, C. W. E. Miller, Editor of the American Journal of Philology as successor to its founder, classical-languages grammarian B. L. Gildersleeve, who had founded it in 1880 and established the tradition that the AJP should maintain autonomy by not allowing itself to become the organ of any group apart from its own subscribers.) [See, in Hockett's biographical pages of the Esper book Analogy ... which Hockett published (University of Georgia Press, Athens: 1973) the framing of what Esper wrote parenthetically in reporting to Hockett what he knew about Bloomfield, Bolling, and others, from the years beginning in 1914 when Esper became a Bolling pupil at Ohio State University in Columbus, as Hockett prints it on page ix: '(I think that the hostility between Bolling and Miller was one of the reasons for the founding of Language.)' Or on page 538 of A Leonard Bloomfield Anthology.]
Shortening the printed text by deleting fully redundant words, we quote:
The Committee ... has conferred by correspondence, and while not unanimous on all points, agrees in making the following report:
1. We think it desirable that the meetings of the LSA should be held in conjunction with those of other societies ... It would be natural not to hold the meetings ... on precisely the same days as those of the other society, but if possible to begin one day earlier, or to end one day later ...
Of 214 paid members of the LSA on March 13 [1925],
   17 belong to the American Anthropological Association,
   61 belong to the American Oriental Society,
   77 belong to the American Philological Association,
   88 belong to the Modern Language Association of America,
   18 belong to none of the four societies,
   13 have not sent in their data.

... we should, if meeting regularly between Christmas and New Year's, meet normally with the APA and the MLA alternately, yet sometimes with the AAA, and once in a while separately; the AOS does not have to be considered, since it holds its sessions in Easter Week. No hard and fast bargain or agreement should be made, but the decision should be made in view of the merits of the case each year.
2. [On abortive proposals for reduced dues for members of two or more societies:] The LSA at the outset needs all the money which it receives.
3. Eligibility to the LSA should not be conditioned upon membership in any other society of a preferred list, which would be difficult to draw up and would arouse jealousies. But the LSA should by every means discourage scholars from withdrawing from other societies because they join the LSA.
4. [Terms (otiose and soon forgotten) for joint publication of bulky items.]
This Kent report, and his others as Secretary, as Treasurer, etc., were on the agenda for the Business Meeting which ran 10:03 a.m. to approximately noon and without a break was followed by the reading of three papers before the 12:52 adjournment; re-convening at 3:05 p.m., some three dozen members heard six more papers before the 5:48 adjournment; and so on until on Tuesday evening, 29 December, Hermann Collitz, in 1925 President of both the LSA and the MLA, delivered his joint presidential address on 'World Languages' printed finally in Language 2.1–13 in the Spring of 1926.
Of the 52 members recorded as present in the Chicago meeting, three went by train to Ithaca, New York, for a final day's meeting at Cornell University along with 13 others who were already there for the APA meeting. Those three were of course Kent and Sturtevant, plus University of Wisconsin Professor Arthur G. Laird, Leonard Bloomfield's 1906–1908 teacher for Advanced Greek and Sanskrit as Professor of Comparative Philology and the man who got him an Assistant's appointment under Francis A. Wood in the University of Chicago Department of Germanic Philology. Weather on the Atlantic-coast regions was bad just then: the Prokosch paper 'The Hypothesis of a Pre-Germanic Substratum' is listed as read by title only because his train up from Bryn Mawr was snowed in.

Returning our attention, from 31 December 1925 to 28 December for other matters of permanent interest dealt with in that morning's Business Meeting, we quote segments from pages 68 and 69 of the Proceedings which provide a lead-in to the two decades when the Linguistic Atlas was always part of the LSA picture and to many of us the most significant part of all. At that time Professor William Frank Bryan in the Department of English of Northwestern University (Evanston, Illinois, the suburb next north of Chicago) where Hans Kurath was Assistant Professor of German and George Oliver Curme, Professor of Germanic Philology, was working towards a second edition of his 1905 Grammar of the German Language and somehow formed a permanent alliance with Kurath which eventually embraced English too, Kurath for Phonology in their Curme & Kurath Historical Grammar of Modern English, Curme for the Syntax which did eventually get published. Now in Chicago in the days leading up to the LSA Business Meeting, W. F. Bryan handed in a letter to the Executive Committee asking for LSA endorsement of an appeal for financial support to the MLA Research Group for Present-Day English for a survey, 'primarily linguistic, of English as spoken in this country, to disclose its particular characteristics and their distribution.' The Executive Committee's recommendation to the Society as placed before the Business Meeting and there approved as we see on page 69 employed an altered wording, no longer as we printed it just above here within the quotation-marks but instead as we now quote from the bottom of page 69:

> The Linguistic Society of America, recognizing the value of a scientific survey of American Speech, particularly of the character of its sounds and their distribution, expresses its approval of the plan formulated by the Committee on a Survey of Spoken English in America, a committee of the Modern Language Association of America. The Society therefore endorses an appeal to one of the philanthropic and scientific foundations for funds with which to begin a survey according to this plan.

Before returning to the last Sunday of December 1924, we pause here to quote the first half of page 62 in Language Vol. 2, 1926, as a supplement to the report that Carlos Everett Conant had died a suicide on 27 January 1925, with a prompt obituary (Language 1.63–64) by Frank R. Blake, who had 'met him only once, over ten years ago' at the time of its writing: There on that page 62, we find an unsigned message to LSA members from Roland Kent:

> Members of the Society will be glad to learn that the Indonesian collection of the late C. E. Conant is not to be dispersed but will remain, as its self-denying founder would have wished, available as a unit for the use of scholars. Its home is to be the Library of Williams College, to which it has been presented by an alumnus of the institution, Mr. Herbert H. Lehman of New York.
> [Born 28th March 1878, Lehman received the B.A. in 1899. Banker and philanthropist before the 1914–1918 Great War, he served on the General Staff (Captain to Colonel) before leaving Washington in 1919 to resume his 1908 partnership in Lehman Brothers. In 1928 he was elected Lieutenant Governor and re-elected 1930; then elected Governor in 1932 and in each biennium before 1942; then made the State Department's Director of Foreign Relief and Rehabilitation, his continuing international service eventually led to his election as Senator. He died 5 December 1963, just 13 days later than his protégé John Fitzgerald Kennedy. We do not know how he learned of the plight of Conant's widow . . .]
> The collection, which includes some sixty of the Indonesian languages and dialects, contains an immense amount of material on the Philippine languages, much of which cannot be duplicated. Of its formation Mr. Joel Hatheway writes: 'Most of the books were purchased by him at the cost of very real sacrifice. A few were gifts from friends, Spaniards and Filipinos, fellow-enthusiasts in linguistic studies. I well remember the days, twenty-five years ago, when his collection was started; when together we visited the monasteries of Manila and Cebu, and Conant would spend his last peso for grammars and dictionaries of the native languages. Within even a week of our arrival in the Islands he had embarked upon the comparative study of the native languages which was to be his life work.'

Secretary Kent's Obituary on Joel Hatheway is in Language 10.227 (1934).

Returning to the inaugural issue of <u>Language</u>, which by design contained just the least number of pages that could be called one quarterly issue of a learned society's full-scale journal, we find it beginning with a unique sort of introductory article by Leonard Bloomfield: 'Why a Linguistic Society?' is its title, and insiders used to call it a "Frontispiece" because it precedes the bulk of the 36-page first issue. The story of why and how it was written comes to us from many sources, but always in the form of oral tradition and most discreetly cloaked, apparently because there was some embarrassment about seeming to reject much of the message of the Hermann Collitz pages (14–16) on 'The Scope and Aims of Linguistic Science.' The tradition is that Bloomfield had to be persuaded by the combined eloquence of at least Bolling, Edgerton, Sapir, and Sturtevant, who prevailed upon him to write 'an expansion of the Call' detailed enough to counterbalance certain archaic messages and implications in the senior man's presentation, lest the younger recruits give up in discouragement. Given some deadline for Bloomfield to meet a month or more later, he wrote his contribution twice: he scrapped his first form of it after the news came that Carlos E. Conant had died in lamentable circumstances 27th January 1925, and the printed text still shows signs of the consequent mental and emotional strain, for instance two bits of first draft text in one sentence (midway on the printed page 4) which cry out for a rewriting to make the sentence fully readable by every literate reader: 'The notion seems to prevail that a student of language is merely a kind of crow-baited student of literature.' By a sequence of accidents, the present historiographer happens to be prepared to convert this into plain American English. My own English was determined by that of my mother, who was born in 1882 within 17 miles (27 km) of the Wisconsin village of Elkhart Lake where Leonard Bloomfield attended the village elementary school alongside rural children—and at each recurrence of his birthday suffered the mockery of every boy, younger and older boys both, who on that day was licensed by immutable custom to call him 'April Fool' and to subject him to often violent abuse.

His father's being a Chicago Jew and the owner of the local 'resort hotel' made the boy entirely an outsider among the schoolchildren during the winter season; he was, moreover, relatively frail and sickly and wore strong glasses; thus he was never a participant in the winter sports and the concomitant horseplay among the local schoolchildren, nearly all of whose parents were members of the Lutheran or at least some other proper church. The well-known shyness and fastidiousness in the adult Leonard Bloomfield was the obverse of the resultant ambivalence, the upper side of the character decisively shaped in Elkhart Lake where he had been cruelly squeezed between the millstones; beneath it was hidden the dark underside of what that milieu taught him in forcing him to survive as best he could.

Midway in the 1930's Bloomfield published (<u>Language</u> 11.97–115, 1935) 'The Stressed Vowels of American English' displaying a remarkably elaborate dialect which, I must now emphatically say, was startlingly at variance with his relaxed conversational English; by personal observation, confirmed in detail by Bernard Bloch's reports to me in numerous conversations, I was convinced that what he published was a conflation designed to embody all possible answers to critics who might accuse Bloomfield of ignorance of this or that bit of data; and furthermore there is evidence aplenty that he was answering Morris Swadesh's paper 'The Vowels of Chicago English' officially published just after it, at pp. 11.148–151 in our journal, although Editor Bolling had had it somewhat earlier.

His 'crow-baited student of literature' belonged to both rural Wisconsin and rural Ohio in a use of 'crow-bait' as a pejorative word for a horse and also (by an obvious extension) a human specimen who likewise was defective in some comparable way. None of us rural witnesses would have found any puzzle in the definition in the 1890 <u>Century Dictionary and Cyclopedia</u>, where the wording is 'An emaciated or decrepit horse, as likely soon to become carrion, and so attractive to crows' plus 'Colloq.' Apart from Bloomfield's 1925 Frontispiece, no attestation is known for any adjectival use. Our latest dictionary, <u>Webster's Third New International</u>, 1961, has lost touch with rural meanings and instead defines the noun as an item of race-track and betting parlance without roots in the soil. Finally the Bloomfield use of its '-ed' derivation belongs rather to the derivation-techniques of Classical Greek, Sanskrit, or Esperanto.

The Collitz paper can be sketchily explicated here. Its printed form, called an Abstract where it appears on pages 14—16 of the initial issue of Language, is not truly an abstract as we understand such things today. Instead it is substantially complete. It does lack the exordium, naturally enough, since that was not to be included (as Truman Michelson perfectly understood beforehand) in eventually drafted Proceedings, and we are sure that that was read off from a separate piece of paper inscribed no earlier than the preceding evening when the final planning was done at the MLA meeting; thus we are in the dark about its content but can safely assume that it was designed to be a personal sort of greeting for each of the several categories assumed to be present in the room according to expectations. (Not that Collitz actually observed such details, since the room was poorly illuminated and he was extremely near-sighted.) As ultimately printed for us, it is (after its unnumbered preliminary half-page stating what 'science' will mean in its English title) presented to us in three subdivisions numbered 'I' and 'II' and 'III' and a terminal half-page which deserves a 'IV' but is unnumbered as we find it.

This much is obvious; the underlying earlier German text contains all the real Collitz message and must be at least partly reconstructed if we are to grasp what Collitz thought he was saying to a far more heterogeneous group than he had ever previously addressed. The earliest text of all was the talk he gave at age 27 when he participated in the 1883 inaugural semester of the southernmost of the Seven Sisters—Radcliffe, Wellesley, Bryn Mawr, Vassar, Barnard, Smith, and Mount Holyoke College—which today our East Coast displays as a mixed string of pearls, rubies, emeralds, but no rhinestones... Beginning as a very junior member of the Bryn Mawr faculty, he escaped to The Johns Hopkins in Baltimore at his earliest opportunity; some time in the late 19th Century, says the gossip, his Umfang und Ziele der Sprachwissenschaft achieved its definitive form and got its English and its (somewhat better) French versions: he had been thoroughly taught French in Gymnasium, along with Latin and Greek, but naturally no English: that belonged in other sorts of schools, where no Greek and but little Latin could be studied. Now at the same time, as we can easily demonstrate, Professor Collitz assiduously collected American words and locutions, all of which he enunciated in an extremely thick North German phonology and an obvious conviction that he had no German accent whatever.

In the Summer of 1931, Bernard Bloch and the present writer (Martin Joos) were exposed to an almost identical performance when Collitz was a Visiting Lecturer in that year's Linguistic Institute, and both took notes and afterwards discussed what we had heard with each other and with other experts. Thus it is with some confidence that the present reconstruction of the Collitz message can be offered: Not the whole text, but only the peroration with inserted glosses:

'[IV.] A matter worthy of our particular attention is the study of ancient and modern languages in our [= American] public schools and colleges. It is not saying too much [when we say] that as a vehicle of general culture the study of languages [plural!] stands unrivalled among the various branches of instruction. Linguistics [= Sprachwissenschaft as already defined], to be sure, cannot in this respect boast of any exclusive merits, [Joos note: here we emphasize:] for the reason that it is impossible to study any particular [written!]language without perusing at the same time specimens of the literature written in that language. The study of [Classical] Greek, e.g., means the study of the Greek language and Greek authors. Obviously it is the combination rather [= rather the combination (= vielmehr...)] of these two subjects than the nature of either one of them singly which renders them valuable for educational purposes. This Society, in any case, has every reason to join hands with the educators endeavoring [= those endeavoring] to secure for the study of languages the place due to it—in the interest both of mental and of moral culture—in the curriculum of our schools.'

Now what is most needed here is a sketch of the Collitz presuppositions: the things he did not say, simply because he assumed that all civilized persons had the same interests and values; plus the presuppositions specifically belonging to an academic world where he felt most at home. One crucial presupposition was that there would always be money: research subventions, scholarships for students, and supplements to professorial salaries for supervising those advanced enough to be prospective doctoral candidates. The ultimate beneficiaries—like all professors that he knew, Collitz was altruistic about academic life—were the populace, all the people whose lives were being enriched by all the studies [= Wissenschaften] which they admired from afar. From the populace at large, school prizes and even university scholarships would draw recruits to scholarly studies from families lacking adequate means; and again, there ought to be an uncle or other patron with money, or at least the connections which would facilitate finding a wife with a dowry.

For documentation we can refer to Thomas Mann's Buddenbrooks, 1900, and the Immensee of Theodor Storm, 1852, which both Franz Boas and Hermann Collitz had read in boyhood years and had been told was realistic orientation for intelligent boys. Finally, we can quote Nicholas Murray Butler's 1944 Annual Report as President of Columbia University. When Maxim Newmark was assembling Twentieth Century Modern Language Teaching, 1948, New York: The Philosophical Library, he requested permission to use three pages from that Report (finally printed as pp. v–vii) as the book's Introduction. Butler gave permission in 1947, and died within a few weeks. Young Nicholas Murray Butler had earned his doctorate in philosophy in 1884 and then studied for a year in Paris and Berlin; from 1887 to 1891 he was the first President of the New York College for the training of teachers (later named the Teachers' College of Columbia University) which he had personally planned and organized. In 1944 his message was, in part, 'The steady decline in the study of foreign languages in American secondary schools and colleges has been a matter of deep concern to everyone interested in liberal education. This has resulted chiefly from the pressure of social studies upon the curricula. It is a part of the theory held by many professors of Education that subjects which require competence in a particular field of subject-matter should give place to [Germanism for "cede their place to"] a program of 'general education' which introduces the student to a wide range of subjects but provides no opportunity for a systematic and well-founded knowledge in any one of them.'

From various dates appearing close above here, we immediately see that on the 28th of December 1924 the mixed audience facing Collitz must have understood him when he began his peroration with 'This Society, in any case ...' as stating theses which ought to sound familiar to every academic person in that decade; on the other hand we can also see that the Collitz message was, by comparison with what the LSA promptly developed into, archaic in the extreme.

Events of 1925, 1926, and 1927 are to be followed from the pages of Language and the earliest of the Monographs which will be listed together on later pages; thus it will be logical to date Chapter II from 1928 onward. From Franklin Brunell Krauss we learn that when Bolling had edited the printer's copy for the second Language issue and released it to the Waverley Press in the second week of April, 1925, he left the correcting of its galley proofs to the University of Pennsylvania group that clustered around Secretary-Treasurer Kent—who also went to Europe for the long summer vacation whenever possible and this time went first to Mâcon to arrange with Protat Frères for the printing of LSA Dissertation No. 1, Associative Interference by Erwin Allen Esper, and from there went on into Switzerland and Italy. Krauss says of Kent that 'His untiring services in this office over a long period of years, during which I assisted him with correspondence, dues, mailing of specific issues, notation of new members, and so forth, were little short of Herculean, and far beyond what most scholars of his professional stature would be willing to contribute. The steady growth of the LSA during its early years is to be credited to his efficiency and dedication to his official duties.'

In 1925 a non-profit journal could assume availability of the cheap Second Class mailing privilege if only it did not print paid advertisements. Also, a modicum of loose advertisements could be enclosed in the same wrapper (or laid in loose in the journal if not caught in its stapling or sewing or glue) if consonant with the official aims of the journal. Members and libraries accordingly saw them in the four 1925-dated issues of Language and in the Esper Dissertation. Thereafter, the practise was abolished as beneath our dignity. Such loose items are regularly discarded in the binding of journal volumes and can be found only in special circumstances.

II: INSTITUTES: 1928 — 1931

For all ordinary observers the emergence of the Linguistic Institute to public view with the end of 1927 altered the Society's significance enormously. Insiders had been expecting something without anticipating its impact or just what it would turn out to be when it arrived; outsiders had never really noticed anything. Only the most prescient of historians of science could have predicted any of its real qualities—and as late as 1936 even those were largely unrecognized. For some useful understanding of what happened, we begin by listing four dichotomies:

1. Winter was, as it has remained, our Annual Meeting season. The months of warm weather were before 1928 principally a time-out period, and variously according to one's age and status among all who were involved with language. For some members (and prospective recruits) it was a vacation and an occasion for decamping; for others it was a period of preparation for two hard-working semesters before the next hot-weather slack season. Once the Institute had been added to the American academic scene, each serious linguist's summer centered around those six or eight weeks as the whole year's center of gravity—or levity. For eager youngsters it was a time of either frenzied or perfunctory study on the margins of one's interests and competencies; for the middle-aged or elderly it was both exhilarating and exhausting: each time, one or more of them were prostrated, but even then they did not seriously regret their involvement. Faculty and students both found the Summer/Winter dichotomy radically altered.

2. Students generally had had their advanced schooling confined to a single 'home' campus: the European tradition of alternating two or more universities' residence-years of lecture-attendance, and the concomitant pattern of getting essentially no 'credits' or 'grades' but only the signatures testifying that that person had been present at lectures: that Wanderjahr(e) tradition had been only marginally there in student consciousness, only dimly half-understood. We are emphasizing the junior half of the Student/Professor interrelation here. When we combine this with the Summer/Winter contrast, we see that the logical result of filling much of a Summer with activities that bring Faculty and students into close association without those Winter-time deadlines and other urgencies must be a new kind of symbiosis with only fractionally predictable results.

3. For one thing, there was a swift burgeoning of talents in those recruits who profited from such concentrated work—while serving also to deflect (perhaps into literary studies or into psychological ones, or into the non-academic world) those others who within six weeks were self-persuaded that Linguistics was Not Their Game after all. (From an Administration's point of view, the latter was a valuable service: in the ordinary way, a student failure might easily consume two or three years of public money instead of a mere two months.) The failures automatically drop out of our reckoning; the permanent effects upon the American developments in consequence of the Linguistic Institutes have been especially the improved self-confidence and mutual respect among linguists, and between the old and the young within their community, henceforth seen as a continent-wide community. Of course it remains impossible to measure this effect precisely in this paragraph, but the career of Bernard Bloch alone may be taken as a sufficient demonstration.

4. To these three points, finally, we need to associate one more which by itself for the 1928-1931 Institute Faculty and their families and friends could outweigh all the others. We state this fourth point explicitly because modern readers, who are mostly accustomed to Institutes staffed with a mixture of age-levels, need to be told that for those families and friends it could be a matter of sheer survival for scholars who as scholars were sustained more by the company of eager youngsters preparing for the future, and preparing the future for the whole community, than by kudos accruing to themselves.

In continuing we may, after a blanket acknowledgement, freely paraphrase, or even copy verbatim without warning, the History of the Linguistic Institute which Archibald A. Hill had published in 1963 at the Indiana University Press as a 15-page pamphlet; our source is the ACLS reprint filling the first 12 pages in its March 1964 Newsletter (15.3) which the Council used for a good many years as one exhibit accompanying appeals for foundation funds, and we begin by quoting Hill.

Two of the main aims of the Linguistic Society have always been (a) the spreading of knowledge on the nature of language into the populace, and (b) the recruitment and training of linguistic scholars. Both were recorded in the Proceedings of the 28 December 1924 Organization Meeting: 'An important suggestion was made by Professor J. L. Gerig, that the Secretary [R. G. Kent] draw the attention of graduate students to the Society, in the hope of securing their memberships early.'

The first step towards recruitment and training was a survey of colleges published as Bulletin 1, 'Survey of Linguistic Studies: Opportunities for Advanced Work in the United States' signed by Kent and Sturtevant as authors. The meat of the slim booklet is a set of tabulations which we have found all but impossible to interpret: constructed by Kent, they show his passion for succinctness unchecked and would have to be expanded threefold before they could be read today. Instead, we find all that really matters in the page of corrigenda, Language 3.26, 1927:

> A survey of Linguistic Studies was issued late in November, 1926, as a Bulletin of the Executive Committee. A few words to correct and to supplement the statements in it may not be out of place. The Survey was intentionally limited to graduate courses in the institutions which are members of the Association of American Universities, although, as was said in the Survey itself, this definition, made for purely practical reasons, causes the omission of certain distinguished schools. Yet it can hardly be disputed that the institutions considered in the Survey, twenty-five in number, include at least twenty of the twenty-five institutions giving a full graduate curriculum, on whatever basis the rating might be made, and therefore the general impression which it creates is not essentially wrong.
>
> But the strictures upon the failure to make American English the subject of instruction seem not to be fully justified. We may criticize the fact that the published announcements of the courses do not indicate that the phenomena and the peculiarities of American English are dealt with or otherwise utilized; but apparently the courses on the English Language are actually so conducted, in a number of institutions where no such credit is given in the Survey. For example, Prof. William A. Craigie of Chicago and Prof. Kemp Malone of Johns Hopkins have courteously sent the information that their courses on the English Language do make American English the basis of the work.

That was the whole page; what we today find most illuminating is that a Survey said to cover all manner of advanced studies that can be called 'linguistic' is found to need correcting only as to the American English focus in courses 'on the English Language' and otherwise is treated as flawless.

In that decade it was generally assumed that a Linguistic Society of America would automatically devote its efforts to language improvements, popularly seen as improvements in grammar, spelling-reform, Esperanto, and similarly motivated tinkerings with the languages 'of civilization' and perhaps Chinese to be generous. The notion of investigating a language without trying to change it, or examining the inner workings of Choctaw as if it were a respectable fashion of speaking like French, was never contemplated seriously by well-educated knowledgeable persons who read The Saturday Evening Post or the Atlantic or Harper's or Scribner's. That would rather be the sort of thing that appealed to H. L. Mencken. Hadn't he authored an iconoclastic book, The American Language (first published in March, 1919; the rewritten Second Edition, December, 1921, and finally the Third, February, 1923) and wasn't that just like Mencken? Public reactions ranged from moral outrage to guffaws over the silliness of scholars. (Note: In the Ann Arbor Linguistic Institutes, 1936–1940, Mencken's was one of the basic books: it shared pride of place with the Linguistic Atlas of New England data-sheets and the Craigie Dictionary.)

In the late Spring of 1927, presumably sometime in April, Dr. Reinhold Eugene Saleski, Professor of German in Bethany College, wrote to Kent as Secretary of our Society to suggest the holding of a Linguistic Institute (his naming!) in the Summer of 1928. In his letter he described an Institute as a gathering of scholars

for interchange of ideas rather than for the holding of courses, though the latter
was not excluded. Kent sent copies of the Saleski letter to all members of the
Executive Committee, and asked them whether they approved the holding of such
an institute under the patronage of our Society. So far, a vague and rather foreign
notion which Kent neither smiled nor frowned upon, and an Executive Committee
whose members were equally divided; but that 1927 Committee's membership
included Vice President Edgar Sturtevant, and that made all the difference. He 'took
up the idea with energy' as Secretary Kent's printed final Report said afterwards.

To anyone who ever observed Sturtevant self-committed to an idea of any
considerable magnitude, the six words tell the whole story. Not much of the tale
is available to us, but enough is in print to make the plot clear in outline. The
Saleski ideas were dealt with almost entirely by letter-writing. Sturtevant saw
that detailed plans would have to be developed, and Committee consent procured
for each detail, in advance of the Annual Meeting at the end of December; in the
course of the 1927 summer months, he got unanimous and hearty approval for an
outline of Linguistic Institute events to fill six weeks during the 1928 Summer,
and finally filled in all details and alternatives to constitute a document which
he presented in many copies to the Executive Committee for consideration on the
eve of the Annual Meeting held in Cincinnati, Ohio, the only occasion when the
Society was to meet in plenary session with a Business Meeting competent to
legislate matters of such moment and thereby protect the daring schemers. He
had gained the approval of the Yale University authorities for the proposed use
of certain campus facilities, and accommodations for visiting staff members
and students of various sorts and even their spouses if any: details are best seen
as laid out in the columns of the descriptive circular which we reproduce at less
than its original size from the exemplar preserved in the Charles Carpenter
Fries Museum. The circular, worded as a letter of invitation, was printed on a
single sheet of thin tough paper exactly an English foot (12 inches) square (30.5
cm wide and 30.5 cm high exactly) from hand-set type. Apart from the box at
the top of its first page, which is set in Bookman type, the fonts used were the
cheapest available in New Haven and lacked even the resources for printed
French, let alone German or Turkish; no explanation for such penny-pinching
is known, and we can only guess that Sturtevant was determined not to waste a
penny of our Society's precious funds.

Our printing of that circular is of course reduced in size; the original size
can be deduced from the original width of the 'box' heading its first page, which
was 5.13 inches or 20.2 cm wide. The proof-correcting was flawless; the given
name 'Edward' for Eduard Prokosch was taken over from the List of Members,
and it was not replaced by the correct form in our publications before the year
1938, where Bloomfield used 'Eduard' in his Prokosch obituary, and it must be
remarked that Prokosch himself never bothered to alter the spelling of the
name and usually called himself simply 'E. Prokosch' in print.

Not all Germans among our members were as easy-going as that, and readers
are warned that correct spellings for any doubtful syllables will be used on later
pages of this History and can be found in the Index. We have paginated the pages
of the circular, of course, and its eight columns are therefore referred to as 19a,
19b, 20a [COURSES], 20b, 21a, 21b, 22a, 22b. The sequence in which the courses
are listed will strike most modern readers as somewhat odd; actually it is more
easily derivable from the shelving sequence of books governed by the Cutter system of 'call numbers' (abandoned, even in the Library of the University of Wisconsin, midway in the 20th century) than from any other single source. Anyhow,
there could not be any 'course numbers' for two reasons at least: first, Yale had
only descriptive names for courses, and there had never been any Summer School
at Yale, so that there was no traditional way to number the fractional-year pieces
of advanced studies that we see listed here.

Linguistic Institute
of the
Linguistic Society of America

You are invited to participate in the Linguistic Institute, to be held at Yale University from July 9th to August 17th, 1928, by the Linguistic Society of America.

ADMINISTRATIVE COMMITTEE

Edgar Howard Sturtevant, Yale University. Director.

Reinhold Eugene Saleski, Bethany College, Assistant Director.

Roland ~~Ronald~~ Grubb Kent, University of Pennsylvania, Secretary of the Linguistic Society.

FACULTY

Frank Ringgold Blake, Associate Professor of Oriental Languages, The Johns Hopkins University.

George Melville Bolling, Professor of Greek, Ohio State University.

Herman Collitz, Professor Emeritus of Germanic Philology, The Johns Hopkins University.

Raymond Philip Dougherty, Professor of Assyriology and Babylonian Literature, Yale University.

Joseph Dunn, Professor of Celtic Languages and Literatures, Catholic University of America.

Franklin Edgerton, Professor of Sanskrit and Comparative Philology, Yale University.

Herbert Charles Elmer, Professor of Latin, Cornell University.

George T. Flom, Professor of Scandinavian Languages and Literature, University of Illinois.

Pliny E. Goddard, Curator of Ethnology, American Museum of Natural History in New York.

Raymond Thompson Hill, Associate Professor of French, Yale University.

Roland Grubb Kent, Professor of Comparative Philology, University of Pennsylvania.

Henry Roseman Lang, Professor Emeritus of Romance Languages and Literature, Yale University.

Angelo Lipari, Associate Professor of Italian, Yale University.

Kemp Malone, Associate Professor of English, The Johns Hopkins University.

Otto Mueller, Professor of Romance Languages, Gettysburg College.

Walter Petersen, Assistant Professor of Ancient Languages, University of Florida.

Louise Pound, Professor of the English Language, University of Nebraska.

Edward Prokosch, Professor of Germanic Philology, New York University.

Frank Otis Reed, Professor of Spanish, University of Arizona.

Karl Reuning, Lektor fuer Anglistik, Breslau.

G. Oscar Russell, Assistant Professor of Romance Languages, Ohio State University.

Daniel Bussier Shumway, Professor of Germanic Philology, University of Pennsylvania.

Edgar Howard Sturtevant, Professor of Linguistics and Comparative Philology, Yale University.

PURPOSE—It is intended to provide for students of linguistic science facilities similar to those afforded biologists at Woods Hole. Scholars who wish to carry on their own researches where they will have access to the needed books, and where they can experience the stimulus of discussion with scholars of similar interests, will find the Institute of advantage. There will be courses for graduate students, for high school and college teachers of language who feel the need of acquaintance with linguistic science or with the history of a particular language or group of languages, and also for scholars who wish to familiarize themselves with more or less remote bits of linguistic territory in the most economical way. The session of the Institute will last six weeks; but scholars may pursue their researches on the spot during all or any part of the summer.

PLACE—The Linguistic Institute is very fortunate in having secured the cooperation of Yale University for its session in 1928. The University has generously put its dormitories, classrooms and library at our disposal. The librarian has consented to consider the purchase of additional books on linguistic science. There is no summer school at Yale, which might interfere with our work. The sea breezes are very agreeable in summer, and a number of salt-water bathing beaches are within reach.

FEES—Each member of the Institute, except instructors, is subject to an Institute Fee of twenty dollars; this is to cover printing and postage, rental and library fees charged by Yale University, and other overhead expenses. There will also be a Tuition Fee of forty dollars for each course. All fees are payable on or before the first day of the session. Members resident outside the United States and Canada are exempt from both fees.

LIVING EXPENSES—Rooms in Yale dormitories will be available both for men and for women. The occupants of these rooms must furnish bedding and towels; the rental will be $4 per week. Rooms in town may be had for $4 per week and up. Double rooms cost $6 per week and up. Furnished apartments may be secured at corresponding rates. Meals may be had at an average cost of about 60 cents. Application for accommodations, with specifications of the kind desired, should be made to the Director.

COURSES—Classes will meet five times a week, and a student will be expected to take no more than two courses. Any one of the courses described below will be given for three or more students; courses for fewer than three students may be given at the option of the instructor. From the descriptions printed below students will probably be able to determine which courses they can pursue most profitably, but the Director will be glad to confer with them by letter. Upon petition from three or more prospective students accompanied by tuition fees, the Institute will endeavor to secure instruction in such other subjects as are in harmony with the purpose of the Institute.

Since most of the necessary books are not kept in stock at the book stores, students should order them at least three weeks ahead, and foreign books should be ordered six weeks ahead. They may be ordered through the Yale Cooperative Corporation, 237 Elm St., New Haven, or Whitlock's Book Store, Inc., 219 Elm St., New Haven.

CREDIT — Several prominent graduate schools have already agreed to accept work done in the Institute as counting toward the M. A. or the Ph. D. on the same terms as work done in other graduate schools.

REGISTRATION—The Institute cannot be held unless a sufficient demand appears by Feb. 1, 1928. Consequently, all interested should register at once as members of the Institute, and indicate which courses, if any, they plan to take. If desired, this preliminary registration may be cancelled later.

REQUEST—It will be greatly appreciated if you will post this notice where it can be seen by any who may be interested.

ADDRESS—The Linguistic Institute, Box 1849, Yale Station, New Haven, Conn.

COURSES.

INTRODUCTION TO LINGUISTIC SCIENCE. MR. PROKOSCH.

A survey of the history of the science; a classification of languages with special consideration of the Indo-European group; phonetic trend, phonetic law and analogical drift; word structure, principles of etymology, outline of comparative syntax. Reading knowledge of German and French essential, acquaintance with Latin and Greek desirable.

PHILOLOGICAL PHONETICS. MR. RUSSELL.

Special attention will be paid to recent x-ray and other experimental evidence which tends to disprove certain of the traditional ideas as to tongue position in the pronouncing of vowels and also of continuant and stop consonants.

EXPERIMENTAL PHONETICS. MR. RUSSELL.

Individual research upon problems of interest to the members of the course; especially problems presented by language intonation, poetic rhythm or metrics, stress or accent, etc. Some recently devised apparatus, which considerably facilitates such investigation, will be available.

SEMANTICS. MR. PETERSEN.

Consideration of the general principles of Semantics, of the psychic basis of interpretation of language, and of semantic change. Study of selected topics in detail, including the semantics of some word groups, of selected stem-suffixes, and inflectional endings. A knowledge of Greek and Latin is desirable, of one or the other necessary.

SOME RECENT THEORIES OF LINGUISTIC SCIENCE. MR. REUNING.

Critical lectures on recent theories about such topics as: "laws" of sound-change; phonetic change; decay of flexions and syntactic change; analytic and synthetic tendencies; profit and loss; root and stem; root-creation; derivation; changes of meaning; analogy; combinative changes; birth and death of words; loan words; inflection and agglutination; individual peculiarities of speech; langue et langage; Sprechen, Gespraech, und Sprache; etc. A knowledge of several foreign languages and of linguistic science is desirable but not necessary. Prospective students should consult the Director about preliminary reading in preparation for this course.

LINGUISTIC ANTHROPOLOGY. MR. GODDARD.

Language a cultural acquisition. Methods of transmission from generation to generation. Internal changes. Changes due to contacts with other languages. Problems of distribution. Types of languages. What is a linguistic family? To be illustrated chiefly from Indo-European and American Indian languages.

METHODS OF STUDYING UNRECORDED LANGUAGES. MR. GODDARD.

The study of unrecorded languages involves certain difficulties not encountered in literary ones. First it is necessary to be able to perceive and distinguish sounds which may be quite new. These new sounds must be studied until they can be imitated and the manner of making them precisely described. They are then to be noted down with appropriate and unequivocal symbols. The facts as to duration, stress and pitch must also be ascertained and also the role they play in the language. When sufficient material has been accumulated meanings must be defined and the words and phrases analyzed into their significant parts. The course will take up these problems in detail and by discussion and practice give the students the

training required for their solution. Lectures and drill in phonetics and grammatical analysis will be the methods employed.

SANSKRIT. MR. EDGERTON.

Elements of the grammar. Lectures on the phonology and morphology from the historic and comparative standpoint. Analysis of easy texts. Text-books: Whitney, *Sanskrit Grammar*, 2nd ed., Leipzig and Boston; Lanman, *Sanskrit Reader*, Boston.

PALI. MR. EDGERTON.

Reading of simple texts; careful analysis of the phonology and morphology of Pali with reference to Sanskrit. A knowledge of Sanskrit is required. Text-book: Andersen, *Pali Reader*, Copenhagen and London.

COMPARATIVE GRAMMAR OF GREEK AND LATIN. MR. STURTEVANT.

An introduction to Indo-European comparative grammar with especial reference to the classical languages. A knowledge of Greek and Latin is assumed. Students must be able to read scientific German and French. Required book: Niedermann, *Outlines of Latin Phonetics*, edited by Strong and Stewart, London, 1910.

GREEK DIALECTS. MR. PETERSEN.

A study of the characteristics of the Greek dialects, their relation to each other, and the light shed by them on the history of the Greek Language. Reading of selected dialect inscriptions. A reading knowledge of Attic or Homeric Greek is presupposed. Required book: Buck, *Introduction to the Study of the Greek Dialects*, Boston (Ginn).

THE LANGUAGE OF THE HOMERIC POEMS. MR. BOLLING.

The course will consist partly of lectures and partly of a linguistic discussion of the third book of the *Iliad* in the manner of E. Hermann, *Sprachwissenschaftlicher Kommentar zu ausgewaehlten Stuecken aus Homer*, Heidelberg, 1914. Special problems will be assigned for investigation to such students as desire them, and opportunity will be given for the presentation and criticism of the results attained. Students will be expected to be able to read the Homeric dialect, and also scientific German and French. Students should own a text of the poems, preferably Ludwich, *Homeri Carmina*, Leipzig, 1889-1907.

OSCAN AND UMBRIAN. MR. KENT.

Interpretation of the chief extant inscriptions of these ancient Italic dialects, with especial attention to etymological method and to the light which they throw on the history of Latin. Prerequisites: a fair knowledge of the history of the Latin language, and ability to read German philological books. Text-book: Buck, *Grammar of Oscan and Umbrian*, Boston (Ginn).

OLD LATIN AND ITS DEVELOPMENT INTO CLASSICAL LATIN. MR. KENT.

A careful study of the inscriptions and of selected literary remains of Latin before the age of Caesar and Cicero, as an introduction to the history of the Latin language. Prerequisite: a good knowledge of the usual Latin forms, syntax, and vocabulary. Text-books: Lindsay, *Handbook of Latin Inscriptions*, Boston (Allyn and Bacon); *Plautus, Comoediae*, vol. 1, edited by Lindsay (Oxford University Press).

LATIN SYNTAX. MR. ELMER.

A course designed primarily for teachers and prospective teachers of Latin, but open to all interested students. This course aims to eliminate altogether many of the difficulties of Latin syntax as usually taught, to simplify many other difficulties, and to correct the numerous and serious violations, found in existing grammars, of fundamental principles of pedagogy. Text-books: Bennett, *New Latin Grammar* (Allyn and Bacon); Bennett, *The Latin Language* (Allyn and Bacon).

VULGAR LATIN AND INTRODUCTION TO ROMANCE PHILOLOGY. MR. HILL.

A study of the phonology, morphology, vocabulary and syntax of popular Latin. The development of the language in the different parts of the Roman Empire will be traced and texts will be used to illustrate the changes. This course is intended to give the background needed for a study of early French, Spanish and Italian. It will also be important for Classical students who wish to know how the Latin language developed. A knowledge of Latin, French and one other Romance Language, and the ability to read German are required. Text-books: Grandgent, *Introduction to Vulgar Latin*, Boston (Heath), 1907; Meillet, *La Methode Comparative en Linguistique Historique*, Cambridge (Harvard Univ. Press), 1925; Meyer-Luebke, *Einfuehrung in das Studium der rom. Sprachwissenschaft*, 2nd ed., Heidelberg (Winter), 1909; Bourciez, *Elements de Linguistique Romane*, 2nd ed., Paris (Klincksieck), 1923; Heraeus u. Morf, *Silviae vel Potius Aetheriae Peregrinatio ad Loca Sancta*, 2nd ed., Heidelberg (Winter), 1921; Morf, *Auswahl aus den Werken des Gregor von Tours*, Heidelberg (Winter), 1922. These books are inexpensive.

OLD FRENCH PHONOLOGY AND MORPHOLOGY. MR. LANG.

The development of the French language from the Vulgar Latin period to the fourteenth century. Prerequisites: a knowledge of Latin; of general phonetics; some practice in reading Old French; a correct pronunciation of Modern French; proficiency in reading scientific German. Text-books: (1) either Schwan-Behrens, *Grammaire de l'ancien francais* (1re et 2me parties, 2me edition: 3me partie, 1re edition), Leipzig (Reisland), 1913; or Luquiens, *An Introduction to Old French Phonology and Morphology*, 2nd ed. (Yale University Press), 1919; (2) Grandgent, *Introduction to Vulgar Latin*, Boston (Heath), 1907; (3) either *La Chanson de Roland*, Oxford Version, by Jenkins (Heath), 1924; or *Extraits de la Chanson de Roland*, publies par G. Paris, 11me edition, Paris (Hachette), 1911; or *La Chancun de Guillelme*, herausgegeben von H. Suchier, Halle (Niemeyer), 1911 (*Bibliotheca-Normannica*, VIII).

HISTORICAL SYNTAX OF THE FRENCH LANGUAGE. MR. MUELLER.

This course will trace the development of French sentence-structure from the Latin through the Old French period up to the Renaisance. Stress will be laid on the Old French word-order. Students should have a reading knowledge of Modern French and should know the essentials of Latin Grammar.

OLD PROVENCAL. MR. HILL.

Special attention will be paid to the linguistic differences between *la langue d'oc* and *la langue d'oil*. Some study will be made of the different dialects of Southern France. The early literary monuments will be used for illustration and practice will be given in the interpretation of the works of some of the troubadours. This course is primarily linguistic, but at the same time aims to give the foundation needed by those who desire to read the poetry of the troubadours. The course may be taken in conjunction with those in Old French, Old Spanish, Old Portuguese, or History of the Italian Language. A preliminary acquaintance with Vulgar Latin is desirable. A reading knowledge of German is essential. Text-books: Grandgent, *Outline of the Phonology and Morphology of Old Provencal*, Boston (Heath), 1905; Schultz-Gora, *Altprovencalisches Elementarbuch*, 3rd ed., Heidelberg (Winter), 1915; Anglade, *Grammaire de l'Ancien Provencal*, Paris (Klincksieck), 1921; Appel, *Provencalische Chrestomathie*, 4th ed., Leipzig (Reisland), 1912.

HISTORY OF THE ITALIAN LANGUAGE. MR. LIPARI.

Although the primary object of this course is to trace the origin and development of standard modern Italian as to pronunciation, vocabulary, forms, and syntax, it also aims to explain the factors that led to the supremacy of the Tuscan dialect over the other dialects of Italy, as well as to bring out the other elements—historical, cultural, and popular—that have contributed to the formation, stability, and flexibility of the "idioma gentile"; and it will include a discussion of the so-called language question, which from the thirteenth century almost to our own times has puzzled the Italian people and vexed men of letters. Informal talks and discussions based on outside assignments and accompanied by reading exercises in texts of the various periods, especially the early. A thorough command of modern Italian is presupposed, a good knowledge of classical and vulgar Latin is essential, and a reading knowledge of the other principal Romance languages as well as German is desirable. Text-books: (2) either F. D'Ovidio e W. Meyer-Luebke, *Grammatica Storica della Lingua e dei Dialetti Italiani*, translated by Polcari, 2nd ed., Milan (Hoepli), 1919; or Grandgent, *From Latin to Italian*, Cambridge (Harvard University Press), 1927; (2) Monaci, *Crestomazia Italiani dei Primi Secoli*, Citta di Castello (Lapi), 1912.

OLD SPANISH. MR. REED.

A study of the phonology and morphology with especial reference to the *Poema del Cid* and the *Conde Lucanor*. Text-books: Grandgent, *Vulgar Latin*, Heath. Ford, *Old Spanish Readings*, Ginn. M. Pidal, *Cantar de mio Cid*, Clasicos Castellanos edition, Editiones de la Lectura, Madrid; and *Gramatica elemental*.

OLD PORTUGUESE. MR. REED.

A study of its relation to the Spanish and Vulgar Latin and of its development from the early lyric through *Os Lusiadas*. Text-books: Grandgent, *Vulgar Latin*, Heath. Camoes. *Os Lusiadas*, Brockhaus, Leipzig. Hills. *Portuguese Grammar*, Heath.

EARLY IRISH. MR. DUNN.

This course will serve as an introduction to Celtic Philology. It will comprise an outline of Old Irish Grammar and the study of selections, beginning with the *Ogam* inscriptions of the fifth and sixth centuries, the glosses—chiefly from the Wuerzburg Manuscript—and the earliest literary texts, and extending to about the tenth century. If time allows, some portions of the heroic saga, *Tain Bo Cualnge*, as preserved in its earliest extant version, the Yellow Book of Lecan, and a Middle Irish text from the Book of Leinster will be interpreted. Text-books: *A Historical Reader of Old Irish*, by Pokorny, Halle, 1923; *An Early Irish Reader*, by Chadwick, Cambridge, 1927.

EARLY WELSH. MR. DUNN.

This, as well as the course in Early Irish, is an elementary class and will suffice as an introduction to the British group of Celtic, consisting of Welsh, Cornish, and Breton. It will include an outline of the grammar of mediaeval Welsh, with references to the older and more modern forms of the language, and the reading of selections in prose and verse from the ancient books of Celtic Britain. *An Introduction to Early Welsh*, by Strachan, Manchester, 1909, contains all the material needed.

GOTHIC AND COMPARATIVE GERMANIC PHILOLOGY. MR. COLLITZ.

Gothic is the most archaic branch of the Germanic group, and has been granted the place of honor among the Old Germanic tongues. Having largely retained the simple features of Primitive Germanic it serves to explain the more complicated conditions met with in languages like Old Norse, Anglo-Saxon, and Old High German. Hence we must turn to Gothic in order to gain a clear insight into matters of fundamental importance in the history of the Germanic languages, such as Grimm's, Verner's, and Westphal's Laws, the Germanic Ablaut, vowel "fracture," the "weak" declension, the "weak" conjugation, etc. While due attention will be paid to topics like those mentioned, the course will not be confined to a discussion of problems in Germanic grammar. It will be conducted primarily as a course in Gothic philology, so as to include, e. g., the necessary information on the Goths and the translation of the Bible into Gothic, as well as practice in pronunciation and critical reading. Students must be familiar with Latin, and they will perhaps find a knowledge of German and Greek no less helpful. As regards the latter, the Greek text of the New Testament has been called the best commentary of the Gothic translation, and the order of the Gothic letters is based on the Greek alphabet. Hence students should make an effort to master at least the Greek alphabet. W. Braune's *Gothic Grammar* will be used as a text-book, preferably in the latest German edition: *Gotische Grammatik, mit Lesestuecken and Wortverzeichnis*, 9 Auflage, Halle (Niemeyer), 1920 (price in publisher's binding $1.75). This edition may be procured from A. Bruderhausen, 47 W. 47th St., New York. An English translation of this grammar (*A Gothic Grammar*, with selections for reading and a glossary, by W. Braune, translated from the fourth German edition by Balg. Milwaukee) appeared in 1895. It may be had for $1 from B. Westermann-Lemcke and Buechner, New York.

OLD NORSE. MR. FLOM.

Phonology and grammar, in connection with the language of the oldest Runic inscriptions, 3rd-9th century; exércises; reading of selections from the sagas; script and orthography of the earliest manuscripts. A reading knowledge of Gerñan is desirable. Text-books: Noreen, *Altnordische Grammatik* 1. 4th ed., Halle, 1923; Gordon, *Introduction to Old Norse*, Oxford (Clarendon Press). Books recommended will be available on reserve.

OLD HIGH GERMAN. MR. SHUMWAY.

Lectures and detailed study of the grammar and dialects, and the interpretation of important prose and poetic monuments. Text-books: Braune, *Althochdeutsche Grammatik*, 3rd and 4th ed., Halle, 1925; Braune. *Althochdeutsches Lesebuch*, 8th ed., Halle, 1921.

HISTORY OF THE GERMAN LANGUAGE. MR. SHUMWAY.

Lectures and collateral reading on the development of the German language from the Indo-European through Primitive Germanic, West Germanic, Old High German, Middle High German, down to New High German, including the development of the New High German literary norm. No text-books required.

OLD ENGLISH. MR. MALONE.

The beginnings and early development of the English language will be studied. The study will be historical and comparative. No previous knowledge of Old English is required, but some knowledge of German is desirable. Textbooks: Moore and Knott. *Elements of Old English*, Ann Arbor (Wahr), 1919; Sedgefield, *Selections from the Old English Bede*, New York, 1917.

HISTORY OF THE ENGLISH LANGUAGE. MR. MALONE.

A study of the development and characteristics of the language from the earliest times to the present day, with particular attention to the modern period. Text-book: Jespersen, *Growth and Structure of the English Language*, 4th ed., Leipzig.

AMERICAN ENGLISH. MISS POUND.

A study of the development of the English language in the United States. The following are among the topics to be given attention: beginnings, relation to the mother tongue, pronunciation, expanding vocabulary, divergent usages, dialects, the common speech, slang, present tendencies, outlook. Lectures, reports, recitation. Text-books: Krapp, *The Pronunciation of Standard English in America*, New York (Oxford University Press), 1919; Mencken, *The American Language*, 3rd ed., New York (Knopf), 1923.

LITHUANIAN AND CHURCH SLAVONIC. MR. PROKOSCH.

An introduction to Balto-Slavic comparative grammar, based on the reading of Lithuanian and Church-Slavonic texts. Reading knowledge of German essential, acquaintance with Latin and Greek desirable. Text-books: Leskien, *Litauisches Lesebuch*, Heidelberg, 1919; Leskien

Handbuch der Altbulgarischen Sprache, Weimar, 1905.

HITTITE. MR. STURTEVANT.

Study of Hittite grammar in connection with the reading of texts; consideration of the relationship of Hittite to Indo-European. Students must have a reading knowledge of Latin, Greek, German, and French. A knowledge of Assyrian is desirable, but not necessary. Textbooks: Goetze, *Hattusilis, der Bericht ueber seine Thronbesteigung*, Leipzig (Hinrichs), 1925 (*Mitteilungen der Vorderasiatisch-Aegyptischen Gesellschaft*, 1924. (3); Sommer and Ehelolf, *Das Hethitische Ritual des Papanikri von Komana*, Leipzig (Hinrichs), 1924 (*Boghazkoei-Studien* 10); Hrozny, *Code Hittite*, Ire partie, Paris (Guthener), 1922. Students who desire practice in reading cuneiform texts should own also *Keilschrifttexte aus Boghazkoei*, fuenftes und sechstes Heft, Leipzig (Hinrichs), 1921; and Forrer, *Die Boghazkoei-Texte in Umschrift*, erster Band, Leipzig (Hinrichs), 1922.

COMPARATIVE GRAMMAR OF THE SEMITIC LANGUAGES. MR. BLAKE.

This course, after an introduction giving a general account of the various members of the Semitic family of speech, of the elements of phonetics, and of change in language, will comprise a comparative discussion of the most important phonetic laws, the most important forms, and the most important constructions of the Semitic languages, followed by the intensive study of some special topic of Comparative Semitic Grammar. Special stress will be laid on the acquisition by the student of the ability to reach independent conclusions on the basis of the linguistic material presented. A knowledge of at least one Semitic language is a prerequisite. No text-book is absolutely essential, but it is recommended that all students have Brockelmann, *Grundriss d. Vergleichenden Grammatik d. Semitischen Sprachen*, 2 vols., Berlin, 1908-1913.

HEBREW. MR. BLAKE.

This course will comprise a systematic study of the main features of Hebrew grammar (script, diacritical marks, phonology, morphology, and syntax), accompanied by grammatical explanations (descriptive and historical) based on Hebrew texts, and supplemented by the systematic study of vocabulary and idiom. Students will be trained in independent handling of grammatical and linguistic material. Text-books: (1) Gesenius-Kautsch. *Hebraeische Grammatik*, 28th ed., Leipzig, 1909 (or earlier edition, English or German); (2) either Gesenius-Buhl, *Handwoerterbuch ueber d. Alte Testament*, 17th ed., Leipzig, 1921 (or earlier edition); or Brown-Driver-Briggs, *A Hebrew and English Lexicon of the Old Testament*, Oxford, 1906.

ELEMENTARY ASSYRIAN. MR. DOUGHERTY.

An introduction to the main features of the Assyrian language. The course will include a consideration of the origin and development of cuneiform writing, a study of cuneiform signs, the reading of Assyrian historical texts, and a brief survey of Assyrian grammar. The text-book, Delitzsch, *Assyrische Lesestuecke*, 5th ed. Leipzig (Hinrichs), may be obtained from G. E. Stechert and Co., 33 E. 10th St., New York.

ELEMENTARY ARABIC. MR. DOUGHERTY.

An introduction to the general principles of the Arabic language. Stress will be placed upon the elements of Arabic grammar and upon the reading of selected passages which will familiarize the student with the written and linguistic forms of the Arabic branch of Semitic speech. The text-book will be Socin. *Arabic Grammar*, English edition, revised by W. H. Worrell, New York (Stechert).

TURKISH. MR. REUNING.

An elementary course in Ottoman Turkish, which will provide a foundation for a scientific study of Turkish grammar. Text-book: Hagopian. *Ottoman-Turkish Conversation Grammar*, Heidelberg (Groos), 1907.

Bulletin 2, dated September 1928, is entirely devoted to the Record of the First Session of the Linguistic Institute and is 20 pages long, far too bulky for complete printing here; still, since LSA Bulletins are not included in the arrangements for re-printing Language itself and the Monographs, we cannot avoid reporting its messages sufficiently to enable our readers to form a usable picture of the events. We present rearranged details, including who taught what to whom, and the Public Lectures — one feature of this and every subsequent Institute to the present day which had not been promised but instead emerged from current planning during the months of January through May 1928, with re-planning week by week during the whole six weeks as one promised Lecture had to be cancelled and replaced on short notice, generally without leaving a trace of the sequence of events in the materials available to us today. Just one eyewitness is known to have survived into 1974 at least: Dr. Karl Reuning wrote to Martin Joos from his retirement home in Sarasota, Florida, in response to Joos queries, and is our authority for certain matters of emphasis and clarification. He is our witness that Carl Darling Buck (University of Chicago) had long previously decided to spend the whole Summer of 1928 in New Haven in any case, Institute or no Institute, and arrived early with the fixed purpose of teaching gratis if needed. And Reuning turns out to have been a close friend of the remarkable Reinhold Eugene Saleski and has assured us that no promise of pay was ever needed to induce Saleski to offer any of his numerous specialities. Finally, Reuning's letter of February 1974 says, 'I have reason to believe that Aurelia Scott, wife of Kenneth Scott, is alive. I lived in the same house with them at 516 Orange Street.' [See below for the name.]

The following Faculty membership list replaces that printed on page 19 above; a + sign is prefixed to a name added, = marks a name duplicated, * for special notes:

= Frank Ringgold Blake, Ph.D., Associate Professor of Oriental Languages in the Johns Hopkins University, Baltimore, Maryland; Courses 35s, 36.

= George Melville Bolling, Ph.D., Professor of Greek in the Ohio State University, Columbus, Ohio; Courses 11, 12.

* Carl Darling Buck, Ph.D., Professor of Comparative Philology in the University of Chicago, Chicago, Illinois; *no scheduled course, but Public Lecture 27 July.

= Hermann Collitz, Ph.D., Professor Emeritus of Germanic Philology in The Johns Hopkins University, Baltimore, Maryland; Course 25; Lecture 10 Aug.

= Raymond Philip Dougherty, Ph.D., Professor of Assyriology and Babylonian Literature in Yale University, New Haven, Connecticut; Courses 37, 38.

= Joseph Dunn, Ph.D., Professor of Celtic Languages and Literatures in the Catholic University of America, Washington, D.C.; Courses 23, 24.

= Franklin Edgerton, Ph.D., Professor of Sanskrit and Comparative Philology in Yale University, New Haven, Connecticut; Courses 8, 9°; Lecture 7 Aug.

= Herbert Charles Elmer, Ph.D., Professor Emeritus of Latin in Cornell University, Ithaca, New York; Course 15.

= George T. Flom, Ph.D., Professor of Scandinavian Languages and Literature in the University of Illinois, Urbana, Illinois; Course 26.

* Pliny E. Goddard, Curator of Ethnology, American Museum of Natural History in New York. Died Friday 13 July; see later notes.

+ Willem L. Graff, Ph.D., Assistant Professor of Germanics at McGill University, Montreal, Canada. No registrant in his course 29.

= Raymond Thompson Hill, Ph.D., Associate Professor of French at Yale University, New Haven, Connecticut; Courses 16, 19.

= Roland Grubb Kent, Ph.D., Professor of Comparative Philology at the University of Pennsylvania, Philadelphia, Pennsylvania; Courses 13, 14; Lecture 'The Conquests of the Latin Language' Friday 13 July.

= Angelo Lipari, Ph.D., Associate Professor of Italian in Yale University, New Haven, Connecticut; Course 20.

* Henry Roseman Lang, Professor Emeritus of Romance Languages and Literature, Yale University; Course 17 announced, resigned: See Mueller!

= Kemp Malone, Ph.D., Associate Professor of English in The Johns Hopkins University, Baltimore, Maryland; Courses 30, 31; Lecture 20 July.

+ John Alden Mason, Ph.D., Curator of the American Section of the University of Pennsylvania Museum, Philadelphia, Pennsylvania; Course 7.

= Otto Mueller, Ph.D., Professor of Romance Languages at Gettysburg College, Gettysburg, Pennsylvania; Courses 17, 18.

= Louise Pound, Ph.D., Professor of the English Language at the University of
  Nebraska, Lincoln, Nebraska; Course 32s.

= Edward Prokosch, Ph.D., Professor of Germanic Philology at the New York
  University, New York City; Courses 1, 1s, 33s; Lecture 24 July.

= Frank Otis Reed, Ph.D., Professor of Spanish at the University of Arizona,
  Tucson, Arizona; Courses 21, 22.

= Karl Reuning, Ph.D., Lektor für Anglistik at the University of Breslau,
  Breslau, Germany; Course 5; Lecture 31 July.

= G. Oscar Russell, Ph.D., Assistant Professor of Romance Languages at the
  Ohio State University, Columbus, Ohio; Courses 2, 3; Lecture 17 July.

* Reinhold Eugene Saleski, Ph.D., Professor of German at Bethany College,
  Bethany, West Virginia; No Course, but Lecture 3 August.*Volunteered.

= Daniel Bussier Shumway, Ph.D., Professor of Germanic Philology at the
  University of Pennsylvania, Philadelphia, Pennsylvania; Course 28.

= Edgar Howard Sturtevant, Ph.D., Professor of Linguistics and Comparative
  Philology at Yale University, New Haven, Connecticut; Courses 10, 34.

COURSES AND REGISTRANTS

1. Prokosch: Introduction to Linguistic Science. Registrants: Bauer, Schuster,
   Stimson, Wyatt, Zieglschmid; also, 1s only, Flom, Miss Franklin.
2. Russell: Philological Phonetics. Reg: Miss Avery, Schuster.
3. Russell: Experimental Phonetics. Reg: Miss Avery.
4. Petersen: Semantics. Withdrawn, Petersen unable to come: illness.
5. Reuning: Some Recent Theories of Linguistic Science. Reg: Schuster, Stimson.
6. Goddard: Linguistic Anthropology. Withdrawn, Goddard fatally ill.
7. Mason: Methods of Studying Unrecorded Languages. Reg: Stimson.
8. Edgerton: Sanskrit. Reg: Stimson.
9. Edgerton: Pali. Reg: none [presumably because offered as an 'alternate']
10. Sturtevant: Comparative Grammar of Greek and Latin. Reg: Griffin,
    Miss Kinnirey, Owen, Miss Turnbull.
11. Bolling: Greek Dialects. Reg: Miss Franklin, Griffin, Latimer, Miss McCarthy,
    Rowell.
12. Bolling: The Language of the Homeric Poems. Reg: Miss Franklin.
13. Kent: Oscan and Umbrian. Reg: Cross, Scott.
14. Kent: Old Latin and its Development into Classical Latin. Reg: Miss Kinnirey,
    Owen, Poynter, Strodach, Miss Turnbull.
15. Elmer: Latin Syntax. Reg: Miss Jones, Murray, Poynter.
16. Hill: Vulgar Latin and Introduction to Romance Philology. Reg: Miss Allsop,
    Darby, Will.
17. Mueller: Old French Phonology and Morphology. Reg: Miss Alsop, Darby,
    March, Miss Wright.
18. Mueller: Historical Syntax of the French Language. Reg: Richardson.
19. Hill: Old Provençal. Reg: Bates, Rowell.
20. Lipari: History of the Italian Language. Reg: Mangano.
21. Reed: Old Spanish. Reg: Goldiere.
22. Reed: Old Portuguese. Reg: none.
23. Dunn: Early Irish. Reg: Miss Greer, Kerns, Miss Miller.
24. Dunn: Early Welsh. Reg: Rice.
25. Collitz: Gothic and Comparative Germanic Philology. Reg: Bauer, Mrs. Col-
    litz, Cross, Miss Field, Kerns, Stutzmann.
26. Flom: Old Norse. Reg: Peterson.
27. Shumway: Old High German. Reg: none.
28. Shumway: History of the German Language. Reg: Frantz, Stutzmann, Ziegl-
    schmid.
29. Graff: History of the Dutch Language. Reg: none.
30. Malone: Old English. Reg: Peterson, Riker.
31. Malone: History of the English Language. Reg: Riker.
32. Miss Pound: American English. Reg: for 32s only, Flom, Miss Greer, Miss
    Miller, Peterson.
33. Prokosch: Lithuanian and Church Slavonic. Reg: for 33s only, Kerns.
34. Sturtevant: Hittite. Reg: none.

35. Blake: Comparative Grammar of the Semitic Languages. Reg: for 35s only, Saleski, Sturtevant.
36. Blake: Hebrew. Reg: Wyatt.
37. Dougherty: Assyrian. Reg: none.
38. Dougherty: Arabic. Reg: Bellinger.
39. Reuning: Turkish. Reg: Mrs. Collitz, Rice.

REGISTRANTS: Backgrounds & Choices

Grace W. Allsop, M.A. (Brown), graduate student at Brown University; 55 Roslyn Avenue, Providence, Rhode Island. Reg: 16, 17.

Elizabeth Avery, Ph.D. (New York University), Professor of Spoken English at Smith College; 370 Sanford Ave., Flushing, New York City. Reg: 2, 3.

Robert C. Bates, A.B. (Yale), graduate student at Yale University; 139 E. 66th St., New York City. Reg: 19.

Charles F. Bauer, A.B. (Franklin and Marshall), teacher of Latin in William Penn Charter School, Philadelphia; Slatington, Pennsylvania. Reg: 1, 25.

Alfred R. Bellinger, Ph.D. (Yale), Assistant Professor of Greek and Latin at Yale University; 234 Fountain St., New Haven, Connecticut. Reg: 38.

Klara H. Collitz, Ph.D. (Heidelberg), author; 1027 N. Calvert St., Baltimore, Maryland. Reg: 25, 39.

Ephraim Cross, A.M. (Columbia), teacher of Modern Languages in the New York High Schools; 1299 Franklin Ave., Bronx, New York City. Reg: 13, 25.

George Odell Switzer Darby, M.A. (Wisconsin), instructor in Harvard University; 50 Linden St., Wellesley, Massachusetts. Reg: 16, 17.

Georgia L. Field, Ph.D. (University of Colorado), Professor of English Literature in Elmira College; 32 N. Prospect St., Amherst, Mass. Reg: 25.

George T. Flom, Ph.D., Professor of Scandinavian Languages and Literature in the University of Illinois; 611 W. Green St., Urbana, Illinois. Reg: 1s, 32s.

A. Mildred Franklin, Ph.D. (Columbia), Professor of Classics at Wilson College; Atlantic Highlands, New Jersey. Reg: 11, 12, 1s.

Adolf I. Frantz, M.A. (Stanford), graduate student in German at Yale University; 146 Tremont St., Ausonia, Connecticut. Reg: 28.

Augustin V. Goldiere, A.M. (Yale), Associate Professor of Spanish in Davidson College; Davidson, North Carolina. Reg: 21.

Willem L. Graff, Ph.D. (Louvain), Assistant Professor of Germanics at McGill University; 1421 Queen Mary Road, Montreal, Canada. Research.

Ida May Greer, M.A. (Iowa), Instructor of English and German at the South Dakota State College; Brookings, South Dakota. Reg: 23, 32s.

Mack Hall Griffin, M.A. (North Carolina), Instructor in Latin and Greek at the University of North Carolina; Chapel Hill, North Carolina. Reg: 10, 11.

Mildred Hathaway Jones, A.B. (Middlebury), teacher of Latin in the Mansfield High School; 74 Pleasant St., Mansfield, Massachusetts. Reg: 15.

J. Alexander Kerns, A.M. (Michigan), Assistant Professor of Latin at Whitman College; 123 Park St., Walla Walla, Washington. Reg: 23, 25, 33s.

John Francis Latimer, M.A. (Chicago), Instructor in Classics at Vanderbilt University; Clinton, Mississippi. Reg: 11.

Helen Kinnirey, M.A. (Columbia), instructor at Trinity College, Washington, D.C.; 186 Liberty St., Middletown, Connecticut. Reg: 10, 14.

Mary S. Lee, A.M. (Pennsylvania), teacher of Latin and Greek in the West Philadelphia High School; 879 Wynnewood Ave., Philadelphia, Penn. Research.

Barbara P. McCarthy, A.M. (Missouri), graduate student in classics as Yale University; 30 Armington Ave., Providence, Rhode Island. Reg: 11.

Antonia Mangano, A.M. (Columbia), teacher of Italian in the Colgate Theological Seminary; Hamilton, New York. Reg: 20.

H. M. March, A.B. (Princeton), Instructor at Yale University; 6 Barnett St., New Haven, Connecticut. Reg: 17

Anna Irene Miller, Ph.D. (Radcliffe), Associate Professor of English in Goucher College, and Instructor in the College for Teachers of The Johns Hopkins University, 1919 Eutaw Place, Baltimore, Maryland. Reg: 23, 32s.

Francis King Murray, A.B. (Stanford), instructor in the Phillips Andover Academy; 23 Salem St., Andover, Massachusetts. Reg: 15.

Eivion Owen, M.A. (Oxford), graduate student in classics at Harvard University; Cambridge, Massachusetts. Reg: 10, 14.

Frederick W. Peterson, M.A. (Michigan), Assistant Professor of Rhetoric at the
    University of Michigan; Foster Road, Ann Arbor, Mich.   Reg: 26, 30, 32s.
Horace Martin Poynter, A.B. (Yale), Instructor in Latin at Phillips Academy,
    Andover; Phelps House, Andover, Massachusetts.   Reg: 14, 15.
Allen Lake Rice, M.A. (Pennsylvania), graduate student in Germanics at the
    University of Pennsylvania; 4217 Osage Ave., Philadelphia. Reg: 24, 39.
Henry Brush Richardson, Ph.D. (Yale), Assistant Professor of French at
    Yale University; 50 Pendleton St., New Haven, Connecticut. Reg: 18.
Charles Cook Riker, Jr., B.A. (Kenyon), head of the department of English,
    DeVeaux School, Niagara Falls, New York; 500 E. Erie St., Painesville,
    Ohio.   Reg: 30, 31.
Henry Thompson Rowell, B.A. (Yale), Instructor in Latin at Yale University;
    242 York St., New Haven, Connecticut.   Reg: 11, 19.
Reinhold Eugene Saleski, Ph.D. ([Leipzig/Freiburg]), Professor of German,
    Bethany College, Bethany, West Virginia.   Reg: 35s.
Carl Schuster, A.B. (Harvard), graduate student at Harvard University; 683
    Hackett Ave., Milwaukee, Wisconsin.   Reg: 1, 2, 5.
John Francis Stimson, Research Associate in Ethnology and Linguistics,
    Berenice P. Bishop Museum, Honolulu, Hawaii; Boîte 59, Papeete, Tahiti
    (South Sea Islands).   Reg: 1, 5, 7, 8.
George K. Strodach, A.B. (Pennsylvania), Assistant in Latin at the University of
    Pennsylvania; 6906 Henley St., Mt. Airy, Philadelphia.   Reg: 14.
E. H. Sturtevant, Ph.D. (Chicago), Professor of Linguistics and Comparative
    Philology, Yale University, New Haven, Connecticut.   Reg: 35s.
L. L. Stutzmann, B.A. (Gettysburg), Teacher of German in Schuylkill College;
    125 Railroad St., Palmyra, Pennsylvania.   Reg: 25, 28.
Pauline Turnbull, B.A. (Syracuse), Assistant Professor of Latin at West-
    hampton College, Richmond, Virginia.   Reg: 10, 14.
Samuel F. Will, M.A. (Indiana), Instructor in French at Yale University; 251 E.
    Rock Road, New Haven, Connecticut.   Reg: 16.
Jean Gray Wright, M.A. (Pennsylvania), graduate student at Bryn Mawr College;
    Lincoln University, Pennsylvania.   Reg: 17.
William F. Wyatt, Ph.D. (Harvard), Professor of Greek at Tufts College; Tufts
    College, Massachusetts.   Reg: 1, 28.

PUBLIC LECTURES

The following public lectures were delivered in the evening, at Harkness
Recitation Hall:

July 13: Mr. Kent, The Conquests of the Latin Language.
July 17: Mr. Russell, The Fallacy of the Vowel Triangle (illustrated).
July 20: Mr. Malone, The Problem of Standard English.
July 24: Mr. Prokosch, The Origin and Trend of Vowel Mutation in Germanic.
July 27: Mr. Buck, The History of Ideas and Changes in Vocabulary.
July 31: Mr. Reuning, Syntactical Influences upon the Present Inflection in
                      Middle English.
August 3: Mr. Saleski, Chinese for Grammarians.
August 7: Mr. Edgerton, The Languages of India.
August 14: Mr. Collitz, Some Fundamental Notions in Linguistics.
August 17: Mr. Bolling, Some Aspects of the Homeric Question.

None of those Public Lectures has been published. The notion of presenting
a publishable paper, or one easily edited for publication, is a far later innovation
with only one point in its favor: a neophyte can prepare one. The 1928 Public Lectures were all spoken from more or less detailed notes, and the best of them in
an offhand fashion by men accustomed to give-and-take interaction with both the
make-up and the mood of their audience controlling what they said phrase by
phrase, and ready to drop out blocks of text or to improvise as called for; they
differed mostly in the relative weights they assigned to the several components
of those Linguistic Institute audiences.

Dr. Reuning's letter says, 'the ten public lectures were attended by many
local people'—that is, the 'town' moiety of the New Haven 'town and gown' complex
—'and by reporters for newspapers. One lecture by Kemp Malone drew nation-

wide attention because he had recommended the use of "it is me" instead of "it is I". Some of his mail suggested that Johns Hopkins ought to fire him. I myself, after my own public lecture, was violently attacked by G. M. Bolling because I had doubted "die absolute Ausnahmslosigkeit der Lautgesetze." When Prokosch defended my point of view, which I had illustrated with certain M[iddle] E[nglish] examples, there was quite a row in the best German tradition.'

In the same letter we learn a number of things in response to requests for memories of the 1928 LI personalities; most of those things will be reported in suitable contexts when their careers are dealt with later in this History, such as the Reuning and Edgerton expedition to Ellis Island to extract Alfred Senn from detention while under suspicions of being an impostor or an agent of some foreign power. For the 1928 Linguistic Institute itself, he tells us that Bolling was horrified at hearing the traditional vowel triangle called into question in the Russell Lecture of July 17th. On Daniel Bussier Shumway, Reuning says, 'I knew Professor Shumway well because he was one of our neighbors at the University of Pennsylvania. He was one of the finest and kindest gentlemen I had the good fortune to know. Another scholar who was liked by everybody was Professor [Franklin] Edgerton. — Collitz's theory of the influence of climate on sound changes, e.g. explanation of the second soundshift [which resulted in High German Pfeffer rather than the pepper retained in English and Low German] as brought about by the necessity to breathe harder in the mountains of Southern Germany and Switzerland, was very much debated at that time. ... The Collitz theory was very much supported by [John Francis] Stimson, who claimed that native languages in the South Pacific have those same sounds where the inhabitants are exposed to regular strong winds. Really, the LI was a lot of fun, and I enjoyed it thoroughly, also the one held in New York in 1930, which was quite different in many ways.'

Kent's Report on the 1928 Institute ends with Sturtevant's Financial Report:

Receipts:

Subvention from Carnegie Corporation of New York	2500.00	
Other donations	210.00	
Institute Fees and Course Fees	3440.00	
Interest on bank balances to July 31	6.10	6156.15

Disbursements:

Salaries	5440.00	
Library fees and stipend of attendant	152.00	
Printing and mailing of circulars	377.62	
Office Expenses	52.44	
Interest paid on loans from bank	22.46	6144.52
Balance on hand, August 18, 1928		11.63

No amount of historical research could uncover the significant human events behind this little fraud. For example, there was no accounting made of Sturtevant family cash outlays and unpaid labor, just a laconic acknowledgement in Kent's narrative for August 9th saying that the Director's wife and daughter had rendered 'constant help with the arrangements, clerical and otherwise' at the end of the Institute session and of course the beginning when on the 'evening of Tuesday 10th July the Director and Mrs. Sturtevant entertained' at the Church-Wall Tea Room. There was a traditional tacit assumption that only a man with Family Money could assume the burdens of a Yale Professor's social duties: tales were told of refusals of promotion from Associate Professor motivated by the lack thereof. For us, the thing to remember is that Sturtevant generosity is what made the early Linguistic Institutes appear cheap and simple to manage.

Next we look at Secretary Kent's summary characterization of this the very first Linguistic Institute. We note first that the total 'membership' of this first Institute, after discounting for duplications, was sixty-five. We continue quoting in full, remarking that the statement was surely rewritten and discussed with all the deliberate thought of a Supreme Court decision:

The number is, in one way, not impressive, and yet in another way it is very significant. A school with only two students to every teacher [1976 note: actually 43 students for courses plus two for research only, against 23 listed Faculty plus three members of the Administrative Committee] must be branded a failure. But it was not as a school that the Institute was first conceived; it was planned to be a conference of scholars in a special field, and the courses were an addition to the plan to ensure the attendance of the scholars in some definite capacity, either as teachers or as pupils. And yet, as was hoped, many of the 'courses' took the form of conferences, where in a group of two or three persons every one contributed his share and every one learned from every other, whichever one might be the nominal leader of the group. There was an unusually sympathetic scholarly atmosphere about the courses, and the remarkable earnestness of the students resulted in obviously unusual profits to them. Not the least valuable of the activities of the Institute was the gathering of small informal groups to discuss linguistic problems quite apart from the times and places of the scheduled courses; and in these, from time to time, virtually every one participated.

We pause to remind readers that the Report was written during the long since forgotten Prohibition period and was for the eyes of not simply our own Linguistic Society members and their associates but also for stiffly starched members of the Yale Corporation. Any printed allusion, however discreet or veiled, to the accessibility of 'drink' within or near the sacred precincts could spoil the chances for a 1929 Institute in New Haven. Actually, the hard drinkers were a vanishingly small minority, and 'drugs' were foreign to the scene. Not cannabis indica but nicotiana tobacum was lavishly employed to saturate the air with its incense of good fellowship wherever those 'small informal groups' held their all-hours gatherings, notably just after the break-up of every Public Lecture Discussion period and serving to continue the discussion without restraint and within face-to-face groups; non-smokers were few, and many of 'the girls' had become smokers simply in self-defense. The per-capita ingestion of the forbidden ethanol, suitably flavored and discussed along with linguistic topics, in close sequence or simultaneously, in the course of any one gathering of the sort in which 'virtually every one participated' was what probably would now be called 'two drinks'—nothing to worry a spouse or a parent. The footnote to the Bloch Obituary, Language 43.6 (1967), belongs to a quite different sort of milieu, Chicago's Near North Side, which corresponded fairly well to Greenwich Village in lower Manhattan, that haunt of sin. New Haven was different. Did none of the Faculty ever visit spots where one went for 'serious drinking' such as were numerous within a few minutes' walk from Harkness Recitation Hall? Not many, surely, because they were noisy and crowded and too dimly lighted for phonetic discussions accompanied by suitable diagrams and demonstrations.

That 1928 Institute inaugurated nearly the whole inner form and a good many of the traditional details for the Society's warm seasons generally, even during the Second World War in most respects. While the activities of the cooler and the cold months have tended to run in the patterns established by the first Editor and the first Secretary-Treasurer, with adjustments of course but without any revolutionary alterations before the 1960's, the Linguistic Institutes have been variously innovative and yet have maintained a stable core of traditional doings: whenever the scheduled employments of time seemed about to eliminate one or another of the traditional social events, experienced members seem to create a hiatus-filler almost overnight. In short, the first Linguistic Institute gave us an inner form and a corporate style for all the decades since. Sturtevant, the man who did more than any other person to set the tone of the 1928 'First Session of the Linguistic Institute', looked forward to the Second Session with well-founded confidence; and the Executive Committee and elder statesmen supported all of his schemes as far as we can discover, while he supported and harmonized theirs so smoothly that even the two-day Conference on a Linguistic Atlas on the 2nd and 3rd of August, 1929, which we shall see was an essentially upsetting affair, turns out in retrospect to have been a fullfilment of potentials instead.

For 1929, again at Yale, the advance commitments of philanthropic money were at least $2,000 greater than the Carnegie Corporation's 1928 subvention. The new plans promised to go far beyond the 1928 ones in the sense of surely attracting not merely some forty persons who came for study without a Faculty appointment, but say eighty or a hundred. Instead, the total registration was fifty-two, classed as 26 scheduled teachers plus 26 non-teaching students, not counting those reported as present only for the two-day Atlas Conference: without further evidence, we can still reasonably suppose that a good many of the Conference people arrived some days or weeks earlier, especially because of the Yale University Library's availability (and its extended hours arranged for the sake of Institute students) or even took up residence: on the list of Conference 'Members' included in Bulletin No. 4 we can find key names listed in alphabetic sequence to a total of 52, and in reprinting that on page 32 here we marginally report how many lines of Kurath's report are filled by each man's words: Professor Dorothy J. Kaucher, of Wells College, was the only woman, and she apparently did not speak out in the meeting. Still, we must remind ourselves that the ultimately printed report was derived from more than one source and was drastically condensed.

For this Second Session of the Linguistic Institute, 1929, instead of the 1928 ratio of two students to one teacher, the ratio had become one-to-one: instead of a reasonably anticipated doubling or tripling of just plain students, there was an intensely disconcerting shrinkage, an apparent failure of New Haven drawing power. What had gone wrong? Reasons that actually proved decisive, person by person among the hundreds to whom a Linguistic Institute ought to have appealed, are irrecoverable for obvious reasons: they would lie hidden in private letters and diaries of every sort of person who mostly never got listed as an LSA member anyhow. Fortunately, it is possible to reconstruct some of the motivations in documentable marginal cases. Two factors will suffice on the present pages.

First, there was the crescendo of speculative fever, a rising wave of easy-money hysteria which, still rising, ultimately broke within a few weeks after the end of this 1929 Institute and has become famous as the The Great Crash. A great many students of all ages, especially such as still had relative freedom of choice for the months of July and August, were saying to themselves, 'Institutes and the like we can always visit in other years; this year is the time to get some of that free-floating folding money, perhaps even make a killing!' Second, Director Sturtevant, perpetually young at heart, was twice as old as those youngsters. For all his empathy with them in the contacts he had, he was too remote from their motivations as students (he himself when not yet 18 years old 'had performed the extraordinary task of teaching himself Sanskrit' according to his biography by E. Adelaide Hahn, one of his favorite pupils at Columbia University: See Language 28.418 [1952]) to be able to guess at what they would most like to do when free of scheduled obligations. So confident was Sturtevant of the positive values of a Yale ambience that he failed to see what it meant in August.

New Haven in a warm summer is simply unbearably stodgy, and the University itself cannot make up for that. In 1929, as in 1928, the Residences, and the spill-over into non-Yale rooming houses and apartments, continued their usual pattern of estivation. That pattern distinguished sharply between mid-week and week-end occupations. Mid-week is the time for either doing or neglecting that promised studying; week-end is the time for getting away from all that. Air-conditioning had been heard of, but the normal escape from heat was in mountains or on the sea-shore — see p. 19b, 'place': The sea breezes are very agreeable in summer, and a number of salt-water bathing beaches are within reach. — In the 1920's the city street-cars and the inter-urban electrified rail lines constituted a continuous and fine-meshed network of inland transportation independent of paved highways and extending without a break from the Hudson River over all but the most dismal patches of the six northeastern states ('New England') and personal automobiles and the newly developing Greyhound Bus system traversed most terrain where the electric cars found grades too steep. Thus there was occupation enough for young people to fill the warm week-ends without taking root in New Haven or wherever. Though evening-by-evening attendance statistics have not survived, we have heard that the Friday Public Lecture attendance in 1928 averaged less than half the Tuesday attendance, and from what we know of the tropisms of youngsters generally that does sound likely. Despite all encouragements, the Friday evening Lectures still did not draw: one automatically did what enterprising students do with a free week-end—one decamped with one or three companions, and on the Sunday was distant from Yale by from 30 to 300 miles (or 50 to 500 kilometers). 'That's what everybody does at Yale, and why don't they have the second Public Lecture on Thursdays if they really want us to come?'

Finally, on the more remote campuses from which more students were to be attracted for the 1929 Second Session, there was a complex of a great many sorts of reasons for not going to New Haven, partly jealousy and regional loyalties, partly a sober calculation that revived awareness of local possibilities. We can easily reconstruct a typical case, choosing to center it at the University of Wisconsin at Madison because that campus is familiar to the writer. The prospective but not actual student may be called Mr. Normal, and he is being modeled on two or three close acquaintances of the present writer in those years; Mr. Normal is not Martin Joos, for Joos spent the 15 months June 1928 through August 1929 in the Hawthorne plant on the western edge of Chicago, working as Junior Engineer of Manufacture designing improved telephone equipments in the laboratories of the Western Electric Company and saving up for two final years in Madison.

During the last few months of 1928, and in any case by the middle of December, Mr. Normal learned enough about the Linguistic Institute's First Session so that he set about consulting Madison experts, both Faculty and student experts, since on whatever North American campus you may be you can find plenty of students to tell you about Yale and New Haven and how far it unfortunately is from New York. He finds that three of the four Faculty members he consults readily point out that right there in Madison he can take courses and seminars, even during Summer Session, with Classics Professor Laird who taught Leonard Bloomfield Sanskrit, with English Professor William Ellery Leonard who never leaves the area in any season and teaches Beowulf and Old Norse to groups or to single students who come to him, and in Spanish (and so of course Arabic) an impressive staff headed by Solalinde and including C. D. Cool who brought back from Manila a great deal of Indonesian expertise. Or if Mr. Normal simply wants to get away from Madison for the hot weather, we'll write to introduce him at, say, Ann Arbor where they have the world's most powerful English Department, or Northwestern North of Chicago where the Crerar and the Newberry libraries are way-stations down to the University of Chicago campus where Leonard Bloomfield is located, or even to Minneapolis where the University of Minnesota is very respectable and Professor Stephenson says he'll have a couple of Canadian linguists visiting for the 1929 Summer Session. Still, if you want New Haven after all, . . .

For the 1929 Linguistic Institute, we begin our narrative with the eleven Public Lectures, because this sequence will result in greatest coherence and clarity:

July   13: Mr. Sturtevant, The History and Prehistory of the Hittites
July   16: Mr. Blake, The Practical Value of General Comparative Syntax
July   19: Mr. Jackson, A Sketch of Manichaeism (illustrated [with lantern slides])
July   23: Mr. Müller, The Linguistic Theories of the Geneva School
July   26: Mr. Curme, Historical Relations of American English to British English
July   30: Mr. Kurath, Some Phases of American Intonation
August 2: Mr. Stephenson, The Influence of Movements of Population upon
           Mr. Russell, Mechanical Methods of   American Dialects
                             Recording Speech
August 9: Mr. Kent, 'No Trespass' in Latin Linguistics
           Mr. Fansler, The Development of English in the Philippines
August 13: Mr. Peterson, The Declension of the Indo-European Personal Pronoun

Two head-names will serve to group the memorable students according to those personal interests which attracted each to the 1929 Linguistic Institute:

George Melville Bolling gave two courses: (a) Beginning Greek for Linguists, with two registrants, (1) a New Jersey teacher of Latin, (2) Miles L. Hanley, M.A. (Harvard), Assistant Professor of English at the University of Wisconsin, the only person to register for more than four courses: he was also in Russell's Philological Phonetics, Russell's Speech Articulation and Auricular Training, Edgerton's Sanskrit, and Kent's Comparative Grammar of Greek and Latin; and (b) The Language of the Homeric Poems, with two registrants, both women, who drop out of the reckoning without leaving any trace in our Society's subsequent history.

Hans Kurath, born in Austria in 1891, came to Milwaukee in 1907 to study at the German-American Teacher Seminary, then to Madison in 1912 for the last Wisconsin year in the Prokosch career; in 1913 both men moved to the University of Texas, and Kurath's A.B. from Texas is dated 1914. His Ph.D. from the University of Chicago was awarded in 1920; his teaching during 1920 to 1927 was in the Northwestern University German Department where George Oliver Curme, Professor of Germanic Philology, whose Grammar of the German Language, 1905, New York: Macmillan, pp. xii, 662, was being revised with the help of young colleagues, used Kurath as one of his consultants. Now that German work was a fraction of the total that occupied Curme; the totality apparently was some sort of comparative grammar of the Germanic languages or at least of German and English and perhaps also Dutch, emphasizing their most recent decades, and involving William Frank Bryan in the English Department: see our Index for all the names and note particularly the top half of page 12 above. In 1929 Kurath was a widower twice over and was courting the young daughter of Professor Prokosch, Gertrude, whom he married in 1930. In the 1929 Linguistic Institute, Kurath gave one course, American Pronunciation, with two registrants: (1) Stefán Einarsson, (2) Dorothy Kaucher, Cornell Ph.D. and now Assistant Professor of English in Wells College, who was also registered (a) in Russell's Speech Articulation and Auricular Training where Hanley also was, and (b) in the Experimental Phonetics of Milton J. Metfessel, National Research Council Fellow in Psychology at the State University of Iowa. At the same time, Kurath also registered as a student in two courses, (a) Otto Müller's Linguistic Geography of France where Edwin Carl Roedder was the other registrant, and (b) Roedder's The Study of Dialects, in which Saleski was Kurath's fellow student. By that time, Roedder was Professor of Germanics at the College of the City of New York, his last academic post; his second-last, 1899 to 1928, was where Roedder became a sponsor and admirer of Prokosch, and in the Spring Semester of his last year had Joos as student in Elementary German and taught us all to call him 'Onkel Edwin' and say 'du' to him by rule.

Obviously the recruitment of Linguistic Institute Faculty for 1929 was largely shaped in anticipation of the Conference to be held to fill the first week-end of August. LSA Bulletin No. 4, after printing Kent's secretarial Record of the 1929 Second Session in 20 pages, goes on for 28 further pages signed by Kurath under the agreed title 'The Conference on a Linguistic Atlas of the United States and Canada ... Sponsored by the American Council of Learned Societies' and begins with a cryptic reference to 'a number of scholars' preparing a 25-page typed Circular and sending that out early in May to a large number of linguists with a request for criticism and suggestions which brought a liberal response. With incorporation of materials thus procured, the Circular in its final form was mailed early in June to an unpublished list of addressees. We can guess that invitees were offered travel and subsistence money by the ACLS, and also that there were not many interested persons whose names are absent from the final list of 'Members of the Conference who were present by invitation' to which we have marginally noted the number of lines of print which are credited to each person who spoke in the condensed reports printed by Kurath. We find Kurath listed for (roughly) 121 printed lines, and G. Oscar Russell for 61 lines, Hanley and Moore for 45 lines each, with George Philip Krapp fifth with 41 lines and no one else with more than 25 lines. The Atlas naming that includes Canada fits with the inclusion of Professor H. S. Alexander (mistakenly 'H. T.' there) and Professor C. H. Carruthers whose son was a Toronto student under Joos.

[Pages 21, end, and page 22, of Bulletin No. 4, issued September, 1929, keyed:]

2	Prof. H. T. (for S.) Alexander, Queens University, Kingston, Canada.
11	Prof. Edward C. Armstrong, Princeton University.
16	Prof. H. M. Ayers, Columbia University.
4	Prof. Frank R. Blake, Johns Hopkins University.
21	Prof. Leonard Bloomfield, University of Chicago.
11	Prof. G. M. Bolling, Ohio State University.
15	Prof. W. F. Bryan, Northwestern University.
4	Prof. C. D. Buck, University of Chicago.
0	Mr. P. W. Carhart, Springfield, Mass. [The G. & C. Merriam Company]
10	Prof. C. H. Carruthers, McGill University, Montreal, Canada.
8	Prof. George O. Curme, Northwestern University.
0	Prof. R. P. Dougherty, Yale University.
0	Prof. Joseph Dunn, Catholic University. [Washington, D. C.]
10	Prof. Franklin Edgerton, Yale University.
0	Dr. Stefán Einarsson, Johns Hopkins University.
0	Prof. Dean S. Fansler, Brown University. [Providence, Rhode Island]
5	Mr. Harvey Fletcher, New York City. [Bell Telephone Laboratories]
0	Mr. Mortimer Graves, American Council of Learned Socities.
5	Prof. W. C[abell] Greet, Columbia University.
45	Prof. Miles L. Hanley, University of Wisconsin.
5	Prof. Clark Hopkins, Yale University.
0	Prof. A. V. W. Jackson, Columbia University.
0	Prof. Jess H. Jackson, University of Texas. [Austin: the only campus then]
7	Prof. T. Atkinson Jenkins, University of Chicago.
0	Prof. Dorothy J. Kaucher, Wells College. [Aurora, N. Y.]
8	Prof. R. G. Kent, University of Pennsylvania.
25	Prof. John S. Kenyon, Hiram College.
25	Dr. J. F. Knott, Springfield, Mass. [The G. & C. Merriam Company]
41	Prof. G. P. Krapp, Columbia University.
121	Prof. Hans Kurath, Ohio State University.
4	Mr. Waldo G. Leland, Permanent Secretary, American Council of Learned Societies.
11	Mr. Percy W. Long, Springfield, Mass. [The G. & C. Merriam Company]
0	Prof. Kemp Malone, Johns Hopkins University, Baltimore, Maryland.
5	Prof. Milton Metfessel, University of Iowa.
45	Prof. Samuel Moore, University of Michigan.
19	Prof. Otto Müller, Gettysburg College.
6	Prof. C. E. Parmenter, University of Chicago.
5	Mr. Charles O. Paullin, Washington, D.C.
0	Prof. Walter Petersen, University of Florida.
0	Prof. Louise Pound, University of Nebraska.
22	Prof. Edward [for Eduard] Prokosch, Yale University.
0	Prof. H. B. Richardson, Yale University.
20	Prof. E. C. Roedder, College of the City of New York. [on Convent Ave.]
61	Prof. G. Oscar Russell, Ohio State University.
5	Prof. R. E. Saleski, Bethany College.
5	Mr. J. C. Steinberg, New York City. [Bell Telephone Laboratories]
10	Prof. George M. Stephenson, University of Minnesota.
23	Prof. E. H. Sturtevant, Yale University.
0	Prof. Rudolph Willard, Yale University.
11	Prof. Karl Young, Yale University.

Kurath's report of the speaking of the 'Members of the Conference who were present by invitation' omits names of persons actually present without having been individually invited beforehand, and leaves us to guess that no such person spoke at all; since he reports only on the plenary sessions of the two days, Friday and Saturday, August 2nd and 3rd, 1929, numerous crucial events remain unmentioned in that Bulletin and have had to be reconstructed from knowledge of consequences that followed after intervals ranging from a few hours up to approximately thirty years. Certain of the consequences have borne no direct relation to the motives of the persons present during that 1929 week-end; absent persons with notable impact may already be identifiable to our readers, and one such had better be named now: Charles Carpenter Fries, without whose participation the content and directions of the Linguistic Atlas work in the 1930's would surely have been startlingly different and possibly abortive. But now we consider a condensation of the Conference, with the pair of Public Lectures on Friday August 2nd, Stephenson's and Russell's.

The Minnesota historian, outlining the original American settlement derivations overseas, spoke of 'the West' from the standpoint of the 18th Century, when the word meant anything beyond the eastern mountains, the Appelachians, and said 'New England' and 'Yankee' interchangeably: 'The sparse population of the West deprived the frontiersmen of the guidance of pastors, teachers, and the more cultivated leaders of an older society, and this may in part account for the loose languages of the West that grates on the Easterner to this day.' At the end of that century, the term 'Northwest Territory' had a perfectly definite reference, as in the Northwest Ordinance which legally delimited the area as that which became all of the states presently named Wisconsin, Michigan, Illinois, Indiana, and Ohio: 'Marietta, the first New England settlement in the Northwest Territory, was founded on the Ohio River in 1788.' In contrast, the South [what we nowadays call 'the Old South'] was settled by a people recruited from a somewhat different element, socially and religiously, in the mother country. The "peculiar institution" of slavery evolved a stratified colonial and antebellum [meaning before the War of 1861 to 1865] society, with a local government adapted to large scale agriculture, without a network of railways comparable to that of the free states, without great mobility of population, and with a reverence for birth and titles. The county was the social and political unit. ... The political control of the South was vested in an oligarchy of families, powerful not through wealth, but by virtue of birth, education, and training, which set them apart ... Families in the same community intermarried and the succeeding generation lived in much the same way ... Do these factors suggest the explanation why the South is the richest portion of the country from a dialectal point of view? [Next, with an abrupt shift of topic from our much later point of view but natural in 1929 when the original projections embraced the whole continent and every language-background from Eskimo to Spanish, the latter the peculiar interest of e.g. Professor Russell, we read that] The Germans can perhaps best be studied in Wisconsin. ... The Germans who settled in Wisconsin before the Civil War [1861–1865] were almost universally literate and on the whole better educated than the Swedes [of Minnesota] ... In the schools of a Yankee neighborhood [in Wisconsin] the children of German immigrants in many cases could not be distinguished by their manner of speech from the Yankee children; but in communities where the Germans predominated, the grandchildren continue to have trouble with the th sound. ...'

From the immediate discussion of Professor Stephenson's paper we quote just a little, and remark first that it apparently never strayed from his interests:

Kurath: How much definite information is available regarding the history of the population, for example, of Virginia, or of Ohio?

Stephenson: There is no dearth of material. For the older states a great mass of secondary material exists, and everywhere there are census and parish records.

Krapp: In New England and the South practically no definite information exists regarding the history of the population up to 1800. It would be a tremendous task to get together the sources of information, as nothing of the sort has been done. Orbeck made a start in several communities of New England. It should not be attempted in connection with the Speech Atlas. [Odd, considering what was done!]

Roedder: There is a close relation between history and linguistic geography. In Wisconsin, the various sections were settled from different parts of Germany and from Switzerland. In Green County [south central Wisconsin] settled by Swiss, the oldest generation spoke [as Roedder observed in frequent visits since long before 1914] unadulterated old Bernese; a sort of koiné is used by the second generation; the third generation use a more literary form of German, and the youngest generation speak almost entirely English. The exact provenience of the various groups must be considered, as Low German would have a different effect on [the spoken form of the local spoken] English from that exercised by High German.

Kurath: How many historians are actively interested in the history of population? Is there a history of population which gives definite figures rather than the usual generalities regarding the provenience of the population? Is there any work of this sort in progress? It would be of great help to the linguists in choosing representative communities for the study of dialect.

Knott: This paper is a challenge to directors of graduate students' research. Minute studies of single communities would be valuable. It is important to study three generations of speakers in any given community.

Paullin: There are the following sources of information as to population in the Southern States [meaning the states of Missouri and those southward along the Mississippi River, plus Kentucky and West Virginia and Maryland and their neighbors southward along the Alantic coast down to but not including Florida, and finally the states lying westward from Florida out to Louisiana together with the whole region enclosed by that circle]: (1) County histories for about one-third of the counties; these are scrappy, never more than fair; (2) histories of cities, somewhat better; (3) the Federal Census, useful for family names; (4) foreign archives.

G. Oscar Russell's presentation 'The Mechanical Recording of Speech' filled the rest of the evening hours until well after midnight. We include nearly every word of the Kurath report which he called 'abstract only' as for Stephenson.

The principal reasons for making mechanical acoustic records of speech in an investigation such as that to be discussed by the Conference on a Linguistic Atlas of the United States and Canada are:

Five reasons in favor: (1) Permanence, even after a recorded dialect is extinct. (2) Preservation of fine detail lacking in phonetic notation. (3) Repeated listening always possible, both (a) enabling interpretation of written phonetic symbols, and (b) picking up details which field workers may have disregarded as irrelevant. (4) No limit on the number of experts who can be invited to listen. (5) No time-limit on discussion of disputed or puzzling observations.

Four types of mechanical recording said to be in use in 1929, including two types of cinema sound-on-film: (1) Vertical-cut wax cylinders electrically recorded, many advantages, few disadvantages, notably perishability and 100-playings limit. (2) Wax-matrix lateral-cut disc masters for composition stampings, superb quality but high equipment cost prohibiting use in the field: studio conditions essential. (3) Modulated light-ray (variable-density) or light-valve (variable-width) sound on cinema film, standardized and patented as the Bristol, the De Forest, and the Western Electric types. Here the Kurath report lists still another, 'Metfessel' recording; this derives somehow (and quite mistakenly) from the book which Metfessel had distributed some hours or days in advance of that Friday session, Phonophotography in Folk Music: American Negro Songs in New Notation, Chapel Hill: The University of North Carolina Press, 1928. The thesis was principally that a high-resolution oscillogram (around 100 feet [30 meters] per minute) made automatically by Metfessel from the grooves of a phonograph disc is unsurpass-able in detecting the significant features of the sounds originally recorded. (4) Metal-disc lateral-track discs embossed by an electrically driven spherical diamond stylus: these reproduce very reliably. Today we can add the note that Miles Hanley made hundreds of those discs of aluminum alloy in the re-survey he executed by visiting the same New England informants during 1932 to 1934, and that in the 1970's the usable ones, those not hopelessly noisy, have been dubbed onto modern tapes and extensively transcribed by student groups either at the University of Chicago or in Madison at the University of Wisconsin to serve the Cassidy Dictionary of American Regional English project.

Discussion of the Russell paper was prolonged and so lively that the printed record must have been compiled from several sets of notes and memories. At least nine contributors are found named in Bulletin No. 4: Russell six times for 20 lines total, Kurath five times in speaking about the Russell paper for 15 lines total —and so on down; since the Kurath write-up itself may have omitted mention of a minor comment or two, not much importance should be attached to the line-counts. In this discussion the focus was generally on what any phonographic recording might serve for. Here are characteristic excerpts, in original sequence:

Kurath: Only part of the material can be phonographically recorded; other features must be noted in longhand ... Do Romanic scholars think Edmont heard correctly in collecting material for L'Atlas linguistique de la France?

Müller: Yes, in all but one or two percent of the cases. Such unity is lost if mechanical devices are used in addition to recording by ear the living speech of the subject. [1976 note: No mention of Edmont's decades of previous field-work!]

Moore: If one man does the job there is unity, but no more than if mechanical methods are used to check up on the field workers' hearing.

Sturtevant: Do you recommend that one man collect all the material in the United States and Canada?

Müller: One man might work in the South, one in the East, one in the West.

Roedder: A wrong impression has been given as to lack of recording in Europe. (1) The Phonogramm-Archiv in Vienna has a large collection; (2) there are plans to supplement the Sprachatlas des Deutschen Reiches by records of the 44,000 communities represented on the maps of that atlas.

Hanley (after saying there was mention of such records in France at the last MLA meeting): But our present plan differs in starting with records. The field work must be done by several investigators; this makes records all the more important.

The Second Session of the Conference began at 9:00 o'clock on Saturday, with Sturtevant as its convenor, and Karl Young was elected Chairman, Mortimer Graves its Recording Secretary, while ACLS Chairman Leland sat close by. Discussions began on the eleven agenda items—I, II, ... XI—derived from all the correspondence; we lack that material today, and are forced to guess our way.

I. What is the effect upon dialects of population movements? Krapp and Knott, saying that details must be collected before they can be studied, moved that no action be taken at present; seconded by Long. Kurath granted the major premise, but remarked that 'in order to choose our 500 communities wisely, we must be guided in part by historical information.' (We note that that was the first trace in the printed record of '500 communities' and that the word 'community' itself seems to have been introduced in some casual group overnight. Also, we must point out that the three persons first named, just before Kurath is here named, represented one well-defined group, the professional dictionary staff of the G. & C. Merriam Company, which had already made great progress in their making of the Second Edition of Webster's New International Dictionary in Springfield, the successor to the 1909 First Edition—so named because it was the first to use the title-word International in the Merriam-Webster series of unabridged dictionaries —and we had better add at once the fact that John S. Kenyon was composing the elaborate Pronunciation pages for its Preface.) After Kurath, the speakers named are Sturtevant, Prokosch, Bolling, and finally W. F. Bryan, who moved 'that all readily available information about sources and movements of population should be utilized in deciding upon centers to study.' (Note that this very motion was what led to making the population historian Marcus Hansen a key man even after his death: he is named posthumously in the 1939 Atlas Handbook as a co-author along with Kurath and Bernard and Julia Bloch. Hansen's output was adjusted for ultimate use throughout the editing decade by Carl Bridenbaugh, Professor of History at Brown University, who had been added promptly to the Committee in Charge when Hansen dropped out.)

II. Mechanical methods of recording? Favorable remarks and countervailing worries fill less than a page of print.

Knott: The present Conference is helpless; this question must be left to the Committee. Is this the time to call for the permanent Committee?

The Chair [Karl Young]: Action of this body is merely tentative in any case, and its [= our] function is to express opinions and make recommendations.

Knott: moved that decision on Question II be left to a committee composed of Kurath, Greet, Ayres, Russell, and Steinberg. [Dangerous choices: see below!]

Leland: This could be only [= could only be only] a committee of the [= this] Conference, and not a permanent committee.

(The Permanent Secretary [a title disused after Leland's retirement] of the money-finding ACLS exchanged significant glances with Mortimer Graves before making this remark, his only recorded words in the Kurath text, which he made to defuse the booby-trap: Knott's list put Kurath and his Ohio State colleague together as a pair ostensibly balancing but actually weakening each other by total mutual incomprehension between a grammarian and a laboratory-only phonetician, put Greet and his intimately associated co-worker Harry Morgan Ayres together as another pair, and gave the balance-of-power vote to young J. C. Steinberg at the Bell Telephone Laboratories, a laboratory technician for whom speech sounds had only physical attributes to be sufficiently preserved for intelligibility [as Dr. J. C. Steinberg he collaborated on Visible Speech, by Potter, Kopp, and Green, New York: Van Nostrand, 1947 (first available in 1948), leaving the proposed five-man group without effective representation of lexical, socio-linguistic, and other interests of the present-day LSA].)

Ayres: moved a substitute: That the Conference recommends the use of mechanical devices of recording speech and leaves the choice of [= among] such devices to the permanent Committee.

Knott: withdrew his original motion. Edgerton: seconded Ayres' motion.

Kenyon: [not to be used exclusively] but supplemented by all the records which can be gotten. (We note that the one word records normally was used in several disparate senses, and that equivocations were not avoided that time! Joos while a student under Hanley observed that the word in Hanley's usage in 1930 always meant a disc or a cylinder, and as a field-worker under Kurath, 1931–1932, found it used notably (a) for historical sources in print or longhand, (b) for handwritten entries in our field work-books as the informant spoke for us.)

Chair: Kenyon's idea can be further considered under the question of the training of field-workers.

Ayres' motion, amended to read as follows, was carried: That the Conference recommends, among other means, the employment of mechanical devices of recording materials for the Dialect Atlas.

III. What is the relative importance of pronunciation, morphology, syntax, and vocabulary in constructing a dialect atlas?

Buck: Do Questions III and IV need discussion?

Moore: IV does not. As to III, vocabulary is distinctly secondary for our purpose, and the collection of lexical material would take too much time. Moreover, a Dialect Dictionary is already under consideration by another group. (We remark that that other group must have been the MLA's Group for Present-Day English.)

Prokosch: We cannot tell in advance which of these four points will be the most important. In different localities different points may have peculiar interest.

Sturtevant: Some of the European atlases are based primarily on vocabulary, so there is room for difference of opinion.

Long: Vocabulary is confusing rather than helpful in collecting material for speech maps. Pronunciation is the most important element for defining local areas. Words are carried far from their natural habitat in this country.

Bolling: agreed with Prokosch. All features are of importance. Vocabulary was strongly emphasized in the latest work on Greek Dialects. [The reference is not ascertainable now any more. Was there a monograph 'Dialects of ...' behind this? Greek of what millennium? And so on and on: we must abandon these questions; yet Bolling in Language 10.48–51 (1934) among other statements shows that he was competent in the present-day American English dialects field.] ... Finally, Hanley moved that 'It is the sense of this meeting that the primary emphasis in the Dialect Atlas should be on pronunciation, except in so far as discrimination of class dialects involves morphology, syntax, vocabulary.' Motion carried, 28 to 11.

There is no other vote-count in the printed record, and we are left to guess at the significance of that fact. From before that point, we lift out one illuminating interchange; referring to the four points about to be listed by Hanley, 'Kent and Moore called for a vote on the comparative importance of the four features.' But Bloomfield could not let that pass unchallenged, and is quoted at some length:

> This is an impossible question to vote on. The European atlases are fundamentally unsound: one cannot predict what to study area by area. The ideal is to send out a man for the summer, preferably a native of the region, and have him bring back several hundred pages of text, some phonograph records, and scattered information. From that ideal we must cut down, but not by prejudgment—not by forcing a subject to pronounce a word like 'wharf' which may not exist in his natural dialect. ([Kurath inserts:] Bloomfield pronounces it <u>warf</u>, because he knows it only through speakers who use that pronunciation, though in all other <u>wh</u>-words he uses the unvoiced sound.)

Joos, in agreement with Bernard Bloch, later determined that this Kurath report misses Bloomfield's real message, which was that in familar language the Joos and Bloomfield word is/was <u>pier</u> or marginally <u>dock</u>, so that <u>wharf</u> was bookish. Therefore, investigation of any such speaker to find out such a thing is pointless.

Narrating on this scale through the last Conference day to its 5:00 o'clock Saturday adjournment would fill a dozen pages with materials that are unneeded for our present purpose; most of that would be insignificant, and the significant items will come into our picture in due course. For the present, the importance of the meeting as a whole can be stated very briefly: From August 1929 onward for a whole decade, the Linguistic Institute, the Linguistic Atlas, and the Society had practically a single history.

Hans Kurath after that Conference devoted nearly all his time to the advance preparations for the Atlas. On his own campus, the Ohio State University at Columbus, where Bolling was—and Bloomfield too in those years—Kurath was in the German Department; its Chairman, M. Blakemore Evans, had been in the University of Wisconsin (Madison) Department of German from 1903 to 1911.

> Evans belongs in any realistic picture we can form for the decades of interest to us here, but unfortunately is rather behind the scenes (as he preferred to be) and never joined our Society. He was very much in the MLA and was completely broad-minded about all sorts of scholarly undertakings of juniors like Bloomfield, but gave active support only to projects centered around the German language and the teaching of German in America. When the Atlas scheming began within the MLA, the fate of the German language in North America was central for Evans; when that component dropped out of the ultimately funded Atlas plans (as Spanish, Amerindian, and the other exotica also did) nothing was left to hold his interest. Incidentally, roughly the same could be said of the University of Wisconsin, where Bloomfield first taught in 1906 to 1908; Chairman Hohlfeld kept in touch with LSA doings without being a member, and seemed delighted to have 1930 LSA member W. F. Twaddell added to his staff: see later for the sequels.

We return to the post-1929 Linguistic Institute, 1930 and 1931 in New York City. As the LSA Executive Committee authorized, Sturtevant in September of 1929 set about organizing a 1930 Session, the Third of the Linguistic Institute. The sources of money derived from industry were expected to be absent-mindedly generous: the $10,000 or even less that an Institute would cost corporations would get past a Vice President in charge of minor outlays who knew that there wouldn't be any way to explain such a thing if it came up in a stockholders' annual meeting if one expressed curiosity and accordingly included that anonymously in <u>Miscellaneous</u>. Wasn't that what they were supporting the ACLS for? And although W. G. Leland's reports to corporate contributors were explicit, they simply were not scrutinized in that age of commercial optimism just before the Great Crash in October 1929.

Sturtevant, somehow warned that subventions such as the Carnegie support in the Institute's first two years could not be expected for 1930, had meanwhile been actively canvassing elsewhere and soon got what he was hoping for. The participation of Professor Roedder, late of Wisconsin and now located as a Departmental Chairman in the College of the City of New York (normally spoken as 'CCNY') at its campus on Convent Avenue and 139th Street, in the 1929 Institute established a firm connection between our planners and President Frederick B. Robinson. On the retirement of his German Department Chairman, Camillo von Klenze, Robinson was ready to offer his decades-long acquaintance double his Wisconsin salary plus moving costs to come to New York and reorganize CCNY German. We find the 1929 Announcement of the Linguistic Institute's Second Session, Bulletin No. 3, naming him as Edwin C. Roedder, Professor of Germanic Philology, University of Wisconsin; the September 1929 Record thereof, issued by Kent post facto, lists him as Professor of the German Language and Literature, College of the City of New York. Roedder had been talked to at the MLA meeting at the end of December 1928, within a few weeks thereafter received Robinson's letter offering him the position of Chairman at CCNY, and eventually responded that he meant to spend some time during the early summer of 1929 at Yale University in the Second Session of the Linguistic Institute where he would be teaching and would be available for visits to New York City for consultations.

Meanwhile Eduard Prokosch had been discreetly watching, knew of the approach to Roedder in the MLA meeting, and spoke to Sturtevant about Roedder's reluctance about moving away from Madison. 'Let's invite him to Yale for the Linguistic Institute,' said one of them, and Sturtevant did that by letter within the week. Through that 1929 Institute, Roedder happily taught Old High German and Gothic and the like; on week-ends he perhaps visited New York or perhaps was visited in New Haven; at the end, he accepted a departmental chairmanship in CCNY at more than double his Wisconsin salary and with the promise of a free hand in reorganizing Germanics to install his far more relaxed supervision in lieu of the patriarchal system in force for more than seventy years. When, finally, Roedder retired at age 70, Wisconsin's Monatshefte für deutschen Unterricht dedicated a double number, March−April of 1943, to him—and almost accidentally included evidence on the 1929 atmosphere in which academic budgeting was managed only a few weeks before The Great Crash. [For expert evidence see, e.g., Frederick Lewis Allen, Only Yesterday, 1931; Gerald W. Johnson, Incredible Tale, 1950; John Kenneth Galbraith, The Great Crash 1929, 1954; or read the New York Times and the contemporary novels.] Today we can sum up by remarking that in the crescendo decade, 1919−1929, every sort of wise planner projected a future where each year was to surpass preceding years by ten or more percent in every measure of value—except that Unit Costs remained fixed.

Kent's Record of the 1929 Institute was no exception. When he wrote, the Crash was still beyond the horizon. The consensus was that conceivably there might have to be some belt-tightening but surely no drastic re-planning for any of the LSA, the Linguistic Institute, or the Linguistic Atlas of the United States and Canada. That atlas project had now been estimated to cost many millions; the prevailing view was that things were bound to get better, and 'next summer will be better than last year, just wait and see!'

With its Director now to be from elsewhere, the 1930 Institute and its local staff to belong to CCNY as center of management, the Administrative Committee needed to have a CCNY member; that was Roedder, but without distinct title—the Associate Director emerged in 1936 in Michigan. What was radically new was the financial set-up.

That Administrative Committee had the reserved right to select Institute Faculty and arrange their teaching schedules. That does not mean that CCNY had not had what we today still call 'linguistics' courses in its Summer Sessions; rather, there had long been an abundance of just such summer-time teaching in substantially all the colleges and universities of Greater New York, and those were numerous and many of them academically of the most competent sort. In this respect, Robinson had seized the Institute as a tool for focusing at least 'linguistics' on his CCNY campus in upper Manhattan and thereby collecting all sorts of students there who otherwise would have clustered for those weeks in Columbia University further to the northward, or in the Washington Square neighborhood, close to Greenwich Village, where New York University was burgeoning; now the CCNY offices did the Linguistic Institute planning and paid all the salaries, great and small, of Institute

Faculty, apart from salaries derived from 'special foundations or gifts'—and
the CCNY fiscal office held the money, did the bookkeeping, and wrote the checks
—simple tasks in those days before such terms as 'tax withholding' and 'fringe
benefits' were ever heard of. Further, CCNY paid for printing and distributing
the Announcement of the Linguistic Institute, plus all the other publicity, a tiny
increase in the work of College offices. To the very considerable relief of our
Secretary–Treasurer, the printing and the general distribution (distribution of
all but the copies mailed routinely to the membership) of the 16-page Executive
Committee Bulletin No. 5, March, 1930, was for once hardly any drain on our
treasury; while for CCNY the basic cost was a small price to pay for certainty
that LSA publicity covered CCNY interests. First there was the March-dated
mailing to the almost 500 members, 'and somewhat later over 7000 copies were
sent out by the College of the City of New York. The announcement was repeated
in the City College's own <u>Bulletin of Courses of the Summer Session 1930</u>, page 6
and 42–48.'

There had been grave misgivings about loss of Institute autonomy in the
Executive Committee and then in the Business Meeting of our Society, 30th
December 1929, salted with variants of 'beggars can't be choosers' and 'who
pays the piper calls the tune' in various languages including Roland Kent's
French and Italian and Latin, capped by George Bolling's claim, with citation
in the appropriate language, to the effect that he had been taught by the Greeks.
The counter-measure then and there invented was the creating of a Linguistic
Institute Endowment Fund, and the collecting of a goodly sum on the spot. Twelve
months later, Sturtevant's Report on the 1930 Linguistic Institute includes this:

> Subscriptions to the Endowment Fund of the Linguistic Institute amounted
> to $2720, of which $1214 has been paid in. The Executive Committe has author-
> ized a Fourth Session, and has reappointed the same Administrative Com-
> mittee. Mr. Albert Blum has again promised a donation toward the stipend of
> a scholar of French nationality to lecture in the Institute. The ACLS has
> made an appropriation to secure the services of one of the editors of the
> Italian dialect atlas for a part of next summer to assist in organizing work
> on the proposed Dialect Atlas of the United States and Canada. He will lec-
> ture in the Institute. The remaining financial responsibility for the Institute
> is undertaken by the College of the City of New York. There is now $18.16
> in the Treasury of the Institute, of which $9.74 was the previous balance
> and $8.42 has been received from the LSA as interest on the Endowment Funds.

We return to the 1930 Institute itself, and begin with documentable bits about
the extra work done, beginning half a year at least previous to that Institute, by
our 1930 President Eduard Prokosch, who visited and wrote letters to numerous
colleagues and especially to those resident in all the spots where he had held
appointments himself. He had been a sometime resident in a good many cities
where there was money: Milwaukee 1898–1900, Chicago 1901–1904, Madison
1905–1913, Austin (Texas) 1913–1917, 1918 officially jobless while he hand-set the
type for his elementary Russian textbook, Bryn Mawr 1919–1928, New York University 1927–1929 (beginning with two Summer Sessions), Yale University 1929–.

In Milwaukee Prokosch was one founder of the student club which called itself
the QTS, the Quousque Tandem Society, after the slogan of the language teaching
reform led in Europe by Viëtor, Jespersen, Sievers and others with the German
slogan Der Sprach-Unterricht Muss Umkehren. A man of awesome energy and
intelligence, great pedagogical talent and intense charm which we latterly have
learned to call charisma, he was known in the moneyed families of Milwaukee
(and so presumably also in Chicago, St. Louis, and so on) as the miracle-worker
who had prepared numerous laggard youths (and their sisters) for certification
as German teachers, in favorable instances an M.A. and even a Ph.D. degree.
Joos later learned this directly from sitting in Madison German Department
groups containing several of those late-bloomers who came from teaching to
study towards higher degrees. Bloomfield in his Prokosch Obituary in <u>Language</u>
14.310 (1938) said that he forgot nothing he had attentively heard or read. We add
that his opinion of job-seekers was highly valued because he was attentive to
every sort of person singly in all circumstances.

MEMBERS OF THE LINGUISTIC INSTITUTE, 1930

FACULTY AND LECTURERS

Frank Ringgold Blake, Associate Professor of Oriental Languages, Johns Hopkins University, Ludwig Vogelstein Lecturer in Semitics.

Franz Boas, Professor of Anthropology, Columbia University.

George Melville Bolling, Professor of Greek, Ohio State University.

George William Brown, Professor of Indology, Kennedy School of Missions, Hartford, Connecticut.

Franklin Edgerton, Professor of Sanskrit and Comparative Philology, Yale University.

Erwin A. Esper, Associate Professor of Psychology, University of Washington.

John Lawrence Gerig, Professor of Celtic, Columbia University.

H. B. Hinckley, of New Haven, Connecticut. [For one Public Lecture, nothing else!]

J[ames] Alexander Kerns, Instructor in Classical Languages, New York University.

Hans Kurath, Professor of German and Linguistics, Ohio State University.

Claude Meek Lotspeich, Professor of Comparative and English Philology, University of Cincinnati.

Jules Marouzeau, Professor of the Latin Language and Literature at the Faculté des Lettres of the Université de Paris, Albert Blum French Lecturer.

Henri F. Muller, Professor of French, Columbia University.

Bennett J. Olli, Instructor in German, College of the City of New York.

Louise Pound, Professor of English, University of Nebraska.

Edward [for Eduard] Prokosch, Professor of Germanic Languages, Yale University, F. W. Lafrentz Lecturer in Old Saxon and Old Frisian.

Karl Reuning, Lektor für Anglistik, University of Breslau.

Henry Brush Richardson, Assistant Professor of French, Yale University.

Helen H. Roberts, Research Associate in Anthropology, Institute of Human Relations, Yale University. [For one Public Lecture, nothing else.]

Edwin C. Roedder, Professor of German, College of the City of New York, Germanistic Society Lecturer in Old High German.

Edward H. Sehrt, Professor of German, George Washington University.

Alfred Senn, Docent in Indo-European Linguistics, University of Kaunas, Lithuania.

Winifred Sturdevant, Lecturer in French, Barnard College, Columbia University.

Edgar Howard Sturtevant, Professor of Linguistics, Yale University.

REGISTRANTS FOR COURSES

The 60 registrants nearly all were CCNY Summer School students, and students belonging to other New York City area campuses, whose personal choices of summer studies, they found, in 1930 referred them to CCNY without their having that in mind when originally choosing—perhaps even a year or more earlier—with the consequence that we can find no evidence of continuing interest in what we call 'linguistics' by searching LSA lists of members or of items reviewed except for:

Murray B. Emeneau, B.A., Instructor in Classics, Yale; Reg: Oscan and Umbrian (given by Kerns: see below), and Bolling's The Language of the Homeric Poems in which Kerns also registered and the other registrant was an Ohio State University Instructor in German, Dr. Eugene Gottlieb.

Martha Jane Gibson, A.M., of New Haven; Reg: Esper's Psychology of Language and Kurath's American English.

Theodore Huebener, M.A., 1460 Hammersley Avenue, Bronx, New York City, Chairman of Foreign Languages, Bryant High School; Reg: [only in] Prokosch's Old Frisian, where fellow registrants were Dr. Eugene Gottlieb, J. A. Kerns, Sanford B. Meech (Assistant Professor of English, University of Michigan), and Nathan Süsskind, M.A., 14 West 118th St., New York City, teacher of Hebrew in a parochial school, who registered also in Roedder's The Study of Dialects.
《When Maxim Newmark assembled his 1948 Twentieth Century Modern Language Teaching, which we quoted on page 15 above, the New York City Director of Foreign Languages of its Board of Education was this same Theodore Huebener, who wrote pages 135–138 and 175–177 and 234–236 and finally 394–396 as well as serving on the Advisory Board.》

John Kepke, M[echanical] E[ngineer], Brooklyn, N.Y.; Reg: Esper's Psychology
of Language, Sehrt's Gothic, and Prokosch's German Etymology, where the 14
registrants included Nathan Süsskind and Mary Saleski, Ph.D., Acting Professor of German, Bethany College, Bethany, West Virginia.

J. A. Kerns, A.M., 101 South 12th Street, Newark, New Jersey, Instructor in Latin,
Washington Square College of the New York University: See above!

Alfred Senn, Ph.D., Kaunas, Lithuania, registrant in Olli's Finnish.

Lorenzo Dow Turner, Ph.D., 1612 Fifteenth St., N.W., Washington, D.C., Professor
of English, Fisk University, Nashville, Tennessee, registrant in Lotspeich's
History of the English Language (which had no other) and in Kurath's American
English.

Secretary Kent's Record of the 1931 Linguistic Institute includes most of the
details of what happened between the 1930 Institute and the 1931 Fourth Session
(also in New York, and the last one before the Ann Arbor Institutes beginning in
1936) and will serve to organize our continuing narrative. We condense a little:

The Director of the Institute, desiring to unite with the Institute the plans for
a Linguistic Atlas of the United States and Canada, had approached the ACLS late
in 1930 to request an appropriation to cover travel and an honorarium to Dr.
Jakob Jud, Editor-in-Chief of the Italian Dialect Atlas; then after learning more
of the publication plans for that Atlas which was then going through the press,
he requested a slight increase to enable Dr. Jud to bring with him his field-worker
Mr. Paul Scheuermeier. That increase was granted by the ACLS at its January
1931 Annual Meeting; but that was still uncertain when our Society held its own
Annual Meeting of 1930 in the Willard Hotel, 14th Street and Pennsylvania Avenue,
Washington, D.C.

For that epoch the LSA Meeting had a relatively large attendance, and that
was natural because of its being scheduled in a spot that Americans say they like
to visit; also, because it was timed to coincide with the final day of the MLA's
sessions at a larger hotel a few minutes' walk to the southward, and finally the
attendance of no less than 70 persons at LSA sessions was natural when the hosts
included George Washington University (campus near the center of government),
the American University at the northwestern edge of ten-mile-square District
of Columbia, Georgetown University also at the western edge and rather closer,
and The Catholic University of America at the eastern edge—that was where
George Melville Bolling was Professor of Greek when he moved to Ohio State
University in 1913—and all four strove to increase our attendance: since Kent
never reported the names of those in attendance who were not current members
and did not sign up for a next-year's membership, we can guess the actual size
of the meeting at close to a hundred, especially since the MLA Meeting had been
the scene of considerable discussion of the Linguistic Institute and our Society.
Here, however, we shall name just those 20 LSA Members whose attendance had
interesting sequels, and we mark with an asterisk those 13 who became Members
of the imminent 1931 Linguistic Institute:

*Bolling, Buck, *Collitz, *Dunn, Fries, *Hahn, *Hanley, *Kent, Kenyon,
Knott, *Kurath, Leopold, Lotspeich, *Orbeck, *Prokosch, *Roedder, Mary
Saleski, *R. E. Saleski, *E. H. Sehrt, *E. H. Sturtevant.

We pause for a note on the three Saleskis, two sisters and their older brother.
The name is pronounced //zàhléskĭy//, or always was so spoken in the German
House at the University of Wisconsin where the younger sister resided as a student.
Without this note our readers would surely find it highly puzzling that R. E. Saleski
turns up repeatedly in our Society's history and yet has been practically forgotten
in all the latter half of our five decades. From scattered traces in print and from
a letter to Joos by Karl Reuning, taken together with memories left in Madison—
another Deutsches Haus resident recalls Else Saleski clearly (she is the wife of a
retired Professor of German, John Workman) as a Summer Session resident in the
1930's—it is apparent that the Saleski family was just such a Jewish academic clan
as Leonard Bloomfield came from but was still in Austrian or Polish territory in
the Great War period. His Ph.D. dissertation places him in both Leipzig and Frei-
burg after the War. What we know of Mary Agnes Saleski is just that she came to

be one classmate of John Kepke in the 1930 Linguistic Institute as we have seen
at the top of our preceding page here. Reinhold was a hard-working collector of
exotic languages and always ready to serve in every capacity in the Institutes,
and there must have been plenty of conscientious performance of duties to get
him confirmed through each of the four Institute years (1928—1931) as Assistant
Director, a post in which incompetence can go far towards utterly spoiling six
hot-weather weeks for Institute Members. The original manner of listing LSA
Members in the annual List included rather full specification of fields, and we
find that his listing, after specifying only 'German' as long as he had academic
positions, in the 1938 List reads:

> FM Reinhold Eugene Saleski, Ph.D., Woodridge, Albemarle County, Virginia;
> Germanic languages, and philosophy, sociology, and psychology of
> language.

Plainly, the permissible advertising of a Member who has been side-tracked.
Why? Joos can't even remember Saleski from his own Linguistic Institute of
1931, but gossip says he was a remarkably boring lecturer. He resigned with
the end of 1940, and joined again for 1950, when his address appears as 444 N.W.
23 Place, Miami 36, Florida: the last of his traces in our Index to Language is
his review of Weissgerber Von den Kräften der deutschen Sprache; the first of
the six items is Sturtevant's review of Saleski's doctoral dissertation, Die
Mittel der sprachlichen Mitteilung, which is still worth reading today for many
sorts of reasons; one item is Saleski's write-up of the 1929 Annual Meeting, in
Language 6.104–114 (1930), showing that in late 1929 he was trusted for a difficult
task and that he performed it expeditiously; and the next thing we see (and find
in our reprinted Language volume) is his review of a book about how Chinese
writing is to be interpreted, showing Saleski's mastery of the bibliography and
also why he was ready in the first Linguistic Institute to give a Public Lecture
'Chinese for Grammarians' and in the next one to offer his course 'An Introduction to the Study of Chinese' with one registrant, Frank R. Blake, Johns Hopkins
Associate Professor of Oriental Languages. In the two New York Institutes, 1930
and 1931, Saleski neither taught nor gave a Public Lecture, nor does he appear
among the registered students in the Record; whether he participated otherwise
does not appear in any Bulletin. In 1930, the Record shows Mary Saleski, Ph.D.,
as a registrant in Prokosch's German Etymology and that's all. Her sister Else
got her advanced studies entirely in Wisconsin, it seems, though this seeming
may be an illusion of our perspective. Though not initially listed among the
members joining early, we find her listed among the Addenda on page 68 thus:

> Miss Else M. Saleski, Assistant in German at the University of Wisconsin
> [in Madison], has accepted a call to Milwaukee-Downer College as Professor
> of German.

She had, we must believe, mailed in her $5.00 early, for thereafter she is listed
as a Foundation Member. During 1925 to 1927 she shuttled between Milwaukee
and Madison, 80 miles [130 km] each way, by the electric interurban cars that
ran on city street-car tracks at the two ends and through intervening towns such
as Watertown—impossible ever since that Depression season when its torn-up
rails were sold as scrap steel on the overseas market and fed rearmament programs before 1940—for conferences with Madison Professors and for research
in Madison libraries and Summer School courses while finishing her Ph.D. She
taught in the St. Lawrence University, Canton, New York, 1927 to 1931, and from
1931 on for at least two years she taught at least German and Spanish in the Junior
College at Grand Island, Nebraska, her post when she resigned from the Society
effective with the end of 1932. In 1933 she spent a couple of semesters in the
Madison Deutsches Haus (508 N. Francis Street, since demolished to clear the
ground for the Madison Inn, which does not continue the address but uses 601
Langdon Street at Francis now) taking 'post-doctoral' work and offering deeply
erudite papers to Professor Hohlfeld as Editor of the Monatshefte für deutschen
Unterricht, all rejected as insufficiently attuned to the needs of actual teachers.
As a non-member she could henceforth appear in our printed records only as a

noteworthy speaker at a Summer Meeting. That seems to have occurred only in
1944 and in Madison, when she discussed the Sebeok paper, the Voegelin paper,
and the paper by K. L. Pike (Summer Institute of Linguistics) 'Positional Significance in Grammatical Analysis' which was discussed also by Sturtevant, Julian
Bonfante, Nida, Rubenstein, and Twaddell. By accident we have also learned that
in 1945 she was at the University of Arkansas. As for Dr. Mary Agnes Saleski,
apparently the less difficult of the sisters, the evidence says that with 1932 she
held an appointment at the St. Lawrence University as successor to Else who had
left that spot a twelvemonth earlier, and was there when she resigned from the
Linguistic Society.

Returning now to our narrative interrupted on page 41 for this Saleski note, we
can now, with the advantage of hindsight, say that the chief impact on our history
was the establishing of the fatefully divided leadership of the Linguistic Atlas of
the United States and Canada. We automatically think of it as our Society's own,
but the fact is that that was Sturtevant's doing insofar as he captured it from its
original sponsors, the MLA and its Research Group for Present-Day English in
which Miles Hanley's voice was loudest and Charles Carpenter Fries was quietly
building and winning friends and high-placed supporters. Also, in those days, as
also later on, the American Dialect Society met as a guest of the MLA in Annual
Meetings and functioned as one Section thereof: that was a slightly earlier event
than the LSA Meeting, and at its conclusion the shared membership came to our
sessions at the Willard Hotel.

That provides two centers for our interest here: (1) Miles Hanley representing
the American Dialect Society and the MLA; (2) Hans Kurath representing the LSA.
For details, readers may refer to the Joos Obituary on Bernard Bloch, and to the
last lines under rubric 'I. What is the effect upon dialects ... ?' on page 35 above.
At the moment we are concerned with the remote origin of this schizophrenia in
leadership, which derives ultimately from around the year 1889. The ADS itself
was of multiple origins, research into which is complicated by the irregularity
of its sporadically published organ Dialect Notes, whose first issue appeared,
undatably from evidence available in Madison, soon after the ADS was formed
in 1889 by a group of unknown size that included William Dwight Whitney of
Yale (and of the Century Dictionary and Cyclopedia), Oliver Farrar Emerson
(then at Cornell, in 1924 at Western Reserve University in Ohio), Benjamin Ide
Wheeler (then at Cornell and in 1924 President Emeritus of the University of
California at Berkeley), and most remarkably Harvard Professor of Romance
Languages Charles Hall Grandgent, teacher of an amazing number of notable
linguists of whom just one will be sketched here. That was Miles Lawrence
Hanley, A.B. Wittenberg 1914, A.M. Ohio State University 1916, University of
Kansas Instructor 1916-17, military service 1917-19, University of Texas
Instructor 1919-23, Harvard-Radcliffe English Assistant and Tutor 1923-27,
and in 1927 called to the English Department of the University of Wisconsin,
Madison, as Instructor. To Madison he always returned from all visiting
appointments, of which the longest (1931-34) was as Associate Director of the
Linguistic Atlas of the United States and Canada.

In 1939, when Volume 1, Maps 1-242, of the Atlas was issued, its Handbook
(containing full explanations and documentation) was made the repository of
every detail that could not be fitted neatly onto the maps. Its Preface, signed
by Kurath alone, narrates that

> The Linguistic Atlas project was initiated by members of the Modern
> Language Association of America and of the Linguistic Society of America.
> From the time of its organization in 1921 until the actual launching of the
> Atlas project, the Research Group of the MLA for Present-Day English
> devoted much thought and discussion to the question of a Survey of American
> English. Many scholars participated ... Harry Morgan Ayres of Columbia,
> James L. Barker of Utah, William Frank Bryan of Northwestern, Sir William
> Craigie of Oxford and Chicago, Charles Carpenter Fries of Michigan,
> Charles Hall Grandgent of Harvard, William Cabell Greet of Columbia,
> Miles L. Hanley of Wisconsin, John S. Kenyon of Hiram, George Philip

Krapp of Columbia, Hans Kurath, then of Ohio State, John Matthews Manly of
Chicago, Samuel Moore of Michigan, Allen Walker Read, then of Missouri,
now of Chicago, James Finch Royster of North Carolina, and Fred Newton
Scott of Michigan.   [henceforth condensing and supplementing:]
The first formal proposal was in the Present-Day English Group of the MLA in
December of 1928. The Committee then formed consisted of Fries (Chairman),
Bryan, Greet, Kenyon, and Read. In January of 1929, without awareness of the
existence of the MLA Committee, Sturtevant as one of two LSA Delegates to the
ACLS laid the general proposition before the ACLS Annual Meeting. Learning of
actual and prospective decisions in the ACLS, Fries called a meeting of his
MLA Committee for February 22nd and 23rd, 1929, in Cleveland, and invited
Sturtevant to attend.

Costs of the Cleveland meeting were defrayed by the National Council of
Teachers of English, which was already sponsoring the Fries American English
Grammar, ultimately published in 1940 (reviewed in Language 17.274 [1941]) and
financing graduate-student Research Assistants in their building of the letter-
file analyses from which the book was derived. That Cleveland meeting resulted
in the New Haven Conference of the beginning of August, 1929, reported above,
beginning with page 31.

Toward the end of August, 1929, the Executive Committee of the ACLS set up
an ad-hoc committee, a task-force, to prepare a budgeted plan for a dialect or
English-speech atlas of locally native English derived from on-the-spot surveys
of the United States and Canada. Hans Kurath was and remained Chairman; there
were at first nine additional members: Bloomfield, Carruthers, Grandgent,
Hanley, Hansen, Kenyon, Krapp, Prokosch, Russell. With Marcus L. Hansen of
the University of Illinois (Urbana) as the member located farthest south, and six
of the nine within easy reach of Chicago, the group soon came to feel that the
English of 'the South' was underrepresented; then W. A. Read of Louisiana was
added, and A. A. Hill at the University of Virginia (Charlottesville) plus Kemp
Malone of The Johns Hopkins University in Baltimore, Maryland. When the
ACLS Delegates met, on the 31st of January, 1930, they had before them an
over-all cost estimate of $664,000.00, completed by December, which loftily
disregarded the Great Crash and consequent dislocations—those were treated
as storms which must very soon blow over and be forgotten—and that was not
a dereliction of duty but the only possible view that scholars could take.

The ACLS meeting adopted the plan and directed its central-office staff to
make ready the ACLS presentations, designed somewhat variously according
to which source of funds was being appealed to in each presentation but not
allowing any contradicting between one and any other, for the ACLS was well
aware of the pattern of 'overlapping directorships' among corporations and
banks: that was what Waldo Leland had carefully selected his staff for: with
alternatives and contingency plans, complete with separate pricings and time
schedules to make up fractional fundings easily from, or at least initiate a
useful correspondence between each possible funder and the ACLS. Those
sources temporized and offered fractions or excuses; temporizing was the one
thing that everybody could do during 1930; and step by step the special committee was forced back nine tenths of the way, to the position which prevailed
in the ACLS meeting at the end of January 1931: a total of $60,000 of ACLS funds
could be spent, spread over 27 months from June 1931 to October 1933, and the
three most intensely interested universities identifiable at the moment—Yale,
Brown, and Harvard—would be carrying all the unbudgeted burdens such as
faculty released-time in lieu of sabbaticals, or the use of office-space, or the
salary of some unexpectedly available junior worker.

Now this is not to say that $30,000 annually, more or less, actually was spent
within the planned first period of three summers and the two academic years
between, but we lack the documentation (nearly all, one must suppose, now lying
in sealed archives, principally in Washington) for detailing the modifications. The
plan included preparing the initial corps of field-workers in the framework of the
1931 Linguistic Institute, and that brought Martin Joos into the picture.

MEMBERS OF THE LINGUISTIC INSTITUTE, 1931

FACULTY AND LECTURERS

Henry S. Alexander, Professor of English, Queen's University, Kingston, Ontario.

George Melville Bolling, Professor of Greek, Ohio State University.

Clive H. Carruthers, Professor of Classical Philology, McGill University.

Hermann Collitz, Professor Emeritus of Germanic Philology, Johns Hopkins University.

Joseph Dunn, Professor of Celtic Languages and Literatures, Catholic University of America.

Franklin Edgerton, Professor of Sanskrit and Comparative Philology, Yale University.

Pierre Fouché, Professor of the History of the French Language in the University of Strasbourg, Albert Blum French Lecturer.

Jakob Jud, Professor of Romance Philology, University of Zürich.

Roland Grubb Kent, Professor of Comparative Philology, University of Pennsylvania.

Hans Kurath, Professor of German and Linguistics, Ohio State University.

Ralph Marcus, Professor of Bible and Hellenistic Judaism in the Jewish Institute of Religion, and Lecturer on Semitic Languages in Columbia University.

Anders Orbeck, Professor of English, University of Rochester (New York).

Eduard Prokosch, Professor of Germanic Languages, Yale University.

Henry Brush Richardson, Associate Professor of French, Yale University.

Edwin C. Roedder, Professor of German, The College of the City of New York.

Paul Scheuermeier, Field Worker for the Sprach- und Sachatlas Italiens und der Südschweiz.

Edward H. Sehrt, Professor of German, George Washington University.

Alfred Senn, Professor of Germanic and Comparative Philology, University of Wisconsin.

Edgar Howard Sturtevant, Professor of Linguistics, Yale University.

REGISTRANTS FOR COURSES

Bernard Bloch, M.A., Lawrence, Kansas; Reg: (1) Les Problèmes de la Préparation d'un Atlas Linguistique, Jud & Scheuermeier; (2) German Morphology, Prokosch; (3) History of the English Language, Alexander; (4) History of American Pronunciation, Orbeck; (5) English Phonetics, Harry Morgan Ayres & W. Cabell Greet (by visiting the Columbia University laboratory).

Martha Jane Gibson, M. A., New Haven, graduate student at Yale; Reg: (1).

Miles L. Hanley, M.A. Ohio State University 1916 & M.A. Harvard 1927, Lecturer in English at Yale & Associate Professor of English at the University of Wisconsin, Madison; Reg: (1), (2), (4), (5).

Rachel Sargent Harris, M.A., Haverhill, Massachusetts, graduate student at Brown University; Reg: (1), (3), (3a) Modern British and American Pronunciation, Alexander; (4), (5).

Martin Joos, undergraduate student in Electrical Engineering, University of Wisconsin (Madison); Reg: (1), (2), (4).

Esther R. Keck, M.A., Brooklyn, N.Y., Assistant in English at the University of Wisconsin (Madison); Reg: (1), (3), (3a), (4), (5).

Hans Kurath, Ph.D., Professor of German and Linguistics, Ohio State University; Reg: (1).

Guy Sumner Lowman, Jr., Ph.D. (University of London), Madison, Wisconsin, & Sterling Fellow at Yale University; Reg: (1), (4).

James Frederick Rettger, B.A., graduate student in English, Yale University; Reg: (1), (4).

Charles Cassil Reynard, B.A., Hiram, Ohio; Reg: (1), (3a), (4), (5).

Lorenzo Dow Turner, Ph.D., Professor of English, Fisk University, Nashville, Tennessee; Reg: (1) plus service as demonstrator.

There were a total of 52 registrants listed in the Record, of whom 41 remain unnamed here for reasons analogous to those mentioned on page 40 here; that criterion also makes the above-listed eleven persons just those whom Kurath initially took seriously as possible field-workers on the Linguistic Atlas. But Martha Jane Gibson and J. F. Rettger each found it distasteful to go out into the

field and perhaps far from familiar libraries while it was still possible to stay
another year at Yale. Esther Keck had more than a year to go in completing her
studies toward the Ph.D. while living comfortably on her Teaching Assistant
salary in Madison, which she would risk forfeiting if she interrupted it, perhaps
lost her chance to continue uninterruptedly while others were available to step
into her slot. (In the 1970's she was Esther Keck Sheldon, retired, of Queens
College, Brooklyn, believed to be living still in 1976.) Lorenzo Dow Turner had
prior commitments for at least 1931–32; later, we find him researching Negro
dialects, to a significant extent for the Atlas of the Southeastern areas.

In the Handbook that accompanies its first-published volume of maps of the
New England States, the actually functioning field-workers in late 1931 are on
page v; apart from Kurath and Hanley, our names were: Bloch, Harris, Joos,
Lowman, Reynard. Each of us had come to CCNY on family funds and private
loans: there were no scholarships for us. Each paid the $52.50 CCNY fees and
took care of his own board and lodging, from his arrival to the first week of
August. Roughly one month, or perhaps it was rather less — Joos remembers
it as midway in the third week — after the beginning of classes in the Institute,
Kurath told us that we had been appointed by the ACLS, and that his Yale office
would issue our monthly salary payments on the scale of $2500 per academic
year of ten months beginning with the first day of October, but $187.50 before
that on August 1 and September 1, before the field trips could begin in earnest.
Meanwhile, each of us had better procure an automobile, available second-hand
in those days for between $150 and $200.

The Joos car, found through a New York Times advertisement, cost $100
with its transferable road-license. The letter to the Joos family home, Alma
Center, Wisconsin, reporting this under date 11 August, says, 'The engine and
transmission are excellent, but for the rest it will need some repairing. However, I'll soon collect enough for travelling expenses to cover that. Mr. Kurath
and I are driving up into Western Mass[achusetts] Thursday [13 August] to start
work in my area. He'll spend a week or 10 days with me, ...' That letter came
from New Haven: we field-workers were spending a few days reading up on our
assigned territories in the Yale Library's collections of 'local histories' or else
helping Kurath settle his own files into filing-cabinet folders, which was Joos's
special task for a week while Kurath mimeographed the first version of the
Questionnaire that had been being constructed in the 'workshop' hours, outside
of the above-listed courses, at first planned for three 2-hour sessions but often
cancelled or stretched almost unpredictably week by week until at the end we
were excused from the final-examination days and departed for New Haven.
The reason officially given by Kurath for excusing Joos from the library work
was that he needed to scout a typical territory in the company of a field-worker
and intended to use Joos for that, and would give Joos pointers each half-day,
making the Yale Library research unnecessary in this one case.

Kurath's planned trip with Joos up into the Berkshire Hills was cancelled;
no explanation was ever stated, but among us field-workers it was rumored that
he had to go into New York to protect our prospects for getting more subvention
funds. The Joos cash on hand, and the daily rate of out-of-pocket spending while
lodging expensively in New Haven with a garage for the Joos car, forced Joos to
leave on Thursday, 13 August, driving alone and somewhat randomly on second-
best roads in a generally northwesterly direction. Remembered points to catch
up on map-reading and snacks have now been reconstructed as New Milford and
Canaan in Connecticut, Hinsdale and Cummington in Massachusetts; and that was
the overnight stop, with the first entries in a Joos Field Notebook made in the
morning in the General Store kept by Leon A. Stevens, who is Informant 232.2 in
the Handbook listing, which ends 'J3' on page 198 because it was Joos's third job
to be completed and mailed to the Kurath office; Informant 232.1 was his mother
Emagene [spoken as if 'Emma Jean'] who showed me the autographed book of
verse, poems by Cummington native William Cullen Bryant, given her when she
recited Thanatopsis for him at age fifteen years in 1870.

In Language 8.239 (1932) we find a report that 'A Language [sic] Institute was conducted by the College of the City of New York with Charles Upson Clark as Director. Thirty-nine courses were offered, in General Linguistics, Indic, Greek and Latin, Romance Languages, Celtic Languages, Germanic Languages and English, Balto-Slavic Languages, Semitic Languages, with a teaching faculty of fifteen members. The Linguistic Society was represented by the Director and nine of the Faculty: E. Cross, G. O. Curme, M. B. Emeneau, J. L. Gerig, W. Leopold, O. Müller, B. J. Olli, C. Pharr, E. C. Roedder. Two scholars were called in from abroad: John H. C. Grattan, Professor of English Language and Philology in the University of Liverpool, and André Mirambel, Professor of Modern Greek in the École Nationale des Langues Orientales Vivantes (Paris).' Neither Grattan nor Mirambel joined our Society.

No more convenient occasion has been thought of for following the Monograph series through to the mid-century point; certain items will be mentioned later:

1925 1 Erwin Allen Esper: Associative Interference: 47 pp., $1.00
1926 2 Roland Grubb Kent: Textual Criticism of Inscriptions: 76 pp., $1.25
1926 3 Francis A. Wood: Post-Consonantal W in Indo-European: 124 pp., $1.50
1929 4 George William Small: The Germanic Case of Comparison: 121 pp., $1.75
1930 5 Edwin H. Tuttle: Dravidian Developments: 40 pp., $0.75
1930 6 Edward Sapir: Totality: 28 pp. $0.50
1930 7 The Curme Volume of Linguistic Studies: 178 pp., $2.50
1930 8 Klara H. Collitz: Verbs of Motion in Their
          Semantic Divergence: 112 pp., $1.50
1931 9 Edgar H. Sturtevant: A Hittite Glossary: 84 pp., $1.25
1932 10 Edward Sapir and Morris Swadesh: The Expression of the Ending-Point
          Relation, edited by Alice V. Morris: 125 pp., $1.50
1932 11 Dael Lee Wolfle: The Relation between Linguistic Structure and
          Associative Interference in Artificial Language Material: 56 pp., $1.50
1932 12 Roland Grubb Kent: The Sounds of Latin: 216 pp., $3.25
1933 13 George L. Trager: The Old Church Slavonic Kiev Fragment: 28 pp., $0.50
1933 14 T. Atkinson Jenkins: Word-Studies in French and English: 94 pp., $1.35
1934 15 Charles Goetsch: The Phonology of the Low German Deeds in the
          Oldest Registry at Riga, Latvia: 59 pp., $1.00
1935 16 W. Freeman Twaddell: On Defining the Phoneme: 62 pp., $1.00
1937 17 William Edward Collinson: Indication, edited by Alice V. Morris: 128 pp., $1.75
1938 18 Robert A. Hall, Jr.: An Analytical Grammar of the Hungarian
          Language: 113 pp., $1.75
1939 19 Harold Whitehall: Middle English ū and Related Sounds: 79 pp., $1.00
1940 20 William B. S. Smith: De la toponymie Bretonne: Dictionnaire
          Étymologique: 136 pp., $2.00
1944 21 Robert A. Hall, Jr.: Hungarian Grammar: 91 pp., $2.00
1945 22 Charles F. Voegelin and Zellig S. Harris: Index to the Franz
          Boas Collection of Materials for American Linguistics: 43 pp., $1.00
1948 23 Martin Joos: Acoustic Phonetics: 136 pp., $2.00
1948 24 Robert A. Hall, Jr.: Structural Sketches 1: French: 56 pp., $1.00
1950 25 Einar I. Haugen: The First Grammatical Treatise: 64 pp., $2.00 [[?]]

Monographs by definition are subsidized—that is, published without ultimate cost to the Treasury of our Society; or to put the point in equivalent terms, the Monograph Series was created, coëval with the quarterly journal Language, to accommodate book-length items without stretching the page-count of the journal inordinately. The relative bulk of 'article' and 'monograph' has varied hugely, as anyone can learn from the above listing and the page-counts of articles in the Fifty-year Index. Our three Editors, moreover, have differed in their definitions of the categories, and have differed for inscrutable reasons on occasion; for now, it is enough to know that there must be a positive and defensible reason always.

Subsidized publication has meant various things too, and here the Treasurer is constitutionally responsible. The Editor's readiness to publish comes first; the Treasurer's certification that money has been found releases the manuscript to the printer. For a few of the Monographs the details are adequately known, in each case partly known by accident of personal acquaintance. Hermann Collitz paid the entire cost of his wife's Monograph No. 8, less than $5.00 per page. No. 16 was at first estimated to make 78 pages, so that its author got a refund from the advance deposit he had made from household funds: he had some sort of private reason for not seeking a subsidy from his University, Wisconsin. No. 23 was, exceptionally so far in the Society's history, published without any subsidy whatever, its cost being carried as a deficit item on the Treasurer's books during the decade when its further sales revenues went directly into the single account for that one Monograph until the deficit had vanished; thereafter the annual Treasurer's Report never mentioned it again, its sales simply constituting an anonymous contribution to the general funds of the Society, guessed by its author or discreetly estimated for him by the Treasurer but only orally. There have never been author royalties on a Monograph to our knowledge.

Quite a few members profited professionally from working as Research Assistants on projects which eventually generated a Monograph, gaining both repute and substantial sums of money. Selected cases reported here will shed light on the internal workings of the Society from various angles and in many colors. We begin with a Foundation Member, Alice Vanderbilt Shepard Morris, and her husband, lawyer Dave Hennen Morris, 1927 member. In joining, she said her 'academic interest' was International Language. They were among the more mature members: Dave Hennen Morris, Jr., was in uniform in both World Wars; in the 1960's he was a banker and a trustee of several charities, and listed himself in Who's Who as a Republican.

Addresses given in our Lists of Members for his parents for 1933 through 1936 were 'Embassy of the United States of America, Brussels, Belgium.' The father's name appears, beginning within that period, as The Honorable Dave Hennen Morris, LL.B. He died in May, 1944; and shortly thereafter the International Auxiliary Language Association, Inc., whose address in New York City was for many years the family address of the Morrises, expanded its activities considerably.

Mrs. Morris signed herself as Alice V. Morris, Litt.D., in the Preface to Monograph No. 17, by W[illiam] E[dward] Collinson, Ph.D., Professor of German and Honorary Lecturer in Comparative Philology, University of Liverpool. We quote her Preface extensively as the best documentation for a variety of things that need to be reported within this History anyhow, condensing appropriately:

Indication is the third installment of a series of language studies entitled 'Foundations of Language, logical and psychological, an approach to the international language problem.' [This series is] part of a more inclusive program ... a further part of which comprises a series of Comparative Studies of ... ethnic and constructed language. ... the participants ... share a growing belief that ... the 'ideal' international language ... must be capable of serving as an instrument of direct communication ... must be capable of serving as a standard medium of translation ... finally, it must be capable of serving as an adequate basis for [foreign-] language study. ... a true language of reference, a common denominator, a sort of fixed point or datum from which ... to assess the divergence or convergence observable between equivalent expressions in various languages. ... only a deliberately constructed language can combine these qualifications ... one containing as its nucleus a stock of symbols and rules adequate to express the most commonly used concepts that underlie all languages ... For the sake of convenience, let us call that nucleus the foundation language or nuclear language ... conceived as a language that consists exclusively of means of expression for each and every basic concept:

1. Grammatical implements ... i.e. parts of speech and syntactical relations. 2. Determinants ... which, without modifying the notional meaning of the word to which they are applied, determine the field of reference ... articles, etc. ... near at hand or at a distance ... previously mentioned or about to be mentioned ... singular and plural ... past, present, or future

time ... certain, necessary, contingent, problematical, unrealizable (cf. use of moods, sentence-particles, etc.). 3. Relational devices, whether rules or symbols, which indicate the relations between notions or complexes of notions, e.g. relations of time, places, causality, appurtenance [sic: not apperte-], etc., often expressed in ethnic languages by case-suffixes, prepositions or conjunctions. 4. Symbols designating notions of a high degree of generality, e.g. agent, act, product, which ... serve as sorters or classifiers of the word-material. 5. Symbols of more specific meaning needed to bring the vocabulary and phraseology to the minimum requisite for communication at an ordinary level.

So far, this has preserved the words and phrases of the Morris Preface, and has kept their sequence, only dropping out (and indicating such omissions by [...]) the expanding words which would be deleted by editors aiming at concise style without loss of message components. At this point, contrariwise, Joos finds it necessary to begin rearranging sequences of words, and to incorporate segments of footnotes (here marked 'fn'), to save the message sense; the reason is that the published text, from here to its end, abruptly shifts to a more diffuse and more than a little confused style. We may easily guess the decisive cause: at this point she has left the marked trail of what Sapir taught her and has shifted to things learned from other mentors such as Jespersen, Zamenhof, and still earlier writers.

Now 1, 2, 3, and 4 (possibly amounting all together to less than 200 items) constitute the means for the manipulation of the selected minimum number of symbols of greater specificity (possibly not much more than 1000) and, in fact, for the manipulation of any number of supplementary symbols, including technical terms, that might ultimately be required for a complete language of reference. ... the entire language ... must be free of everything that merely encumbers. Ambiguities, synonyms, irregularities, and idiomatic expressions are to be avoided, and ...

The effort of learning the nuclear language would be merely that needed to learn a limited vocabulary and a few simple rules. (fn: Under the direction of Dr. Edward L. Thorndike, a six years' investigation of the rate of progress in learning the 'synthetic' languages Esperanto and Ido was conducted by Dr. Laura Hall Kennon. Quoting from Language Learning, issued by Division of Psychology, Institute of Educational Research, Teachers' College, Columbia University, New York City, 1933, p. 7: 'On the whole, with expenditures of from ten to a hundred hours, the achievement in the synthetic language will probably be from five to fifteen times that in a natural language, according to the difficulty of the latter.') [Here Joos is about to omit about one page]

As a basis for general language study Esperanto has been used in experimental courses in ten schools in the United States, with pupils from 11 to 15 years of age. The text book was General Language Course, Helen S. Eaton, Banks Upshaw and Co., Dallas, Texas, 1934.

The Foundations of Language series [now quoting verbatim] was launched by Professor Edward Sapir [with LSA Monograph 6 and Monograph 10] and Professor William E. Collinson (University of Liverpool) in consultation with Mrs. Alice V. Morris representing IALA. In 1930 the larger program, both the Foundations of Language and the Comparative Studies, was approved [sic!] by the first International Meeting on Linguistic Research held in Geneva, and in 1931 in Geneva the Second International Congress of Linguists entrusted [sic!] the IALA with the carrying out of the proposed researches. [This ends the use of the Morris text.]

What, presumably, is the factual background for the claims she makes above? The hypothesis we must choose, knowing the other personalities from all other evidence, is that in 1931 Mrs. Morris and fellow enthusiasts for Esperanto put in a proposed agenda item for discussion, as any registered Congress member was free to do, and thereby automatically gained Otto Jespersen's endorsement for investigating the extent to which natural languages employ similar formal devices. On the other hand, Christine Mohrman would have blocked a real endorsement of Esperanto itself, and Jespersen would have advocated his Novial instead.

Exactly one of the Comparative Studies was ever published. In 1940 the Committee on Modern Languages of the American Council on Education issued Helen S. Eaton's Semantic Frequency List for English, French, German, and Spanish: a correlation of the first six thousand words in four single-language frequency

lists. Pp. xxii + 441. Chicago: University of Chicago Press, 1940. Joos reviewed
the book, Language 17.160-162 (1941) and thereby offended Miss Eaton gravely, to
judge from her refusal to acknowledge the existence of the reviewer when we both
attended our Society's Annual Meeting at the end of 1944: she, I was told, expected
unmixed congratulations, while my intent was simply to clearly describe the book,
since the book itself claimed to have been constructed by impossible procedures.
Conceivably the offense could have been avoided if I had suspected the existence
of her 1934 book—see above—published so obscurely that I have never found a copy.

When George Trager joined the Society he stated his academic connection as
Research Associate, International Auxiliary Language Association. That remained
his listing during the three years 1931-1934; then he moved to the Adams State
Teachers College, Alamosa, Colorado. Meanwhile his IALA earnings enabled him
to bring out Monograph No. 13. Naturally he reviewed for our journal and others:
in those days, scholarly journals nearly all paid reviewers, and editors saved
money by cutting each review to minimum length. During the first 15 years of
Language, reviewers (except officers!) were paid, at first $1.00 per page, in later
years more. Ultimately, the rate rose to $1.60 per page with a limit of $12.50 per
issue. That was the high-water mark: when Bolling's tenure ended and Bloch took
his place, he persuaded the Executive Committee to abolish those honoraria and
said what his reasons were: all Members should be glad to review gratis, not just
the officers, for they were all equal 'in the sight of God' and the Editor wanted to
persuade the competent ones to review, not pay them to review. The sudden shift
in policy caused hardly a ripple in 1940 amid the numerous dislocations of imminent war. The Reviewer's Honorarium had outlived its usefulness. But while it was
available, it often made just the difference between being able to pursue cherished
plans and being forced to postpone some plan, perhaps to drop it.

Besides Trager, no doubt a good many others could be named. Joos with the 1936
Zipf review got better than twice the annual dues: it was the longest review Bolling
had so far accepted. Morris Swadesh joined with 1931; he was co-author of Sapir's
Monograph No. 10 and had no doubt been paid for his work; in 1933 he was in the
Yale Institute of Human Relations; by 1934 Mary Haas had joined both our Society
and that Institute and is listed as Mrs. Morris Swadesh.

In sampling the Monographs we have started out from Mrs. Alice V. Morris;
our other personal starting-point will be Louis Herbert Gray, Signer of the Call,
who signed as Professor of Comparative Philology and Oriental Languages in the
University of Nebraska, at Lincoln, where Louise Pound was Professor of English.
Gray was one of many 19th-century philologists who stood firm there while many or
most others moved into the 20th century. Already before 1915 Gray had completed
a book manuscript, Foundations of Language, which remained unpublished for three
decades while accumulating a reputation for being weightier and deeper than the
1914 book by Leonard Bloomfield, An Introduction to the Study of Language, and of
course would surpass Bloomfield's Language of 1933 when Gray had taken time to
incorporate what he saw fit from publications emerging after that war and shelved
in the Library of Columbia University and others in the New York area. In 1925 he
visited England for the purpose of delivering a course of lectures described on
page 22 of the first issue of Language; he did not resume his Nebraska post but
was Professor of Oriental Languages in Columbia University from then on, still
revising his magnum opus when he could find suitable Research Assistants and
could spare the time from his multifarious duties. And he supervised doctoral
candidates with out-of-the-way specialties, for example the author of Monograph
No. 20, of which more anon.

We cannot guess just why Gray's title is identical to the title used by Alice
V. Morris as reported here on page 48 for a series of International Language
studies; that is to say, it is equally likely, on evidence accessible today, that his
title was already 'Foundations of Language' in 1914 or so—and that that famous
wording was appropriated by his 1939 publisher, Macmillan, without Gray's doing
anything more than accepting the proposal of the publisher's functionaries. This
would agree with the fact that 'Foundations ...' is a title almost wildly misfitting

with what the book ultimately turned out to be. In the 1920's, publishers of books for the educated public—that is to say, 'trade' books rather than textbooks—looked for 'selling points' more than they looked for scholarship, for example they wanted flamboyance of the Mencken sort, before accepting one for publication. Now when Bloomfield's 1933 Language appeared, the New York offices of other text and trade publishers began to hear from their salesmen in the field that Henry Holt had stolen a march on them, and how about getting a new language book from some Professor, best of all from one in Columbia University. So there were early approaches to Professor L. H. Gray, and the actual six-year delay until the Gray book came out is to be accounted for by the reclusive working habits of its author (so that we need not focus on the cleft-palate blurring of his speech that made his phonetic demonstrations useless, but can instead point out that his book deals only with orthographies when ostensibly discussing phonetics) delaying the up-dating (it has no postwar bibliography) until the publisher simply printed it from the old typescript.

The review copy sent to the Editor of Language was one of those left for the second Editor to deal with when Bolling bowed out midway in 1939. Bloch could neither ignore the work of the Society's 1938 President nor procure a damning by faint praise, much as he was tempted. What he did, following the counsel of Leonard Bloomfield, was to arrange to have a triumvirate of reviewers. Bloomfield composed a neat description printable on a single page, and sent that off to the most distant of the minor journals that continually importuned him for contributions. Today we find it in Hockett's book A Bloomfield Anthology, credited to Modern Language Forum 24.198 (1939); but Hockett's procedures automatically ignore the facts we next point out: MLF was published (in California) by and for High School Teachers of English and of Foreign Languages, notably Spanish, Italian, French, and German. Meanwhile Bernard Bloch had sent the review copy to Zellig Harris with a note to say that a graduate student at Harris's University had just joined the LSA and used the standard card (designed to inform Editors of a new member's areas of competence as a reviewer) to name a list of topics that almost covered the scope of the Gray book, so would Harris consult Donald Swanson and divide the work with him? Their reviews are in Language 16.216–31 and 231–35. Gray resigned forthwith; we have no information available on how he was persuaded to join again, so that he was listed in 1943 as 'SC' and in 1944 as both 'SC' and an Emeritus Member.

We are still following events of the 1920's here. When L. H. Gray began his Columbia University years, he had Assistants at least for work on Monograph No. 20, one who did enough to be named on its title-page: De la toponymie Bretonne, Dictionnaire Étymologique / par William B. S. Smith, préparé sous la direction de / Louis H. Gray / d'après le manuscrit inédit d'Auguste Brizeux. Now W. B. S. Smith was a neighbor of George Trager's when he joined the LSA in 1934. We cannot know just when he began his Breton work, but we do know that his output included a sketch of Breton historical phonology in its four principal dialects, meant to serve for comparison with Brizeux etymologies. Perhaps because the manuscript turned out to be an omnium gatherum of sound and also unsound etymologies (natural in the decades when Brizeux was compiling it) Gray omitted it from the printed LSA Monograph and returned it to Smith, who kept it as his own and in due course asked George Trager to get it published. Finally, in the Spring of 1942, when the editing of the new-hatched Studies in Linguistics which we thought was going to be mimeographed under Charles F. Hockett was abandoned to Trager and Joos jointly and severally (Trager as now the logical Editor, Hockett having been drafted and sent to Vint Hill Farms in Virginia for basic training which seemed to consist principally of raking dead leaves, and Joos as the busybody who had sold the mimeography idea to the December 1941 organizing meeting and said, when they were about to abandon or indefinitely postpone SIL for lack of printing money, that he in Toronto had prepared a typewriter for such jobs) the half-baked Smith paper, which Trager had intended for stenciling without alterations other than correcting a handful of typing errors, seduced Joos into studying in the Celtic grammar collections in the University of Toronto Library and totally rewriting the Smith pages.

These opening five pages (47–51) of the present Chapter have not maintained narrative sequence; the reasons were stated in various spots, beginning with the listing of the first 25 Monographs, and need not be repeated here. That done, we can return to the 1931 Summer which launched the Linguistic Atlas field-work in New England. Quite a number of additional names have surfaced in the five-page interlude, all significant as almost equally serving to show that our Society meant various things to various sorts of Members. No shorter list of personal factors could adequately demonstrate this History's leading thesis, that The Linguistic Society of America is both a face-to-face group and an open society, not a closed one. Another drafter of these pages would start out naturally from his personal experiences and present a partly disparate list of persons and their interactions; but all history is biography anyhow, and Martin Joos as historiographer has mentioned the name 'Joos' infrequently by comparison with the opportunities that the events offered. The important message is that the inner form of the LSA can be demonstrated as both a social group and a creative enterprise.

The Linguistic Atlas was the defining enterprise of the decade. In the Obituary on Bernard Bloch there is a list of participants in Sapir's 1937 Field Methods that supposedly was complete but actually lacks one name; including that, we get this definitive list of ten young men: Bernard Bloch, John B. Carroll, J Milton Cowan, Jack Autrey Dabbs, Zellig S. Harris, Fred W. Householder, Jr., Norman A. McQuown, Kenneth Lee Pike, Henry Lee Smith, Jr., Morris Swadesh. Nobody seems to have been disturbed by the absence of women among the ten. One, Dabbs, is not much heard of outside of the Southwest. The youngest was Carroll, aged 21; every one of the ten remains individually memorable after more than a generation.

From 1931 onward, our Society's annual Proceedings appear to be giving short shrift to the year-by-year progress of the Atlas, but it would be wrong to deduce that the Atlas work carried on entirely by LSA members meant less to us than to other groups. The whole enterprise was under the ACLS roof. We did our part, but that did not include anything much in financial terms, and the MLA had a prior claim to the kudos. From the start it had been settled that printed reports were to be issued semiannually, the Director and the Associate Director alternating in the preparing and signing of them after the first assignment resulted from a coin-toss. Now our own journal came out quarterly, and Editor Bolling reported in December what had been reported to him in August or earlier; but Dialect Notes printed full reports promptly as often as its typescript was brought to a printer located within a few minutes' walk from Miles Hanley's 1931–1934 office in the Harvard complex. His scheduling for that was twice a year, midsummer and midwinter, and as long as his wife was on hand to keep everything under control the schedule was held to, or nearly. Now Louise Hanley had a superb ear for English rhetoric and technical skill in handling written records including her own shorthand when recording the Staff Conferences: in due course she would be told by Miles to write up her notes accumulated since the last time, and he himself had to get on the road to make some aluminum-disc recordings right away. Louise Hanley never could regard any worker in the 'English' field in any other light than as a competitor to Miles and potentially a plagiarist, and this paranoid attitude led to distortions of all sizes and shapes in the printed record, too many to list here; one, however, will serve to counterbalance Gerald Udell's article 'Responses of Co-Workers to the Word "Informant"', pp. 441–54, Studies in Linguistics in Honor of Raven I. McDavid, Jr., 1972: University of Alabama Press. Beginning in August, we had all discussed the possible terms for designating involved persons and finally had come to a firm conclusion after many false starts. The term ultimately standardized for victims of our interviewing processes—the autochthonous native American-English witness reliably reporting what was said locally in 1931 or perhaps as far back as 1870 and distinguishing between those older forms and the later ones which displaced them recently—was settled by departure from the obvious interviewee that we aimed at but could not allow to be seen or heard by outsiders for at least two separate sorts of reasons: (1) the preposterous intervieweeweewee which was sure to come out of playful or malicious oral transmissions and would be reflected in newsprint to our disadvantage; and (2) the journalistic and educational quibbling over the 'proper' orthographic forms of such words as employé(e)(s), seeing that English lacks gender—or doesn't it? We got rulings from the titular Editor of Webster's SecondNew International Dictionary, the President of Smith College in Northampton, William Allen Neilson, to whom Joos was accredited by letter and whose Secretary, Miss Annetta Clark, became a Joos victim; but that could only confirm our printing uses and those were not our real problem: what was our ultimately adopted word to be in speech—face to face with local journalists as well as in our interviewing—so that we could not be landed in untenable positions. Bernard Bloch composed a set of limericks to test out the range of possibilities, and that finished the game for good and all. We adopted informant(s) definitively, never -ante(s), overriding the Bloch and Kurath principle (which we all agreed with) that science is a universal decontaminant. We argued for a time whether we hadn't better avoid a vocable that is reminiscent of 'informer'—unsavory character!—but abandoned that line by agreeing that no word is ever safe in all contexts from malicious distortions, or innocent ones either.

The one 1931-32 field-worker whose early years (to age 19) were entirely rural was the one who was most apprehensive about how our image was being shaped in the village weeklies. The city words 'linguistic' and 'atlas' meant whatever reader or writer ('correspondent' was the village term for that) took them to mean, and in every newly entered community each of us had to feel his way cautiously—or else try to exploit the prestige of Yale University as Joos did by naming young men who had gone to Yale from there; but that didn't work for the defectively educated informants who were often our best witnesses, since they were many of them contemptuous about people who had been spoiled for farm life by College. In Cummington, the first Joos community, it was easy because of the sponsorship of Joos by Leon A. Stevens, universally trusted in and all around the area of both Cummington and the hamlets and isolated farmsteads which he visited, once each week at least, delivering groceries and taking orders from housebound clients and once taking Joos along to meet possible informants.

When the Handbook was being finally prepared for printing, the discursive text within it was perfected by Bernard and Julia Bloch with difficult points always laid before Hans Kurath for determination; after each shift of policy, the younger members of the triumvirate had to comb the book for residual non-uniformities. One naturally wonders whether their three sorts of components can be sorted out as the book now reads. The answer is that it is always impossible to be confident. The reason is that Bernard was a skillful parodist bent on harmonizing his own contributions with Kurath's, and Julia did the final typing and could be relied upon to return to the strait and narrow path whenever Bernard swerved from parody into caricature: she would query and offer revisions, never silently adjust. She was, after all, an even more subtle parodist than Bernard—and never malicious.

Finally leaving Rutland, Vermont (24 West Street is the address used in letters to Joos in Alma Center) to join Kurath in Providence, Rhode Island, in 1933, they used some of their savings to buy the Oxford English Dictionary. It was some day in 1933 that Bernard wrote to Joos a letter on many aspects of the Atlas and in it pointed out the curious fact that Cummington was almost the only spot in all New England where the local speech used rivulet for a minor tributary to a brook and speculated on whether young William Cullen Bryant picked it up from John Milton, since Milton had substituted it for the usual riveret of his own century. Anyhow, the abundant New England evidence, he said, nowhere contradicted an assumption that Bryant himself, titling an early poem 'The Rivulet' with reference to a stream near his boyhood home, had planted the word in the schools of the neighborhood.

That Oxford dictionary in all its many volumes, which Bernard called 'NED' in writing to Martin Joos—its 19th-century title was 'New English Dictionary' and Miles Hanley always called it that, speaking its title generally as 'NED'—went everywhere with Bernard and Julia Bloch from then on. Its etymology of fetish became a challenge-problem in one such letter—'Something to chew on: the whole external history of that word, and why it has been spelled with ch.'

IV : REVIVALS : 1936 – 1940

After the two Linguistic Institutes at Yale and then the two in New York City, there was none in any state of the Northeast—the region lying between the Atlantic and the Appalachians, not including the Southern States southward of Pennsylvania —until the Institute of 1974 at Amherst in central Massachusetts. Many reasons for that long hiatus are known; here it will be enough to speak of the strongest of them, especially since most reasons are undocumentable. The shift to another region could not take place while the Depression still prevailed. Both 1932 and 1933 were years in which subsidies were unavailable for an enterprise whose charms had faded and vanished during the trial years before that. The Linguistic Society leaders, and especially the Institute's Director, E. H. Sturtevant, found that there was something about the Northeast that was unfavorable to Linguistic Institutes; instead of trying to specify what that might be, we look for favorable factors in the Interior, the area which was tried next. There were and still are a plethora of attractive features about the University of Michigan at Ann Arbor, situated at the comfortable distance of about 30 miles (or 50 kilometers) westward from the Detroit area. Each major University of the Interior—Wisconsin, Illinois, those of the Chicago area, and so on—has its own character, in each case determined at the time of its founding and hardly altered significantly since. Popularly they are called 'midwestern' campuses, implying that they lie in what was called the Middle West and hardly saying anything significant either geographically or in the sociological or cultural sense that must interest us here; our term Interior alludes only to the heartland situation which these campuses share. Anyhow, our word will not be found in use already in ways that could mislead our readers.

Among the campus Departments in the Language and Literature fields, German is the characteristic one for the University of Wisconsin—and Madison is what is normally meant in referring to that University by its state-name, contrary to one misconception held abroad which misplaces it in the state's largest city—just as English is the Language and Literature field that the University of Michigan, ever since its foundation midway in the 19th century, has most notably developed. And Charles Carpenter Fries, 33 years of age at the time, had joined its Department of English in 1920 while still at work on his Ph.D. Dissertation treating of drifts in grammatical usage in the Middle English and Early Modern periods with a view to altering our American school treatments of 'English grammar' and 'correct English' by exerting pressure towards realism, away from prescriptivism. He was the most single-minded personality in all the Linguistic Institutes during the 1930's when he had them under control; details will emerge all along, readable in the successive brochures handsomely printed by the University of Michigan as Official Publications each mid-summer, and on this present page Joos remarks only that a pattern of anonymity prevails in them in contrast to the full naming characteristic of the Sturtevant-operated Institutes of the pre-hiatus four years; for example, Institute-enrolled students as such are never named except that a student who served in a conspicuous capacity as some sort of aide is named on an appropriate page; and again, Albert Henry Marckwardt, principal academic aide to Fries, remains anonymously in the background of the daily operations and gets named here mostly by implication. Marckwardt's letter of 21 November 1974 is the answer to Joos requests for more light on how Michigan's English Department got to be what we found in the Institutes of 1936 to 1940 inclusive, and again in those years after the Second World War that A. A. Hill will report on in due course: the Marckwardt information has been carefully sprinkled into the following pages, and his phrasing only rarely emerges by itself: the reason is that he was writing in the absence of his files of papers and simply omitting what he could no longer certify.

The preëminence of Michigan in English derives from the late 19th century and is assignable to a number of Professors as well as an enterprising Administration which in 1915 brought in Samuel A. Moore to replace J. S. P. Tatlock (who had left for Stanford) and then, promptly after the War, when Louis Strauss became the English Department Chairman, the Literature side of English recruited at least three notable scholars, Professors Campbell, Hanford, and Bredvold, to supervise the very large number of advanced students. Meanwhile Fries acquired a number of Research Assistants; it is not certain that each of them chose to work for him because of personal attraction to his 'linguistic' types of research into English of earlier centuries, but we do know that when the idea arose of investigating usage in letters written to the Veterans Bureau in Washington and Fries got help from at least one Senator from Michigan in gaining access to such letters, it came to seem that this Ann Arbor Professor was worth a student's interest as opening up a less crowded field than Literature, one that could buy some tickets to Washington and pay for snooping in files and a chance to learn the ropes in the Library of Congress. Finally, in 1928 Marckwardt joined the English Department, and soon Fries made use of him as his closest aide in all sorts of enterprises.

The finances of the University of Michigan were on different bases than in other states of the region. Since the 19th century it had its own secure revenues without needing to get its money by legislative appropriation biennially as in Wisconsin: instead, a regular levy was established (called 'millage' because reckoned as so many mills per dollar or equivalently dollars per thousand dollars) payable on all 'real property' in the state according to its official valuation and collected by the taxation offices for the account of the University. In the decades before Detroit's automobile manufacture began to grow explosively, all was serene, and Ann Arbor and the University prospered without incurring rural or urban jealousies; and in the 1930's, finally, the University budget was gradually shifted onto a negotiated fraction of the new sales tax: the state had no personal income tax. These things kept the campus atmosphere quite cheerful right along, until the 1940 Summer Session (of course including the Linguistic Institute) suddenly found itself with severely restricted revenues for political reasons which we need not investigate.

When the Linguistic Institute was suspended in a way that was tantamount to an abrupt termination after its 1931 Fourth Session in New York, Professor Fries saw New York's loss as possible Michigan gain. Promptly he started spreading the thesis that Ann Arbor has outstanding qualifications for undertaking an expanded Summer School program—Summer School Sessions lasting eight weeks regularly were a Michigan feature of long standing, so that expansion was all that was called for, with adjustments managed by experts—in all branches of Linguistics plus the established Michigan specialties, English linguistics and pedagogy and lexicography embracing Middle English and Early Modern English. The National Council of Teachers of English had long been financing the Fries studies of letter-writing English mentioned above: see the review of the Fries 1940 book American English Grammar in Language 17.274 f (1940). In the MLA, where Fries sat on committees and chaired certain of them, such themes were familiar, but he also cultivated his LSA contacts; and to the latter he emphasized the great value which he and the campus Administration in Ann Arbor attached to sponsorship by the Linguistic Society of America, so that even an initial trial session could be announced as 'The' Linguistic Institute of the Linguistic Society of America.

By Christmas of 1934, when before New Year's Eve our Annual Meeting had accidentally brought Bernard Bloch and George Trager together in a corner with an informal conference on the status of oddities such as the item which later came to be transcribed /eh/, in the high-level conclaves tentative agreements had been reached which were encapsulated in the Announcement for the Linguistic Institute of 18 months later. There were altogether five of those handsomely printed booklets, for the Ann Arbor Linguistic Institutes of successive years, 1936 to 1940, each self-titled as a University of Michigan Official Publication and a numbered item of one fiscal year's series beginning with the beginning of July. Now after 1936 everybody got effective information from mimeographed sheets and letters, and the remaining four brochures are dated each within its Summer Session:

June 10, 1936: 37.54: Session June 29 to August 21; June 30, 1937: 38.79; August 13, 1938: 40.13; July 15, 1939: 41.5; July 3, 1940: 42.1: June 25 ...

Contents of the brochures are reported here rather fully, for several sorts of reasons. For one thing, they are Official Publications only in the sense that their printing at State Government expense was authorized and their manufacture took place in the University's printery on the Ann Arbor campus; they were, however, not incorporated into the Archives, so that today they cannot be found in a central Library of State documents or even of University documents, for evidently there is no obligation to file or preserve them at all. A Department, of course, could be interested enough to preserve them in a departmental file, but no such department was found by persons who were interested and searched in Ann Arbor for Joos in 1974. Our evidence comes entirely from the brochures in the Fries family files, some of them duplicate copies presented to Joos, plus letters from A. H. Marckwardt. Also, contemporary newspaper reports have been drawn upon, supplied by Carleton T. Hodge, who sent Joos a file of xeroxings from his personal archives; any other source will be named on the page(s) where it comes into the picture.

The full-time Faculty will be listed by their calendar years of Institute teaching, abbreviated as '36' for 1936, etc. Administrative Committee members remained unaltered throughout the five years before the War:

Charles C. Fries, University of Michigan, Director
Edgar H. Sturtevant, Yale University, Associate Director
Roland G. Kent, University of Pennsylvania, for the LSA
  Norman L. Willey, University of Michigan: see below:
  William H. Worrell, University of Michigan: see below:

				40	Harold B. Allen, Lecturer in English
			39		William Berrien, Instructor in Portuguese
	38			40	Leonard Bloomfield, Professor of Linguistics
37				40	Bernard Bloch, Lecturer in English
				40	J Milton Cowan, Lecturer in Linguistics
37					Franklin Edgerton, Professor of Sanskrit
			39		William F. Edgerton, Professor of Egyptology
			39		Murray B. Emeneau, Lecturer in Oriental Languages
36	37	38	39	40	Charles C. Fries, Professor of English
36	37			40	Vernam E. Hull, Lecturer in Irish
36		38			[R] Hayward Keniston, Professor of Spanish
	37	38	39		George A. Kennedy, Assistant Professor of Chinese
		38			Roland G. Kent, Professor of Comparative Philology
37			39		Thomas A. Knott, Professor of English
37			39		Charles A. Knudson, Professor of French
36					Hans Kurath, Professor of English
36	37	38	39		Albert H. Marckwardt, Assistant Professor of English
36	37	38			Clarence L. Meader, Professor of General Linguistics
36	37				Ernst Alfred Philippson, Assistant Professor of German
36	37	38	39		Walter B. Pillsbury, Professor of Psychology
36	37	38			Leo L. Rockwell, Professor of English
37					Edward Sapir, Professor of Linguistics
37					Chih-pei Sha, Lecturer in Chinese
36					John W. Stanton, Lecturer in Chinese
36	37	38	39	40	Leon H. Strong, Assistant Professor of Anatomy
36		38		40	Edgar H. Sturtevant, Professor of Linguistics
			39		George L. Trager, Lecturer in Slavic Languages
36	37		39		Leroy Waterman, Professor of Semitics
36		38	39	40	Norman L. Willey, Professor of German
				40	Lloyd S. Woodburne, Lecturer in Psychology [[& Assistant Dean]]
36	37		39		William H. Worrell, Professor of Semitics
36	37	38	39	40	Joseph K. Yamagiwa, Lecturer in Japanese

1940 Courses will be listed in a second alphabet after listing the 1936—1939 Courses because of a partly mysterious reorganizing of them all between 1939 and 1940!

TIME SCHEDULE

8:00-9:00	9:00-10:00	10:00-11:00	11:00-12:00	12:00-2:00	2:00-3:00	3:00-4:00	4:00-5:00
Old English (English 103s) Rockwell TuWThF 2215 A.H.		*Rise and Development of Standard English* (English 201) Fries and Marckwardt TuWThF 3217 A.H.	*Modern English Grammar* (English 152) Fries and Marckwardt TuWThF 1209 A.H.	Luncheon Conferences TuTh Michigan Union	*American English* (English 109s) Kurath TuWThF 2003 N.S.	*Linguistic Survey of New England* (English 117) Kurath TuTh 2003 N.S.	
						Methods and Practice of Recording a Living Language (English 118) Kurath WF 2003 N.S.	
Old Icelandic (German 213) Willey MTuWTh 305 S.W.	*History of the German Language* (German 205) Philippson MTuWTh 203 A.H.	*Introduction to German Dialect Study* (German 209s) Willey MTuWTh 305 S.W.	*Introduction to Indo-Germanic Linguistics* (German 183s) Willey MTuWTh 305 S.W.				
Arabic (Oriental Lang. 163s) Worrell MTuWTh 2023 A.H.	*Coptic* (Oriental Lang. 171s) Worrell MTuWTh 2023 A.H.	*Assyrian* or *Aramaic* or *Hebrew* Waterman MTuWTh 2021 A.H.	*Ethiopic* or *Comparative Semitic Grammar* (Hour tentative) Worrell MTuWTh 2023 A.H.			*Old Irish* (English 110) Hull MTuWTh 3209 A.H.	
Japanese (Oriental Lang. 191s) Yamagiwa MTuThF 2019 A.H.	*Hittite* (Oriental Lang. 197s) Sturtevant TuWThF 2029 A.H.	*Chinese* (Oriental Lang. 181s) Stanton TuWThF 2019 A.H.	*Comparative Grammar of Greek and Latin* (Greek 166 or Latin 166) Sturtevant TuWThF 2014 A.H.		*Introduction to Linguistic Science* (English 151) Sturtevant TuWThF 3209 A.H.		
Spanish Syntax (Spanish 167s) Keniston TuWThF 210 R.L.			*Psychology of Language* (Psychology 108s) Pillsbury and Meader MTuWTh 1121 N.S.			*Study of Language as Biological Process* (Gen. Ling. 135s) Meader MTuWTh 2019 A.H.	

Anatomy and Function of the Vocal Apparatus (Anatomy 210) Strong Daily, 8-12. 3528 E. Med.

COURSES OF INSTRUCTION IN THE LINGUISTIC INSTITUTE*

AMERICAN ENGLISH. The chief types of cultivated pronunciation and their relation to local dialect and popular speech. Geographic distribution and social stratification of words and idioms. Professor KURATH. TuWThF, 3. 2003 N.S.

Elect as English 109. Two hours credit.

ANATOMY AND FUNCTION OF THE VOCAL APPARATUS. Following an introductory survey of the phylogenetic and developmental history of the vocal organs of man, the course proceeds to an intensive study of their gross and microscopical anatomy. The nervous mechanisms associated with speech and the influence of the endocrine glands on the larynx receive special consideration. In the laboratory the students dissect the neck and oropharyngeal region in minute detail, the thorax fairly comprehensively, and the abdomen and pelvis only insofar as these latter regions contain structures involved in the production of speech. Assistant Professor STRONG. Daily, 8-12. 3528 E.Med.

Elect as Anatomy 210. Six hours credit.

ARABIC. Arabic is the most characteristic, the most copious, and the best known of Semitic languages. Apart from its importance to mediaeval studies and modern life, it is the best means of acquaintance with the Semitic type of language. Textbook: Socin, *Arabic Grammar*, reprint, New York, 1920. Later editions of Socin, *Arabische Grammatik*, Berlin, several dates, in German or in English, may be used; but the first English edition, above mentioned, is greatly preferred. Copies may be had of the publisher, Stechert, New York. A limited number may be bought in Ann Arbor. Professor WORRELL. MTuWTh, 8. 2023 A.H.

Elect as Oriental Languages 163. Two hours credit.

ARAMAIC. Grammar and reading, with emphasis upon structure and phonology. Textbook: C. R. Brown, *Aramaic Method*. The reading will cover the Aramaic portions of Ezra and Daniel together with selections from non-Biblical texts. Professor WATERMAN. MTuThF, 10. 2021 A.H.

Elect as Oriental Languages 161. Two hours credit.

* ABBREVIATIONS.—A.H., Angell Hall; E.Med., East Medical Building; N.S., Natural Science Building; R.L., Romance Language Building; S.W., South Wing; U.H., University Hall; W.Med., West Medical Building.

HITTITE SEALS

American English

1936: Kurath: The chief types of cultivated pronunciation and their relation to
local dialect and popular speech. Geographic distribution and social stratification of words and idioms.

1937, 1938: Knott: The course in American English will study the various forms
of behavior of the English Language in America: The sources of vocabulary
in immigrating European populations and in the native languages. The adap-
tations and coinages to meet American conditions both colonial and national.
The achievement of cultural conditions in which standard English became
more widely adopted. The influence of dictionaries and schools on usage.
Present-day differences and relations between the standard American and
the standard British vocabularies and usages. Colonial, national and present
regional pronunciations, especially the spreading of what Krapp calls "Gen-
eral American." The materials studied will be found largely in Kenyon's
American Pronunciation, Krapp's The English Language in America,
Mencken's [The] American Language, American Speech (a quarterly journal),
Dialect Notes (annual [sic! actually quite irregular] publication of the Dialect
Society), and A Dictionary of American English [presumably Craigie's
Historical Dictionary is meant by this cryptic mistitling].

American Dialect Geography

1937: Bloch: The Linguistic Atlas of the United States and Canada: general plan
of the project. Problems, methods, and results of the New England survey;
preparation of the work sheets; selection of communities and informants;
field work; editorial procedure. The historical interpretation of regional
and social variation in American English. The discussions will be supplemented by laboratory demonstrations of field work and by practice in the
phonetic recording of dialects. Students will have an opportunity to investigate selected specimens of American speech at first hand, and to prepare
one or more field records.

Anatomy and Function of the Vocal Apparatus

1936 37 38 39: Strong: MTuWThF 8–12: Elect under a Medical School number
and for 6 semester-hours of credit, three times the usual credit-value of
Linguistic Institute courses.
Following an introductory survey of the phylogenetic and developmental
history of the vocal organs of man, the course proceeds to an intensive
study of their gross and microscopical anatomy. The neck and oropharyngeal region in minute detail, the thorax fairly comprehensively, and the
abdomen and pelvis only insofar as these latter regions contain structures
involved in the production of speech.

Arabic

1936, 1937, 1939: Worrell: Arabic is the most characteristic, the most
copious, and the best known of the Semitic languages. Apart from its
importance to mediaeval studies and modern life, it is the best means of
acquaintance with the Semitic type of language. Textbook: Socin, Arabic
Grammar, reprint, New York, 1920. Later editions of Socin, Arabische
Grammatik, Berlin, several dates, in German or in English, may be used;
but the first English edition, above mentioned, is greatly preferred. Copies
may be had of the publisher, Stechert, New York. A limited number may
be had in Ann Arbor. This course is an alternate to 'Egyptian: Coptic'

Aramaic

1936: Waterman: Grammar and reading, with emphasis on structure and
phonology. Textbook: C. R. Brown, Aramaic Method. This reading will
cover the Aramaic portions of Ezra and Daniel together with selections
from non-Biblical texts.

Assyrian: Waterman

  1936, 1937, 1939: Grammar and reading, with emphasis upon structure and phonology. The course will be directed toward gaining control of the Assyrian sign list as rapidly as possible so as to begin the reading of easy historical texts. Textbook: Delitzsch, Assyrische Lesestücke.

Chinese

  1936: Stanton: An introduction to the grammar and syntax of Chinese (kuan hua). The method of learning Chinese will receive more emphasis than the acquisition of a vocabulary. Textbook: Aldrich, Practical Chinese.

  1937: Kennedy and Sha: MTuWThF 8–10, 11–12, 2–3: Six semester-hours, intended to be the student's only registration for credit! An intensive, introductory course in reading modern Chinese. Emphasis will be on the acquisition of vocabulary and on extensive reading practice. Students are expected to devote full time to this course, which will meet four hours daily, with additional individual instruction to be arranged. Reading materials have been specially prepared and printed for this course. Admission is only by consent of the instructor. This course is offered by the American Council of the Institute of Pacific Relations, in association with the Linguistic Institute.

  1938: Kennedy: MTuWThF 8–9:30, 10–12: Six semester-hours… [wording is identical with the 1937 wording from here to end…]

Chinese (Advanced Course), 1938: Kennedy: MTuWThF 10–12, 2– 4, 2 semester-hours of credit for each of the sections a, b, and c. This course meets four hours daily, each hour constituting a separate unit. The first hour is devoted to pronunciation drill and conversation practice. In the other three hours are read selections respectively from Chinese (a) newspapers, (b) stories of historical characters, and (c) standard novels. Students may elect the whole course, if sufficiently well prepared, or any portion of it.

Chinese. Beginning Chinese: 1939: Kennedy: MTuWThF 11, other hours to be arranged: 6 semester-hours of credit. A concentrated course in modern colloquial Chinese. No prerequisites.

Chinese. Selected Readings in T'ang Dynasty History and Literature: 1939: Kennedy: MTuThF 10. An intensive course in classical Chinese, using texts from the dynastic history and from two of the most important essayists, with collateral readings of later historical material. For advanced students only. Class limited to nine students.

Comparative Grammar of Greek and Latin

  1936: Sturtevant: TuWThF 11. Elementary course on the methods and results of linguistic science as applied to Greek and Latin. A reading knowledge of French and German is required, as well as training in Greek and Latin.

Comparative Semitic Grammar

  1936: Worrell: MTuWTh at an hour to be arranged. The purpose of this course will be to systematize and supplement the knowledge of those who have studied one or more Semitic languages; but it may be profitably taken by those who are experienced in linguistic studies, without having previously mastered a Semitic language. Textbook: Brockelmann, Semitische Sprach- wissenschaft, Leipzig, 1916. (This belongs to the Sammlung Göschen, and is not to be confused with two larger works by the same author and with similar title.) A limited number of copies may be bought in Ann Arbor.

Egyptian

  Coptic Dialects: 1939: Worrell: MTuWTh 8. Reading of Bohairic, Fayyumic, Achmimic, and sub-Achmimic texts, with attention to characteristic dif- ferences of phonology, morphology, syntax, and vocabulary, and with dis- cussion of their interrelationship and relative geographical position. Text- books: Till, Koptische Dialektgrammatik; Till, Akhmimisch-Koptische Grammatik. [Stechert] This course is an alternate to that in Arabic.

Egyptian
   History of the Ancient Egyptian Language
      1939: William F. Edgerton: TuWThF 9. A lecture course primarily for
      students of linguistics who have no previous knowledge of Egyptian.
      After a brief description of the kinds of source materials available the
      lectures will attempt a systematic analysis of Old Egyptian, the literary
      language of the Fifth and Sixth dynasties, followed by an attempt to trace
      the history of the language from predynastic to Coptic times.

Egyptian
   Middle Egyptian
      1939: William F. Edgerton: TuWThF 11. An introductory course for students
      who wish to learn to read hieroglyphic. Required textbooks: Gardiner,
      Egyptian Grammar (Oxford, 1927), and Sethe Aegyptische Lesestücke,
      Leipzig, 1924, or second edition, 1928.

English Courses Note: Before 1939, certain of these were placed in the alphabetic
   lists in the brochures according their first titling word, often a word which we
   now treat as a sub-title—as for the two W. F. Edgerton courses just above—so
   that in 1936, 1937, 1938 the Fries and Marckwardt jointly taught Modern English
   Grammar followed 'Methods ...' and their Rise and Development ... followed the
   unrelated 'Psychology ...' of Pillsbury and Meader!

English
   Rise and Development of Standard English: Fries and Marckwardt
      1936: TuWThF 10 — 1937: TuWThF 8 — 1938: TuWThF 10. [Joos note: Certain
      topics were treated as Fries specialties, others as Marckwardt topics.
      When Fries lectured, Marckwardt attended to take notes; Fries usually
      did not reciprocate, and Marckwardt had a student note-taker instead.]
      After a survey of the chief developments in the major English dialects from
      the eleventh to the fourteenth centuries, the class will give particular atten-
      tion to the London dialect of East Midland from the end of the fourteenth
      century to the eighteenth century. A knowledge of Old English is essential.

English
   Modern English Grammar: Fries and Marckwardt
      1936: TuWThF 11 — 1937: TuWThF 10 — 1938: MW 2—4. The types of gram-
      matical processes used in Modern English and their historical relation.
      A consideration of the grammatical ideas expressed in the English
      language since 1500 (a) by the forms of words, (b) by function words, and
      (c) by word order.

English
   Introduction to Modern English
      1939: Marckwardt: TuWThF 8. An inductive study of the sounds and gram-
      mar of present-day English, with a brief consideration of syntax.

English
   Rise and Development of Standard English: Inflection and Syntax
      1939: Fries: Hours to be arranged.

English
   Old English
      1936, 1937, 1938: Rockwell: TuWThF 8. The elements of Old English gram-
      mar, with some consideration of Germanic antecedents and subsequent
      developments.
      1939: Knott: [Identical days & hours, identical description as Rockwell's]

English
   English Phonetics
      1937: Bloch: MTWTh 11. The mechanism of speech. English sounds in isola-
      tion and in context. The phonetic structure of cultivated speech. Intensive
      ear training and practice in the phonetic notation of speech. Textbook:
      John S. Kenyon, American Pronunciation, 6th Edition, Ann Arbor, 1935
      [the revised edition which Joos indexed and put through press in 1934!]

Ethiopic

1936: Worrell: MTuWTh, hour to be arranged. Ethiopic is a primitive southern variety of Semitic, which is usually studied in connection with Arabic as contributing to the general picture of the Semitic type of language. As the language of Christian Abyssinia, its importance is similar to that of Coptic. Textbook: Chaine, Grammaire Éthiopienne, Beyrouth, 1907. A limited number of copies may be bought in Ann Arbor.

Field Methods in Linguistics

[Introduced by Sapir in 1937; next given by Bloomfield in 1938; replaced in 1939 and 1940 by distinguished scholars invited to Ann Arbor by the week or longer.]

1937: Sapir: TuWThF 11. It is hoped to make this course as inductive as possible. The task will be set the members of the class to find out all they can about the phonetics and morphology of some language which is entirely unknown to them. The materials are not to be obtained from books but by direct questioning, the phonetic notations of the class corrected by the instructor being the final authority. No reference to printed literature will be allowed. It is hoped to show that a perfectly adequate grasp of any language, even a complex one, can be obtained by the direct phonetic approach. The phonetics needed to carry on the course will be developed as need requires. It is believed that the fear which so many students of written languages have of the direct phonetic method is entirely unwarranted, and it is hoped that this course may do something to make real the oft-repeated statement that languages exist primarily as oral phenomena, not as written symbols.

1938: Bloomfield: TuWThF 11. Studies in the Central type of the Algonquian languages (Fox, Ojibwa, Cree, Menomini). It is hoped to make this course as inductive as possible. There are no prerequisites; in particular, no previous knowledge of Algonquian languages will be expected. The material will be presented orally; if possible, some of it will be presented by native informants. Phonetics will be developed as needed. The work will consist in determining the phonetic structure of the forms, the word structure, syntax, and categories, and the relationship between the several languages.

French: History of the French Language

1939: Knudson: TuWThF 11. External history: the Romanization of Gaul; the rise of dialects; the development of national unity and the spread of a national language; French as a product and as an instrument of French civilization. Internal history: the sources or modern French pronunciation, syntax, and vocabulary. Trends of scholarship in this field, past and present. Textbooks: Wartburg, Evolution et structure de la langue française (Chicago, 1937, second edition); Holmes and Schutz, History of the French Language (New York, 1938).

German Dialect Study, Introduction to

1936: Willey: MTuWTh 10. A general survey of the field of continental West Germanic dialects.

German Etymology

1937: Philippson: MTuWTh 10. Lectures on the modern German vocabulary, its origins and development, stressing derivation, word formation, and semantics, with constant reference to English. The students will use Ernest Wasserzieher's Woher? Ableitendes Wörterbuch der Deutschen Sprache. Reports on assigned readings.

Gothic

1937: Philippson: MTuWTh 11. Study of Gothic phonology and morphology with constant reference to Indo-European and primitive Germanic conditions. Wright's Grammar of the Gothic Language, readings in Ulfilas' Bible translation.

1938: Willey: MTuWTh 8; 1939: Willey: MTuWTh 10. Study of Gothic phonology and morphology with constant reference to origins and to developments in cognate languages. Streitberg's Handbuch der gotischen Sprache, readings...

Hebrew
  1936: Waterman: Grammar and reading with emphasis upon structure and
    phonology: MTuThF 10. Textbook: Davidson, Hebrew Grammar.
  1937: Worrell: Elementary course in Biblical Hebrew: MTuWTh at hours to
    be arranged. Textbook [identical].

Hittite
  1936: Sturtevant: TuWThF 9. Reading and interpretation of texts. Lectures and
    discussions on Hittite comparative grammar. No previous knowledge of
    Hittite or of cuneiform writing is required.
  1938: Sturtevant: TuWThF 11. A study of the grammar in connection with the
    reading of texts; special attention will be paid to the relationship of Hittite
    to Indo-European. Texts: E. H. Sturtevant and G[eorge] Bechtel, A Hittite
    Chrestomathy (1935); E. H. Sturtevant, A Comparative Grammar of the
    Hittite Language (1933). It will be helpful to own also E. H. Sturtevant,
    A Hittite Glossary, 2nd ed. (1936).

Indo-Germanic Linguistics, Introduction to
  1936: Willey: MTuWTh 11. A consideration of the phonological and morphological
    characteristics of the Indo-Germanic parent-tongue with special attention to
    the methods of reconstructing the forms and roots.

Introduction to Linguistic Science
  1936: Sturtevant: TuWThF 2. The origin of the science and some of its chief
    results. Phonetic law: its importance and some suggested explanations.
    Analogy: contamination, creation, analogy in syntax. Change of vocabulary,
    including word-formation. Change of meaning. A survey of the known
    languages.
  1937: Sapir: TuWThF 3. The place of general linguistics in social and biological
    science. Speech from the point of view of behavior and language from the
    point of view of cultural patterning. A survey of the fundamental processes
    used in language; fundamental categories generally or frequently selected for
    grammatical treatment. Phonetics and phonemics. Factors making for change
    in linguistic form and content. Classifications of language, genetic and mor-
    phological. Brief characterization of selected languages. The importance of
    linguistics for the social sciences, psychology, and an analysis of literature.
    Textbooks: E. Sapir, Language (1931), and L. Bloomfield, Language (1933).
  1938: Bloomfield: TuTh 7–9 p.m. The biological and social place of language.
    The meaning of speech-forms; semantics. Speech-sounds and phonemes.
    Word structure and syntax. Relationship of languages; speech families; the
    comparative method. Writing. The distribution of dialects. Change in lan-
    guage: phonetic change, creation of new forms, borrowing; the rivalry of
    forms. Standard languages; local dialects, jargons, slang; literary language;
    linguistic superstition, tabu, normative grammar. Applications of linguistics:
    teaching children to read; composition; the teaching of foreign languages;
    logical and mathematical systems. Textbooks: [the same books as in 1937!]
  1939: See the several entries under the general heading 'Linguistics' below!

Japanese: Yamagiwa
  1936: MTuThF 8. The purpose of this course will be to furnish a fundamental
    understanding of the Japanese language. There will be a survey of the gram-
    matical forms used in familiar and polite discourse, and a study of the Japan-
    ese system of writing. This course is designed both for the student seeking
    practical knowledge of Japanese for use in speaking, reading, and writing,
    and for those who are more interested in its purely linguistic aspects. An
    attempt will be made to compare the grammar of Japanese with the grammar
    of western languages. Textbook: Arthur Rose-Innes, Conversational Japanese.
  1937: MTuThF 9 and 2: Two or four semester-hours of credit. The purpose ...
    fundamental understanding ... both for ... practical knowledge ... and ... its
    purely linguistic aspects. The morning class will be devoted to intensive
    study of the grammatical forms used in familiar and polite discourse, and

the afternoon class to practical work in speaking, reading, and writing. The student may elect the grammatical work only, for two hours credit; or the grammar and practical work together, for four hours credit. Text: Rose-Innes, Conversational Japanese, supplemented by Japanese readings.

1938: [The 1937 listing reprinted identically!]

1938: Japanese (Advanced Course). A brief, intensive review of the grammar, followed by graded readings in modern writing. This course is designed for students who wish to read more or less technical materials in their respective fields.

1939: [The two 1938 course-listings repeated, the second slightly retouched!]

Language as a Biological (Physiological) Process, Study of

1936: Meader: MTuWTh 3 — 1937: 2 — 1938: 3 p.m. again

Human speech will be treated as a form of communication which was gradually evolved throughout the entire evolutionary history of the earth, emerging in the animal kingdom from the simpler vegetative, food-securing activities of the alimentary organs until it became an extremely intricate system of indirect life-serving processes. The production of speech sounds and the phenomena of meaning will be discussed from this (the genetic) point of view. Textbooks: a standard textbook of anatomy, such as Piersol's, Cunningham's, Gray's, Toldt's, or Sobbota and Murrick's; Arey, Developmental Anatomy; Luciani, Physiology, Vol. III; Bechtevew, Human Reflexology.

Latin Morphology: 1938: Kent: TuWThF 10. The declensional and conjugational forms of Latin will be traced as they developed from the primitive Indo-European and as they changed within Latin itself. Special attention will be given to the regular phonetic developments as leading to irregularity of the paradigms, and to the analogical changes as tending toward the restoration of regularity. Some older Latin inscriptions will be studied in detail. Textbooks: R. G. Kent, The Sounds of Latin (1932), and one of the following: A. Ernout, Morphologie historique du Latin, 2d ed. (1927); E. Kieckers, Historische Lateinische Grammatik, 2d part, Formenlehre; W. M. Lindsay, Short Historical Latin Grammar, 2d ed. (1915). The first named may be obtained from the instructor.

Linguistic Survey of New England: 1936: Kurath: TuTh 3—5. The results of the work done upon the Linguistic Atlas of the United States and Canada during the last six years. The general plan. Preparation of the work sheets. Selection of communities. The field work. Preparation of map manuscripts. The historical interpretation of regional and social variations in American English.

Linguistics

1939: Introduction to the Scientific Study of Language

Fries and members of the staff of the Linguistic Institute: TuTh 7—9 p.m. A series of lectures and discussions to illustrate the principles and methods of modern linguistic science in dealing with language materials. The particular topics to be discussed in the weekly bulletins of the Linguistic Institute.

Linguistics

1939: Voegelin, Emeneau, and Trager: Recording and Analysis of a Living Language: MW 2-4. A number of small groups will work co-operatively at recording and analyzing several living languages as employed by native speakers of those languages.

(a) American Indian. Two kinds of students are contemplated: (1) linguists who want the experience of working with an unwritten "primitive" language; (2) ethnographers who want to learn how to record speeches, prayers, and texts in general, and at the same time know how to distinguish between a "native name" and a more or less descriptive commentary.

An Indian informant, probably a Delaware, will be brought to Ann Arbor. Lists of words containing only simple phonemes will be dictated by the informant. These words will be followed by lists containing consonant clusters.

Having acquired an alphabet for writing, the class will take down sentences given by the informant to illustrate word classes and the paradigms of each word class. These preliminary sentences will be generally based on the same words used for working out the phonemes, so that each member of the class may prepare card files of given words appearing with various inflectional affixes and thus arrive at an inductive discovery of Delaware grammar (phonology and paradigms).

The procedure up to this point will parallel the technique used by Americanists in the field, except that the examples given by the informant will be pointed toward the analysis to be made by the class. For the remaining time, about half of the session, the informant will dictate texts, at first slowly, but finally in units of normally spoken phrases. Further linguistic analysis (derivation, composition) will be based on the texts indicated.

The group taking dictation from the Indian informant will be limited to twelve students. A second section for students working with copies of Delaware dictation can be formed if desired; this second section would have the experience of analyzing but not of recording Delaware speech.

(b) Similar opportunities for recording and analysis will be available in a Slavic language and (c) some other language to be announced at the beginning of the session.

Linguistics: Practical Semantics
1938 & 1939: Knott
  Registration is restricted to twelve students [in 1938, but eight students in 1939]; a conference with the instructor is suggested prior to registration.
1938: TuWThF 3 — 1939: 9 o'clock, with laboratory hours to be arranged. Two, four, or six semester-hours of credit.
    Some knowledge of Old English and Middle English language and literature is required. Using primarily the quotations in the collections of the Middle English Dictionary, together with those found in Bosworth-Toller and in Godefroy, the students will study the historical development of the meanings of several hundred words. The work done will constitute a direct contribution to the Middle English Dictionary. Occasional lectures, frequent group discussions, personal instruction, and from twenty to twenty-five laboratory hours a week will be the normal schedule.

Linguistics: Psychology of Language (1939): See below at 'Psychology ...'

Methods and Practice of Recording a Living Language
  1936: Kurath: WF 3–5: A laboratory course based upon the principles and methods employed by the Linguistic Atlas of the United States and Canada. Phonetic recording of specimens of American English. Preparation of one or more field reports. A continuation of the work of the Linguistic Atlas in a portion of the Middle West.
  1937: See 'American Dialect Geography' above!

Modern English Grammar: 1936: See under 'English' above!

Old French Phonology and Morphology (Introductory Course)
  1937: Knudson: TuWThF 10. This course will trace in outline the development of the sounds and forms of spoken Latin into Old French, as of the time of the Chanson de Roland. [Textbooks:] [(Bruno Paulin) Gaston] Paris [1839-1903], Extraits de la Chanson de Roland (Paris: Hachette); Luquiens, Introduction to Old French Phonology and Morphology (New Haven: Yale University Press). [Joos note: The cryptic and supercilious condensing of bibliography information, and in particular omission of nearly all dates, edition-numbers, and so on indefinitely, with the result that these facts are reserved to the Professor's own students as a matter of principle, was and long had been the custom among scholars in the Romance Languages and Literatures field and also the custom of printeries. One must feel apologetic about clarifying the original print, we are given to understand, but after all, this is History!]

Old French Phonology and Morphology (Second Course)
> 1937: Knudson: Hours to be arranged. (Tentatively announced. May be offered
> as an alternate to [the Introductory Course] if the number of students war-
> rants.) This course, intended for students who have completed a year's work
> in Old French, or the equivalent, will study in some detail the language of an
> early thirteenth-century text. Bourciez, Précis historique de phonétique
> française (Paris: Klincksieck); La queste del saint graal, ed. Pauphilet
> (Paris: Champion).

Old Icelandic
> 1936: Willey: MTuWTh 8 — 1938: Hours to be arranged. The elements of Old
> Icelandic phonology and morphology and a comparison with cognate dialects
> in the Germanic group. Textbook: E. V. Gordon, An Introduction to Old Norse.

Old Irish
> 1936, 1937: Hull: MTuThF 3. This course will serve as an introduction to Celtic
> philology. It will consist of an outline of Old Irish grammar and a study of
> one of the oldest literary texts. The linguistic and literary relationship of
> the Celtic languages will be stressed and continual reference will be made
> to topics of investigation. Textbooks: R. Thurneysen, Handbuch des Alt-
> Irischen (C. Winter, Heidelberg, 1909); J. Strachan and Osborn Bergin,
> Stories from the Tain (Hodges, Figgis and Company, Dublin, 1928).

Pali, with an Introduction to the Middle Indic Dialects
> 1937: Franklin Edgerton: TuWThF 10. Either this course or 'The Veda ...' will
> be given, whichever is requested by a greater number of students, but
> not both. Prospective registrants are therefore urged to communicate
> with the Director of the Linguistic Institute as soon as possible. The
> textbooks must be ordered from abroad.
>
> Analysis of easy Pali texts, particularly from the standpoint of Sanskrit,
> some knowledge of which is required. The history of the sounds and
> inflections of Pali, and their derivation from Sanskrit, will be studied, with
> incidental reference to other Middle Indic dialects and to the Hybrid Sanskrit
> of the Buddhists. Textbooks: Dines Andersen's Pali Reader with Notes and
> Glossary (London and Copenhagen, 1910), and W. Geiger, Pali Literatur und
> Sprache (Strassburg, 1916).

Phonetic Basis of Romance Phonology
> 1938: Keniston: TuWThF 8. A study of the changes in sound between Latin and
> the Romance languages, and an interpretation of the physical processes
> involved. An elementary knowledge of Latin and of phonetics will be useful
> for those electing this course.

Practical Semantics: See page 63 above, at 'Linguistics: Practical Semantics'

Problems in Indo-European Comparative Grammar
> 1938: Sturtevant: TuTh 3, F 2-4. The new evidence from Hittite apparently
> requires fairly extensive revision of the reconstructions in the handbooks.
> A search will be made for tentative solutions of the problems thus raised
> which shall harmonize as closely as possible with generally accepted
> doctrine. Lectures and discussion.

Psychology of Language
> 1936, 1937, 1938: Pillsbury and Meader — 1939: Pillsbury alone
> 1936: A survey of the facts in psychology which bear upon linguistic problems.
> Textbook: Pillsbury and Meader, Psychology of Language, 1928.
> 1937: Among the subjects treated are: the laws of thought and language, the
> history of linguistic theory, language as a form of expression, the genesis
> of tissue integration in language, the psychology of syntax, the psychology
> of attention and persuasion.
> 1938: [The 1937 listing unaltered!]
> 1939: [The unaltered listing again, but 'Meader' deleted!]

Rise and Development of Standard English: 1939: Fries: See above under 'English'

Russian
   1937, 1938: Professor Meader and Madame Pargment
   1937: MTuWTh 3 — 1938: MTuWTh 11. A practical introductory course
      designed to familiarize the students with the inner mechanism of the
      language and a sufficiently large vocabulary to enable them to read
      Russian with no other aid than a dictionary.

Sanskrit
   1937, 1939
   1937: Edgerton: TuWThF 9. Rapid survey of the essentials of the grammar,
      with introduction to the historical study of the language and its relation to
      Indo-European in general. Detailed study of easy texts, with careful
      analysis from grammatical, historical, and cultural viewpoints.
      Whitney's Sanskrit Grammar and Lanman's Sanskrit Reader should be
      owned by students.
   1939: Emeneau: MTuWTh 9. [Identical description!]

Slavic: Church Slavonic
   1939: Trager: TuWThF 10. An introduction to the comparative grammar of the
      Slavic languages.

Spanish Syntax
   1936: Keniston: TuWThF 8. An introduction to the methods of syntactic analysis.

Study of Language as a Biological (Physiological) Process: See page 62 'Language'

Sumerian
   1937: Waterman: MTuWTh 2. Beginning course. Grammar and reading with
      emphasis upon structure and phonology. Textbook: C. J. Gadd, Sumerian
      Reading Book.

The Veda, Introduction to its Language and Literature
   1937: Edgerton: TuWThF 10. Selected hymns of the Rigveda; critical analysis of
      the text, with introduction to Vedic exegesis. Some knowledge of Classical
      Sanskrit required. Whitney's Grammar and Lanman's Reader will be used.
      Either this course or 'Pali ...' will be given, whichever is requested
      by a greater number of students, but not both.

= =

   As remarked at the bottom of our page 56, the 1940 list of courses and their
teachers need to be registered separately, and they appear accordingly on pages
66-68, condensed by back-referencing the unaltered items.
   This arrangement is, of course, deceptive enough so that readers need some
such explicit warning as this present paragraph to protect against confusion.
   Also, readers can profit from thoughtfully considering the little tabulation,
next here, showing the number of persons involved in the teaching, summer by
summer, in each of the five Ann Arbor Linguistic Institutes of 1936 through 1940:

1936: 16: Only Kurath and Sturtevant as visiting staff, leaving 14 Ann Arbor ones
1937: 18: From elsewhere: Bloch, Franklin Edgerton, Kennedy, Sapir, Sha
1938: 13: From elsewhere: Bloomfield, Kennedy, Kent, Sturtevant
1939: 16: From elsewhere: Berrien, W. F. Edgerton, Emeneau, Kennedy, Trager,
1940: 11: From elsewhere: Bloch, Cowan, Sturtevant, Voegelin   [Voegelin

   The maximum count, 18, may perhaps be partly accounted for by the decision
to make the 1937 Summer Session conspicuously worth having in Ann Arbor, in
ways that will emerge presently, notably by building up one late July fortnight
with visiting lecturers and a final week-end conference that eventually became
the Summer Meeting of the Linguistic Society of America. The official First
Summer Meeting was that of Friday and Saturday, July 29th and 30th, 1938,
and was announced by Secretary Kent's Second Circular from Philadelphia.

<u>The 1940 Linguistic Institute Announcement</u> listed these Courses:

Anatomy and Function of the Vocal Apparatus: Strong: [Identically as in 1936-39!]

Celtic
   Old Irish: TuWThF 9
   [The 1936 and 1937 description repeated, identically as on page 64, plus one
   additional textbook:] Students may also consult H. Lewis and H. Pedersen,
   <u>A Concise Comparative Celtic Grammar</u> (1937).

Comparative Grammar of Greek and Latin
   Sturtevant: TuWTh 10
   An introduction to Indo-European grammar from the point of view of the
   classical languages. The discovery of several pre-Indo-European laryngeal
   consonants has involved some changes in reconstructed Indo-European;
   these changes will be discussed. A reading knowledge of French and German
   is required, as well as training in Greek and Latin. Textbook: <u>Précis du
   Phonétique historique du Latin</u>, M. Niedermann, nouvelle édition, 1931.
      This course will be offered as an alternate with that in Hittite. The
      choice of the course to be given will be determined May 20 on the basis
      of the advance notices of intention to register.

English: American Dialect Geography
   Bloch: TuWThF 11. Historical sketch of linguistic geography in Europe, with a
   description of the chief European dialect atlases. The Linguistic Atlas of
   the United States and Canada: general plan of the project. Problems,
   methods, and results of the New England survey: preparation of the questionnaire, training of field workers, selection of communities and informants,
   field work, editorial procedure. The historical interpretation of regional and
   social differences in American English will be studied in specific examples
   taken from <u>The Linguistic Atlas of New England</u>, Vol. 1 (1939). The discussions
   will be supplemented by demonstrations of field work and practice in the
   phonetic recording of dialects. Students will have an opportunity to investigate selected specimens of American English under conditions of field work,
   and to prepare one or more complete field records. Recommended text:
   Hans Kurath (and others), <u>Handbook of the Linguistic Geography of New Eng-
   land</u> (1939).
      Students who intend to make first-hand studies of spoken English, either
      in connection with this course or independently, are advised to attend
      also the course in Phonetics and Phonemics, where they may receive
      the necessary phonetic training.

English: Modern English Grammar
   Fries: TuWThF 11. A survey of the inflections and syntax of present-day
   American English, with especial attention to social differences. [Formerly
   given as a joint course by 'Fries and Marckwardt' ever since its creation;
   now that the Fries <u>American English Grammar</u> of 1940 had been perfected,
   his principal aide was away from Ann Arbor on sabbatical leave in Mexico]

English: Old English
   Allen: TuWThF 8. The elements of Old English grammar, with some consideration of Germanic antecedents and subsequent developments.

English: Rise and Development of Standard English: Inflections and Syntax
   Fries: Hours to be arranged. After a survey of the chief developments in the
   Southern dialect [= speech in Southern England] from the eleventh to the
   fourteenth centuries, the class will give particular attention to the London
   dialect of East Midland from the end of the fourteenth to the seventeenth
   century. A knowledge of Old English is essential.

Germanic: Gothic: Willey: MTuWTh 11. [The 1938 entry identically as on page 60]

Germanic: Old Icelandic: MTuWTh 8. [The 1938 entry identically as on page 64]

Hittite: Sturtevant: TuWThF 10. [See 'Hittite' on page 61, 1936 and 1938, first the
'Reading and Interpretation' and two years later 'A study of the grammar' for
the two courses which in 1940 appear merged into a single course:]

    Reading and interpretation of texts. Lectures on the bearing of Hittite upon
Indo-European comparative grammar, particularly as concerns the newly
discovered laryngeals. Textbook: E. H. Sturtevant and G. Bechtel, A Hittite
Chrestomathy (1935). It will be helpful to own also E. H. Sturtevant, A Com-
parative Grammar of the Hittite Language (1933) and E. H. Sturtevant, A Hittite
Glossary, 2d ed. (1936). This course will be offered as alternate with that in the
Comparative Grammar of Greek and Latin. Choice of the course will be deter-
mined May 20 on the basis of the advance notices of intention to register.

Linguistics: Introduction to Linguistic Science
    Sturtevant: TuTh 7-9 p.m.
    The position of linguistics among the sciences. Speech and writing. Phonetics
and phonemics. Types of linguistic structure. Speech and animal cries.
"Primitive" languages and the technique for studying them. Phonetic law
and primary phonetic changes. Analogic creation. Contamination. Semantic
change. Change of vocabulary. The method of comparative grammar.
Textbook: L. Bloomfield, Language (1933).

Linguistics: Mechanical Apparatus and Instrumental Techniques
    Cowan: TuWThF 4.
    A laboratory course designed to acquaint students with apparatus and tech-
niques which can be used for the objective study of linguistic problems. The
theory, practice, and application of phonographic recording and reproduction.
Usage of various electro-acoustical devices for the recording of pitch,
loudness, quality (timbre), and duration of speech sounds. Students will be
encouraged to use the laboratory equipment on their own specific problems.
The experimental literature pertinent to linguistics will be reviewed.

Linguistics: Phonetics and Phonemics
    Bloch: TuWThF 9
    (1) Phonetics, the study of speech sounds considered as physical events, is
not properly a part of linguistics, but to linguists it is both an indispensable
tool for linguistic studies, descriptive and historical, and a background for
the understanding of linguistic phenomena. This point of view will govern the
presentation of the following topics: the physiological mechanism of speech;
general phonetic theory and system, with a survey of the chief classes of
sounds occurring in the languages of the world; the construction of a phonetic
alphabet. The discussions will be supplemented by intensive ear training and
practice in the phonetic recording of speech. (2) Phonemics, the study of
speech sounds considered as the signalling units of language, is an important
branch of linguistic science. Topics to be discussed under this head include
the definition of the phoneme; the phonemic structure of English, German,
and French; principles of phonemic analysis; the phonemic interpretation of
a phonetic record; morpho-phonemics and historical phonemics. Students
will be given practice in the phonemic notation of English and other
languages.

Linguistics: Recording and Analysis of a Living Language
    Voegelin: MW 2-4
    A small group will work co-operatively at recording and analyzing a living
language as employed by a native speaker of that language.
    Two kinds of students are contemplated: (1) linguists who want the experi-
ence of working with an unwritten "primitive" language; (2) ethnographers who
want to learn how to record speeches, prayers, and texts in general, and at the
same time know how to distinguish between a "native name" and a more or less
descriptive commentary.
    A Chippewa Indian informant will be brought to Ann Arbor. Lists of words

containing only simple phonemes will be dictated by the informant. These words
will be followed by lists containing consonant clusters. Having acquired an alphabet for writing, the class will take down sentences given by the informant to
illustrate word classes and the paradigms of each word class. The preliminary
sentences will be generally based on the same words used for working out the
phonemes, so that each member of the class may prepare card files of given
words appearing with various inflectional affixes and thus arrive at an inductive
discovery of Chippewa grammar (phonology and paradigms).

The procedure up to this point will parallel the techniques used by Americanists in the field, except that examples given by the informant will be pointed
toward the analysis to be made by the class. For the remaining time, about half
of the [Linguistic Institute's two-month] session, the informant will dictate
texts, at first slowly, but finally in units of normally spoken phrases. Further
linguistic analysis (derivation, composition) will be based on the texts indicated.

The group taking dictation from the Indian informant will be limited to
twelve students.

Linguistics: Seminar
    Bloomfield and Sturtevant: Saturday 10:30 a.m.
        Special problems in linguistics. The seminar is intended to provide for
        advanced students engaged in linguistic research an opportunity for discus-
        sion and criticism of their problems and materials.

Linguistics: Techniques for Investigation of Primitive Cultures
    Voegelin: Tu 2–4, Th 3–4
        A seminar devoted to field methods for obtaining (1) [a] glossary of material
        culture: names for flora and fauna and manufactured articles, place names and
        other geographic terms; (2) the vocabulary of social organization: kinship
        terms, personal and clan names, status terms and titles; (3) religious and
        ethical concepts: terms and stereotypes used in ritual, origin myths, and
        personal contact with the supernatural, as well as ideals of behavior and moral
        estimates; (4) aesthetic judgment and knowledge: arts and crafts terminologies,
        numerical and calendrical systems, pictographic and other writing; (5) texts:
        autobiographical and folkloristic material dictated by a Chippewa Indian. The
        seminar will thus acquire, with the assistance of an ethnographer, a topical
        vocabulary of content (culture in general) to be analyzed on the basis of form
        (linguistic criteria).

Psychology of Language
    Woodburne: TuTh 8: One [semester-] hour of credit
        A review of psychological factors in the growth and use of language.
        [This half-course consisted of selected chips from the primeval
        Pillsbury-and-Meader course of 1936 and later, judged adequate
        for Linguistic Institute purposes and in 1940 taught by their young
        assistant after the retirements of the two inventors in 1938 and in
        1939. In 1940 he was an Assistant Dean; see below, page 93]
==

Above, beginning with page 56, we have taken everything from a single source, the
five Announcements for the Linguistic Institutes of 1936, 1937, 1938, 1939, and 1940.
Next we step back to the Summer of 1937, the time when the LSA Executive Committee set about seeing whether the Ann Arbor developments would, in a second
Summer Session, still bring further successes, perhaps even justify supporting a
further project of Director Charles Carpenter Fries. He projected making the
eight-week Linguistic Institute period the occasion for a Summer Meeting of the
Linguistic Society of America around the end of July each year. To procure full
documentation for his proposal, Fries caused the 1937 Institute to be minutely
recorded by a thoroughly organized pyramid in which his principal assistant,
Marckwardt, enlisted a number of team captains, and so on; finally, some time
in August/September, the English Department's stenographers stencilled six
mimeographed pages which we quote complete beginning with the next page here:

THE LINGUISTIC INSTITUTE
June 28 to August 20, 1937

The Linguistic Institute of 1937, like that of 1936, was a part of the Summer Session of the University of Michigan. Even more than in 1936, however, the Linguistic Institute maintained a unity within itself and the distinct character of the work was not interfered with by the mass of diverse activities with which it was surrounded. On the other hand, the kind of publicity [fn: This publicity was largely the work of Mr. Harold B. Allen, one of the students in the Linguistic Institute] which the L. I. enjoyed in this Summer Session of more than 5,000 students, 55% of whom were graduate students, did well to spread the gospel of linguistics among groups that very rarely hear of linguistic science and the problems with which it deals. This publicity dealt chiefly with the lectures and luncheon conferences arranged for the Institute as a whole. The two lectures each week on Wednesday and Friday evenings were well attended (usually by about 75 although at one 250 were present) and were followed by lively discussions. The subjects of these lectures were as follows:

1. Wed., July 7. The Human Larynx. Prof. L. H. Strong, University of Michigan.
2. Fri., July 9. Tocharian and Its Placement in Indo-European. Prof. Edward
                  Sapir, Yale University.
3. Wed., July 14. Speech and Emergent Specificity. Prof. John Muyskens,
                  University of Michigan.
4. Fri., July 16. Hittite and the Substratum Theory. Prof. Walter Petersen,
                  University of Chicago.
5. Wed., July 21. The Greek "Rough Mutes". The Internal Evidence for Aspirate
                  Pronunciation. Prof. E. H. Sturtevant, Yale University.
6. Fri., July 23. The Greek "Rough Mutes". The External Evidence and the
                  Change to the Modern Spirant Pronunciation. Prof. E. H.
                  Sturtevant, Yale University.
7. Wed., July 28. Hittite numan and manka. Prof. E. Adelaide Hahn,
                  Hunter College.
8. Fri., July 30. The Structure of the Algonquian Languages. Prof. Leonard
                  Bloomfield, University of Chicago.
9. Wed., Aug. 4. The Revival of Hebrew. Dr. Zellig Harris, University of
                  Pennsylvania.
10. Fri., Aug. 6. Linguistic Changes and Tendencies in the New Hebrew.
                  Dr. Zellig Harris, University of Pennsylvania.
11. Wed., Aug. 11. (a) The Menzerath-Janker X-Ray Motion Pictures, with
                   Sound, of the Movements of the Vocal Organs During
                   Speech. Discussion by Dr. Bernard Bloch, Linguistic
                   Atlas, Brown University.
                   (b) Stroboscopic Motion Pictures of the Vocal Cords in
                   Action. Discussion by Dr. [J] Milton Cowan, University
                   of Iowa.
12. Fri., Aug. 13. The Indo-European Laryngeals. Prof. Edward Sapir, Yale
                   University.

The last lecture, a magnificent marshalling of the types of evidence supporting the "laryngeal hypothesis," was given at the request of the L. I. students, among whom this subject had received considerable informal discussion throughout the session. The lectures by Professor Petersen, Professor Sturtevant, and Professor Bloomfield were made possible by the money given the Linguistic Institute by the Linguistic Society.

The luncheon conferences, usually upon such topics as would lend themselves to general discussion, had an average attendance of 85.

[[1976 editorial note: The stencil-cutting typewriter used in the original lacked diacritics and also lacked square brackets [ ]. This explains each Joos correction such as the repair of the damaged Cowan name above or the damaged Sanskrit word rūdhi below in the Fries remarks]]

These luncheon conferences were:

1. July 1. The Problems of the Phoneme. Round table discussion led by Professors Knott, Bloch, and Sapir.
2. July 6. Sound Change and Phonetic Laws. Round table discussion led by Professors Meader, Worrell, and Fries.
3. July 8. The Voice Mechanism. Professor L. H. Strong.
4. July 13. Intonation in English, French, and German. Dr. [J] Milton Cowan.
5. July 15. The Origin of the Alphabet. Dr. Zellig Harris.
6. July 20. Are Linguists Studying Speech? Prof. Edward Sapir.
7. July 22. Etymology and the Interpretation of Texts. Prof. Franklin Edgerton.
8. July 27. Problems in Criminal Argot. Dr. David Maurer.
9. July 29. Problems of "Meaning." Round table discussion led by Dr. L. S.
Woodburne and Prof. H[ereward] T. Price [Associate Editor of
the Early Modern English Dictionary, 1929 LSA Member]
10. Aug. 3. Experiment in Teaching Chinese. Dr. George Kennedy.
11. Aug. 5. Investigating Vowel Length in French. Dr. Pierre Delattre.
12. Aug. 10. Substratum and Linguistic Change. Round table discussion led by
Professors Edgerton, Waterman, Worrell, and Willey.
13. Aug. 12. Linguistic Problems Involved in the Proposal for an International
Auxiliary Language. Round table discussion led by Professors
Meader and Willey, Dr. Harold Rose, and Mr. [Norman] McQuown.

Discussions starting in these conferences were frequently carried further in the
classes, and yoga and rūḍhi, given life by Professor Edgerton, became popular
technical terms in class and in conversation.

The chief work of the Institute, however, was carried on in the courses given by
a faculty of 18 members. In addition, Professor Prokosch of Yale had been provided
for in this faculty but he found it necessary to withdraw because of ill health. The
list of the faculty follows:

Bernard Bloch, Lecturer in English
Franklin Edgerton, Professor of Sanskrit
Charles C. Fries, Professor of English
Vernam E. Hull, Lecturer in Irish
George A. Kennedy, Lecturer in Chinese
Thomas A. Knott, Professor of English
Charles A. Knudson, Assistant Professor of French
Albert H. Marckwardt, Assistant Professor of English
Clarence L. Meader, Professor of General Linguistics
Ernest A. Philippson, Assistant Professor of German
Walter B. Pillsbury, Professor of Psychology
Leo L. Rockwell, Professor of English
Edward Sapir, Professor of Linguistics
Chih-pei Sha, Lecturer in Chinese
Leon H. Strong, Assistant Professor of Anatomy
Leroy Waterman, Professor of Semitics
William H. Worrell, Professor of Semitics
J. K. Yamagiwa, Lecturer in Japanese

This faculty offered 27 courses, as follows: [Note: the underlinings have
been omitted below by Joos!]
1. American English, Professor Knott.
2. American Dialect Geography, Dr. Bloch.
3. Anatomy and Function of the Vocal Apparatus, Assistant Professor Strong
4. Arabic, Professor Worrell
5. Assyrian, Professor Waterman
6. Chinese [fn: The work in Chinese was an intensive course to which the
students devoted their entire time. It was financed by the
American Council of the Institute of Pacific Relations and
brought into association with the Linguistic Institute
primarily through the efforts of Professor Sturtevant.]

Professor Kennedy and Mr. Sha

7. Coptic, Pofessor Worrell
8. English Phonetics, Dr. Bloch
9. Field Methods in Linguistics, Professor Sapir
10. German Etymology, Assistant Professor Philippson
11. Gothic, Assistant Professor Philippson
12. Hebrew, Professor Worrell
13. Introduction to Linguistic Science, Professor Sapir
14. Japanese, Mr. Yamagiwa
15. Language as a Biological (Physiological) Process, Professor Meader
16. Modern English Grammar, Professor Fries and Assistant Professor Marckwardt
17. Old English, Professor Rockwell
18. Old French Phonology and Morphology (Introductory), Assistant Professor Knudson
19. Old French Phonology and Morphology (Advanced), Assistant Professor Knudson
20. Old Irish, Associate Professor Hull
21. Pali, with an Introduction to Middle Indic Dialects, Professor Edgerton
22. Psychology of Language, Professors Pillsbury and Meader
23. Rise and Development of Standard English, Professor Fries and Assistant Professor Marckwardt
24. Russian, Professor Meader
25. Sanskrit, Professor Edgerton
26. Sumerian, Professor Waterman
27. The Veda, Professor Edgerton

Two of the courses here named were offered as alternates, to be given only if a greater number of students applied for them than for the ones first listed. Instead, however, of the 25 courses thus planned for, 28 were given, including both the courses in Old French, an advanced course in Russian, and an additional course in the phonetics of Navaho by Professor Sapir [unnumbered: thus he gave three!].

For these 28 courses there were 356 elections by 258 separate individuals. These figures do not include the staff members who visited courses given by their colleagues. Of these 258 at least 125 came to the University of Michigan primarily for the work of the Linguistic Institute. Among these students were 29 who were holders of the Ph.D. degree and, in most cases, members of the faculties of other colleges or universities [fn: By special arrangement holders of the Ph.D. degree may attend the work of the Linguistic Institute as guests of the University of Michigan without payment of tuition fees]. There were also ten students who, recommended highly by [their former] instructors, were granted scholarships provided by the American Council of Learned Societies. Geographically, students in the Linguistic Institute represented every section of the United States, from New England to California and from Canada to Mexico City.

Although there were serious gaps in the program of studies offered, those who attended the Linguistic Institute for 1937 seemed genuinely enthusiastic concerning the work accomplished. Both Professor Edgerton and Professor Sapir gave unsparingly of their energy and of their time not only to the individual problems of the students but also to making fruitful all the general discussions of the Institute. It was their especial contribution which gave particular character to this session of the Linguistic Institute and made it successful.

More clearly than ever appeared the function of the summer Linguistic Institute. In comparison with the summer weeks, annual meetings of a few days can do but little for the stimulating interchange of ideas and the discussion of the significance of the latest results of linguistic research. Young scholars can profit greatly from the intimate contacts with a few outstanding linguists which each session of the Institutes makes possible. And a summer Institute can provide economically for courses in remote bits of linguistic territory, making them available to those who hold academic positions in widely separated institutions. In some way it should be possible to bring the advantages of the Linguistic Institute more fully to the attention of those mature students who could best profit from the work. Greater num-

bers as such are not desired, for the resources of the Institute do not depend upon
the fees paid; but the success of such an Institute should probably be measured
not only by what is done for those who happen to attend but also, in some part, by
its ability to reach those who should attend.

The Linguistic Institute was revived in 1936 under an agreement whereby the
Summer Session of the University of Michigan provided for it experimentally for
a period of two years. During the two weeks of July when Professor Sturtevant
visited the 1937 session the administrative committee of the Linguistic Institute
(with Professors Edgerton and Sapir instead of Professor Kent) met with Professor L. A. Hopkins, Director of the Summer Session, and other administrative
officers of the University of Michigan to discuss future provision for the Institute.
At that meeting the administrative officers of the University of Michigan agreed
to continue the support of the Linguistic Institute for another period, this time for
three years. Plans are therefore going forward for the sessions of 1938, 1939, and
1940. [To any historically-minded person, one of the more interesting things
   about this document—technically a document only in the sense that it is
   unchallengeably a part of the written documentation, although it had no
   discoverable status as an item of official documents of the University
   of Michigan, nor yet as a document within the Linguistic Society, but
   at most seems to have been introduced privately into LSA conclaves by
   Charles Carpenter Fries and never exposed to the membership at large
   —is that it is totally and absolutely anonymous! Only internal evidence
   such as the patch-work stylistic alternations can serve us here. Segments composed in unmixed Fries Style are few—indeed, only the very
   last paragraph of all is certainly a Fries paragraph, and also the first
   two sentences on our page 69; apart from those pieces of text, only the
   two styles of Harold Allen and Albert Marckwardt are surface-styles
   here, and neither of these casual observations can be confirmed today.]

- -

In the career of the Linguistic Society of America that 1937 Summer Session at
Ann Arbor is of peculiar interest in that it included the first association between
our Society's second Editor, Bernard Bloch, and the second Secretary—Treasurer,
J Milton Cowan, alluded to in the Joos Obituary on Bloch, Language 43.9 (1967): in
the mimeographed narrative which we have just been reprinting, we see that Bloch
must have been in the audience when Cowan gave his Intonation paper on Tuesday,
July 13th, and that the garden party referred to in the Obituary was on Sunday 18th
July—most likely at the home of Charles Carpenter Fries: a harmless guess if not
justified: Joos is thinking of the special attractions of the Fries garden just then—
so that the two 30-year-old youngsters, we see, took only a week or so to agree to
offer the pair of performances described for Wednesday, August 11th, on page 69.
This reminds us that the scheduling of Public Lectures and of Luncheon Conference
speakers was rather tentative as the Summer Session began early in July, and that
there was always room for last-minute alterations. Finally, there had originally
not been any intention of anything of either sort after the Thursday, August 12th,
Luncheon Conference on the last available day before final examinations. Thus we
see that the student request to hear from Edward Sapir on IE Laryngeals, and on
an ill-omened day at that, was and for us today remains an extraordinary tribute
both to Sapir and to that group of students.

The Annual Meeting of December, 1937, was the scene of a massive distribution
of a mimeographed First Circular or prospectus describing the forthcoming First
Summer Meeting. No example is known to have survived: such items, precariously
assembled of sheets of flimsy paper held together by a single staple in the upper
left corner, have been carried off home from the December meeting already in bad
condition—sheets coming away from that staple (which the Department of English
office staff regularly placed horizontally, the neatest-looking and most impractical
stapling, practically guaranteeing that the paper will tear from normal folding)—
and at home either loaded with notes (so that the First Circular could be compared
with Kent's Second Circular) or without useful notes and therefore destined for
oblivion, typically wastebasketed or used for starting a fireplace fire.

𝕷𝖎𝖓𝖌𝖚𝖎𝖘𝖙𝖎𝖈 𝕾𝖔𝖈𝖎𝖊𝖙𝖞 𝖔𝖋 𝕬𝖒𝖊𝖗𝖎𝖈𝖆

FIRST SUMMER MEETING, ANN ARBOR, 1938

SECOND CIRCULAR

THE Linguistic Society of America will hold its First Special Summer Meeting at Ann Arbor, Michigan, on Friday and Saturday, July 29-30, 1938, in conjunction with the session of the Linguistic Institute, on the campus of the University of Michigan.

Those planning to attend the meeting, if not already in Ann Arbor for the Linguistic Institute, should write to Prof. C. C. Fries, University of Michigan, Ann Arbor, Mich., for rooms and prices, stating the accommodations which they need, and for what period of time. Those attending the meeting are cordially invited to arrive somewhat in advance or to stay over after the end of the sessions, that they may visit the classes and see the Linguistic Institute in operation.

The sessions will be held in the Amphitheater on the third floor of the new Horace H. Rackham School of Graduate Studies.

Guests are cordially invited to attend the sessions and other gatherings.

Local Committee: The Local Committee in charge of the arrangements consists of L. Bloomfield, C. C. Fries, R. G. Kent, E. H. Sturtevant.

Attendance: The following members and members-elect of the Society have announced their intention to be present at the Ann Arbor meeting:

H. B. Allen	C. E. Finch	Z. S. Harris	F. K. Li	L. L. Rockwell
G. Bechtel	C. C. Fries	C. T. Hodge	A. H. Marckwardt	Miss H. H. Shohara
Mrs. R. M. Bechtel	Miss F. Gamper	H. Hoijer	R. I. McDavid, Jr.	J. W. Stanton
B. Bloch	A. H. Gerberich	H. Hootkins	C. L. Meader	L. H. Strong
L. Bloomfield	D. M. Gilbert	O. E. Johnson	H. Meier	E. H. Sturtevant
J. M. Carriere	C. R. Goedsche	H. Keniston	D. F. Munro	S. N. Trevino
F. G. Cassidy	A. Goetze	G. A. Kennedy	E. D. Myers	C. F. Voegelin
J. M. Cowan	Miss M. R. Haas	R. G. Kent	Mrs. C. Plumer	R. L. Ward
Miss J. E. Daddow	Miss E. A. Hahn	J. Kepke	H. T. Price	L. Waterman
J. M. Echols	R. A. Hall, Jr.	J. A. Kerns	Miss M. Quay	N. L. Willey
M. B. Emeneau	M. L. Hanley	T. A. Knott	J. F. Rettger	R. D. Williams
	J. K. Yamagiwa		Mrs. A. R. Zollinger	

Dinners and Luncheons: Arrangements have been made to enable the members and their friends to lunch and dine together during the meeting.

PROGRAM OF THE SESSIONS

For the reading of a single paper, the outside limit of time is twenty minutes; some readers have limited themselves to a shorter period. All are urgently requested to observe the time limit, as free discussion of the papers is very desirable.

The Committee on Publications asks that typewritten copy of the papers, in form ready for publication, be handed to the Secretary of the Society during or immediately after the sessions.

With LSA Secretary Kent's Second Circular announcing the Society's First Summer Meeting, Ann Arbor, 1938, we for the first time encounter an exhaustive list of personal names of members foregathering in a setting fully conducive to leisurely exchange of information and prejudices: the Annual Meetings are always too time-limited and otherwise unfavorable to formation of new clusterings. The Second Circular's listing of names is of course tentative; as it says, 'The following members and members-elect of the Society have announced their intention to be present at the Ann Arbor meeting' but that was an intention not always fulfilled, and the ultimately published Proceedings must be consulted to determine whether a particular member did attend. Also, Julia Bloch was always there in Ann Arbor too, and that presence is never mentioned.

First Session, on Friday, July 29, at 2:00 P.M., in the Amphitheater; chairman, Professor Leonard Bloomfield.

Address of Welcome, by Edward H. Kraus, Dean of the College of Literature, Science, and the Arts.

Report of the Local Committee, by Professor Charles C. Fries.

Remarks on the policy of the Society, by the Secretary, Professor Roland G. Kent.

Appointment of Committee on Resolutions.

Reading of Papers:

1. Dr. **Mary R. Haas** (Yale Univ.) : Alternative Syncope in Primitive Muskogean. (15 min.)
2. Prof. **Raven Ioor McDavid, Jr.** (The Citadel, Charleston, S. C.) : An Introduction of Undergraduates to the IPA Alphabet. (10 min.)
3. Prof. **Edgar H. Sturtevant** (Yale Univ.): The Prehistory of the Indo-European Stems in long *a*. (20 min.)
4. Prof. **J. M. Carriere** (Northwestern Univ.) : French Dialectology. (20 min.)
5. Prof. **Miles L. Hanley** (Univ. of Wisconsin) : *Ng.* (10 min.)
6. Prof. **Hermann Meier** (Drew Univ.): The Word Families of the English Language. (10 min.)

Informal Dinner, in the Assembly Room on the third floor of the Horace H. Rackham School of Graduate Studies, at 6:00 P.M.; subscription price, $1.10 (including state sales tax).

Second Session, at 8:00 P.M., in the Amphitheater; chairman, Professor Roland G. Kent. Invitation program:

7. Prof. **Albrecht Goetze** (Yale Univ.): Umlaut in Babylonian.
8. Dr. **J. Milton Cowan** (State Univ. of Iowa): The Vocal Cords in Action (illustrated with moving pictures).

Third Session, on Saturday, July 30, at 9:15 A.M., in the Amphitheater; chairman, Professor Edgar H. Sturtevant.

Reading of Papers:

9. Prof. **Roland G. Kent** (Univ. of Pennsylvania) : A Forged Old Persian Inscription in Cuneiform Characters. (15 min.)
10. Prof. **Albert H. Marckwardt** (Univ. of Michigan): A Survey of English Dialects in Michigan and Indiana. (20 min.)
11. Prof. **E. Adelaide Hahn** (Hunter College) : The Position of the Subordinate Clause in Hittite. (20 min.)
12. Prof. **Leonard Bloomfield** (Univ. of Chicago) : Initial *k* in German. (15 min.)
13. Prof. **Edward Delos Myers** (Trinity College, Hartford, Conn.): The Linguistics Course at Trinity College. (15 min.)

Luncheon, in the Assembly Room on the third floor of the Horace H. Rackham School of Graduate Studies, at 12:15 P.M.; subscription price, payable at the luncheon, 52 cents (including state sales tax).

Fourth Session, at 2:00 P.M., in the Amphitheater; chairman, Professor Charles C. Fries.

Reading of Papers:

14. Dr. **George Bechtel** (Yale Univ.): The Hypothesis of Reduced Vowels in Indo-European. (20 min.)
15. Dr. **Ruth Moore Bechtel** (New Haven) : The Reduced Grade of Original Short Vowels in Greek and Latin. (20 min.)
16. Prof. **Thomas A. Knott** (Univ. of Michigan) : The Middle English and the Early Modern English Dictionaries. (20 min.)
17. Dr. **Harry Hoijer** (Univ. of Chicago) : Two Spanish Words in Chiricahua Apache. (15 min.)
18. Dr. **J. Alexander Kerns** (New York Univ.) : The Tense Categories of Indo-Hittite and Indo-European. (20 min.)

Non-members of the Linguistic Society, who wish information about the work of the Society and the manner of joining it in membership, are asked to hand their names and addresses to Professor R. G. Kent, Secretary, L. S. A., or to write to him at Bennett Hall, University of Pennsylvania, Philadelphia.

All persons, whether or not members of the Linguistic Society, who wish information about the Group for Phonetics or the Group for American Indian Languages, should likewise apply to Professor Kent.

⟦ The foregoing two paragraphs 'Non-members ...' and 'All persons ...' were cut away from the bottom of Kent's short fourth page and inserted at this point, and then the 'ACTIVITIES ...' entries for August 4 and 5 were brought forward from the top of his fourth page; thus nothing is omitted. ⟧

ACTIVITIES OF THE LINGUISTIC INSTITUTE
July 25 to August 6, 1938

Unless another place is named, all the lectures and luncheon conferences here listed will be held in the Horace H. Rackham School of Graduate Studies, in the rooms specified.

Monday, July 25

4:30 P.M., in the Main Auditorium:
Public Lecture: PROF. ROLAND G. KENT (Univ. of Pennsylvania), The Reconstruction of the History of Languages.

Tuesday, July 22= 26

12:10 P.M., in the Assembly Room (third floor):
Luncheon Conference: PROF. J. MILTON COWAN (State Univ. of Iowa), Experimental Linguistic Methods.

4:30 P.M., in the Main Auditorium:
Public Lecture: PROF. EDGAR H. STURTEVANT (Yale Univ.), Lapses and Linguistic Change.

7:00-9:00 P.M., in Angell Hall, Room 231:
Lecture and Discussion: PROF. LEONARD BLOOMFIELD (Univ. of Chicago), Relationship of Languages.

Wednesday, July 27

4:30 P.M., in the Main Auditorium:
Public Lecture: PROF. LEONARD BLOOMFIELD, Linguistic Science and the Problem of "Correct" Language.

7:30 P.M., in the Amphitheater (third floor):
Lecture: PROF. J. MILTON COWAN, Acoustics and Linguistics.

Thursday, July 28

12:10 P.M., in the Assembly Room (third floor):
Luncheon Conference: PROF. J. MILTON COWAN, Recent Experimental Linguistic Results.

4:30 P.M., in the Main Auditorium:
Public Lecture: PROF. C. C. FRIES (Univ. of Michigan), The Changing Grammar of Modern English.

7:00-9:00 P.M., in Angell Hall, Room 231:
Lecture and Discussion: PROF. LEONARD BLOOMFIELD, Phonetic Change.

Friday, July 29, and Saturday, July 30

Sessions of the First Special Summer Meeting of the Linguistic Society of America.

Tuesday, August 2

12:10 P.M., in the Assembly Room (third floor):
Luncheon Conference: DR. MURRAY B. EMENEAU (Fellow of the American Council of Learned Societies for Research in Dravidian Languages), Problems in Dravidian Phonetics and Phonemics.

7:00-9:00 P.M., in Angell Hall, Room 231:
Lecture and Discussion: PROF. EDGAR H. STURTEVANT, Phonetic Change.

Wednesday, August 3

7:30 P.M., in the Amphitheater (third floor):
Lecture: PROF. FANG-KUEI LI (Yale Univ.), The Classification of Chinese Dialects.

Thursday, August 4

12:10 P.M., in the Assembly Room (third floor):
Luncheon Conference: DR. MURRAY B. EMENEAU, Parts of Speech and Types of Predication in Dravidian.

7:00-9:00 P.M., in Angell Hall, Room 231.
Lecture and Discussion: PROF. LEONARD BLOOMFIELD, Creation of New Forms.

Friday, August 5

7:30 P.M., in the Amphitheater (third floor):
Lecture: PROF. E. ADELAIDE HAHN (Hunter College), Hittite *kwitman*.

Bulletin No. 12, issued with the March 1939 Language, includes the Fries report to the December 1938 Annual Meeting; and there we find that nine of the June list of those intending to be present have dropped out (conceivably as not positively known to be present: after all, if one has not been recorded by signature the name could simply have been overlooked despite the urgent requests to register) so as to create a list of these absentees, all current members of course: F. G. Cassidy, Miss F. Gamper, Miss M. R. Haas, H. Keniston, J. A. Kerns, Mrs. C. Plumer, J. W. Stanton, L. H. Strong, S. N. Treviño; since two or more of these are known to have been in residence in Ann Arbor at the time, we are left with a tiny puzzle. We date the memberships of the ten names that had been added to the Kent list: Hugo Broeker (1938), Arthur F. Carlson (1938), Norman E. Eliason (1936), S. I. Hayakawa (1938), Laura E. Heminger (1938), William R. Leete (1938), Herbert H. Petit (1938), Walter B. Pillsbury (1936), Hans Sperber (1935), Albert van Eerden (1938). Other persons who attended, as everybody on the Ann Arbor campus knew they could, remain everywhere unlisted because they were not registered as actual or prospective dues-paying LSA members: to make one's election as a member for 1938 automatic, $5.00 dues were to be paid to Kent promptly, failing which he would strike the name before publication of Bulletin No. 12. We mention this explicitly to keep all the names in correct historical perspective; see the Fifty-year Index for implications. The younger students, as usual, were most likely to save their money; the Friday evening Subscription Dinner at the 1938 Institute was substantial and cost $1.10 including the Sales Tax, and the Saturday Luncheon 52¢; the equivalent meals in 1976 would cost roughly $6.00 and $3.00. (In the 1939 Institute, definitely less!) In sum, it emerges that our Society's membership grew notably in direct consequence of the revival of the Institute beginning with the 1936 Summer Session, and still further increases came with the instituting of the Summer Meetings.

With the complete Second Circular for 1938 before us on pages 73-75, we can reduce the identically constructed 1939 to a bare printing of only what is new and assume that interested readers will take the old from those pages:

Local Committee: The Local Committee in charge of the arrangements consists of C. C. Fries, Chairman; M. B. Emeneau; C. F. Voegelin; and R. G. Kent, ex officio.

Attendance: The following members and members-elect of the Society have announced their intention to be present at the Ann Arbor meeting:

H. B. Allen	J. M. Echols	C. T. Hodge	R. I. McDavid, Jr.	D. F. Sheehan
C. L. Barnhart	Franklin Edgerton	H. Hootkins	C. L. Meader	Miss H. H. Shohara
H. A. Basilius	W. F. Edgerton	O. E. Johnson	H. H. Petit	E. H. Sturtevant
B. Bloch	M. B. Emeneau	H. H. Josselson	E. A. Philippson	G. L. Trager
L. Bloomfield	C. C. Fries	A. P. Kehlenbeck	K. L. Pike	A. van Eerden
Hugo Broeker	Miss F. Gamper	G. A. Kennedy	W. B. Pillsbury	C. F. Voegelin
Miss M. M. Bryant	D. M. Gilbert	R. G. Kent	Mrs. C. Plumer	L. Waterman
F. G. Cassidy	Miss M. R. Haas	J. S. Kenyon	H. T. Price	N. L. Willey
J. M. Cowan	Miss E. A. Hahn	T. A. Knott	Miss Mabel Quay	W. H. Worrell
P. C. Delattre	Miss L. E. Heminger	C. A. Knudson	J. F. Rettger	J. K. Yamagiwa
J. del Toro	C. Hockett	A. H. Marckwardt	L. L. Rockwell	

First Session, on Friday, July 28, at 2:00 P.M., in the Amphitheater. Chairman, Professor E. H. Sturtevant.

Address of Welcome, by Professor Louis A. Hopkins, Director of the Summer Session of the University of Michigan.

Remarks on the policy of the Society, by the Secretary, Professor Roland G. Kent.

Appointment of Committee on Resolutions.

Reading of Papers:

1. Prof. L. L. Rockwell (Colgate Univ.): The Nomenclature of Levels of Speech. (15 min.)
2. Prof. Charles F. Voegelin (De Pauw Univ.) : The Number of North American Indian Languages Actually Spoken Today. (20 min.)
3. Dr. Mary R. Haas (Institute of Human Relations, Yale Univ.) : Men's and Women's Speech in Koasati. (15 min.)
4. Mr. Kenneth L. Pike (Univ. of Mexico): Tonemic Disturbance in the Mixteco Song "The Flea." (15 min.)
5. Dr. Charles Hockett (Worthington, Ohio) : The Stop Phonemes of Ojibwa. (15 min.)

Informal Dinner, at the Michigan Union at 6:00 P.M.; subscription price, 80 cents (including state sales tax).

Second Session, at 8:00 P.M., in the Amphitheater. Chairman, Professor Charles C. Fries, President of the Linguistic Society of America.

Invitation program:

6. Prof. Leonard Bloomfield (Univ. of Chicago): Algonquian Word Formation.
7. Dr. J. Milton Cowan (State Univ. of Iowa) : The Mode of Vibration of the Vocal Cords (illustrated with moving pictures).

Third Session, on Saturday, July 29, at 9:15 A.M., in the Amphitheater. Chairman, Professor Franklin Edgerton.

Reading of Papers:

8. Prof. Pierre C. Delattre (Wayne Univ.): Is the Word a Phonetic Entity in French? (15 min.)
9. Prof. J. S. Kenyon (Hiram College): Distinctive Dialectal Values of the Noun and Verb Endings —ɪz, —əz and —ɪd, —əd. (15 min.)
10. Prof. Albert H. Marckwardt (Univ. of Michigan): The Survey of Folk Speech in Michigan and Indiana. (20 min.)
11. Prof. E. H. Sturtevant (Yale Univ.): The Pronunciation of Latin *qu*. (15 min.)
12. Prof. E. Adelaide Hahn (Hunter College) : The Sequence of Tenses in Hittite. (15 min.)
13. Prof. Roland G. Kent (Univ. of Pennsylvania): The Avestan Instrumental in —*is*. (15 min.)

Luncheon, at the Michigan Union at 12:15 P.M.; price 52 cents (including state sales tax). Prof. Floyd A. Firestone of the department of physics, University of Michigan, will demonstrate the artificial larynx.

Fourth Session, at 2:00 P.M., in the Amphitheater. Chairman, Professor Roland G. Kent.

Reading of Papers:

14. Dr. Murray B. Emeneau (Yale Univ.): The Morpho-phonemic Technique applied to Kolami, a Dravidian Language. (15 min.)
15. Prof. George A. Kennedy (Yale Univ.): Tone-Patterns in a Chekiang Dialect. (15 min.)
16. Prof. Franklin Edgerton (Yale Univ.): Pali *middha*, a Ghost-word Materialized. (15 min.)
17. Dr. George L. Trager (Yale Univ.) : Problems of Baltic Phonemics. (15 min.)
18. Dr. Bernard Bloch (Brown Univ.): The Theory of a Phonetic Alphabet.

Report of Committee on Resolutions, and action thereon.

Members of the Linguistic Society and their friends are invited to tea in the Assembly Room of the Rackham Building at 4:00 P.M.

ACTIVITIES OF THE LINGUISTIC INSTITUTE, JULY 24 TO AUGUST 9

(Lectures will be given in the Amphitheater (third floor) of the Rackham Building; luncheon conferences will be held at the Michigan Union.)

Wednesday, July 19

7:30 P.M. Lecture: PROF. E. H. STURTEVANT, The Phonetic Basis of Rhythm, especially in Greek and Latin.

Thursday, July 20

12:10 P.M. Luncheon Conferences: DR. CHARLES F. HOCKETT, Accentual Systems and Tra-ger's Law.

Friday, July 21

7:30 P.M. Lecture: PROF. LEONARD BLOOMFIELD, Composition and Derivation in Algon-quian.

Wednesday, July 26

7:30 P.M. Lecture: PROF. ROLAND G. KENT, Deciphering the Old Persian Inscriptions.

Thursday, July 27

12:10 P.M. Luncheon Conference: MR. KENNETH L. PIKE, Linguistic Aspects of Bible Translation.

Friday, July 28, and Saturday, July 29

Sessions of the Second Special Summer Meeting of the Linguistic Society of America.

After the Sessions of the Second Special Summer Meeting of our Society, as all
such meetings were called while Kent was Secretary (and Treasurer) there were
three further days accounted for in 1939 with one further Luncheon Conference and
two final evening Lectures:

Thursday, August 3; 12:10 p.m. Luncheon Conference: Prof. E. Adelaide Hahn,
                               Hirt's Theories on Indo-European Syntax
Friday, August 4; 7:30 p.m. Lecture: Professor Leonard Bloomfield,
                            Algonquian Vocabulary
Wednesday, August 9; 7:30 p.m. Lecture: Prof. C.F. Voegelin, Dr. M.B.Emeneau,
                               and Dr. G. L. Trager, Field Work at the Linguistic
                               Institute on Delaware, Tamil, and Lithuanian

   This, we remind our readers, was that 1939 Summer Session at Ann Arbor when
Bernard Bloch took over from the Society's First Editor, Bolling, after the 1938 to
1939 consultations for which the list of names on page 76 can be scanned to find
those dozen or more experts who were available to advise the Nominating Committee towards the official electing of a new Editor that was scheduled for the 1939
Annual Meeting at the end of December.

   For the Summer Sessions and their Linguistic Institutes in Ann Arbor for the
same years as the Kent Second Circulars, we have abundant unofficial documentation from the collectanea of Carleton Taylor Hodge and from C. F. Voegelin's pp.
36, 37, in Language Sciences No. 30 (April, 1974) midway in a review devoted to a
trio of items including A Leonard Bloomfield Anthology, ed. Charles F. Hockett,
Bloomington: Indiana University Press, 1970:

> To me the most engaging facet of Bloomfield's life and work was his interest
> in working with informants. My own training for work in the area of informant-
> based grammar had already been derived (from Uldall, for phonology of the
> Jonesian type, and for syntax from Boas and his students, Kroeber and Sapir,
> and from the latter's students, Mary Haas, Stanley Newman, and Morris
> Swadesh) before I began bringing speakers of Hidatsa, Ojibwa, Delaware, and
> Shawnee to Linguistic Institutes at Ann Arbor and Chapel Hill and Bloomington.
> But I now value no educational experience higher than the opportunity to work
> together with Bloomfield on informant-based grammars. At the early [meaning
> the earlier ones at Ann Arbor] Linguistic Institutes I was elected to show how
> anthropological linguistic field work was done, partly because Bloomfield re-
> fused to teach how he did it—the cook does not want the diners to enter his
> kitchen, he would say, or words to that effect (so much for the erroneous belief
> that 'discovery procedures' were a central concern for everyone in pre-trans-
> formational linguistics); but nothing seemed to fascinate him more, once he had
> completed his 1933 Language, than to attend Linguistic Institutes, give plenary
> lectures on occasional evenings, and otherwise work from early morning till
> night with a speaker of any Ojibwa dialect that I happened to have brought to the
> Linguistic Institute for that summer. Speakers of three different Ojibwa dialects
> were brought in three different summers—one from Walpole Island in southern Onta-
> rio, one from Birch Island in Ontario north of Lake Michigan, as was a more or less
> monolingual Ojibwa grandmother who allowed us to do most of the translation of
> her Ojibwa sentences, though she was able to gloss some words and phrases.
>   Well, this is how we worked (without tape recorders, which postdate World
> War II). The Ojibwa speaker would dictate a text—anecdotal, autobiographic, or
> folkloristic—in non-casual style (slow enough so that we could transcribe, much
> as one dictates a letter to a typist lacking training in shorthand). One had to
> guard against a word by word rendering in which words are said in citation
> form; also against a sentence by sentence rendering which would have overtaxed
> our phonetic memories in transcribing. What was wanted was a phrase by phrase
> rendering which would give us phonetic information to distinguish internal san-
> dhi from external sandhi, and provide a span short enough to remember in tran-
> scription. Repetitions could then be elicited but not replication of the kind that is
> nowadays obtainable by playing back a previous segment on the tape; the phonetic
> repetitions we obtained typically varied from the original model, and it was these
> variants that were classified as 'free variants'.
>   In the evenings, we would sometimes discuss the 'phonemic' distinctions of
> the dialect we were currently working with, and wonder how extensive 'phone-
> mic' variety might be in the vast territory that Ojibwa speakers inhabited—
> about as great as that of Cree in territory, though apparently with less dialect
> differentiation. Bloomfield once suggested that all Algonquianists concentrate

for one summer on a survey of the whole range of dialect diversity from
Plains Ojibwa to easternmost Ojibwa from a strictly 'phonemic' point of view,
thereby providing a new model for dialect atlases, which should be uncluttered
by uninterpretable phonetics, but should instead record only those phonetic
minutiae which are relevant to phonemic distinctions. (Early formulations of
'distinctive features' were supposed to be like 'phonemic distinctions', except
in notation; see now Michael Silverstein's " 'Distinctive Features' in Leonard
Bloomfield's Phonology," to appear in ⟦a projected Festschrift which vanished⟧
      After a text was transcribed, there were two different periods in which
translation was attempted. The first was the less interesting, and was done in
the presence of the informant—at the end of the morning or afternoon session.
The object of this session was to gloss segments, and to distinguish word
boundaries from phrase boundaries, and morpheme boundaries from word
boundaries. We never discussed the terminology or the classification that
Bloomfield advocated for segments (e.g., in "Algonquian" of the Anthology); we
could of course literally point at our transcribed texts if there were any difficulty in determining where morpheme, word, or phrase boundaries were located. (The question of sentence boundaries was not, that I remember, ever raised.)
I gathered from these privileged sessions with Bloomfield that he evaluated
the informant-based grammars of others in Algonquian on whether their morpheme boundaries were at the places that were usable in his comparative work
—in his total accountability for the reconstruction of proto forms; and I remember even now how pleased I was when he said I had made the morpheme cuts in
Shawnee at spots that were relevant to his reconstruction of Algonquian proto
forms. (In the terminology of today, 'morpheme cuts' are made at the boundaries of the ultimate constituents in syntax. These boundaries or 'morpheme
cuts' were essential to Bloomfield's way of reconstructing up to but not beyond
the ultimate constituents or string of constituents, with total accountability.)
Though Bloomfield was inclined to segregate his discussion of comparative-
method linguistics from that of informant-based grammar of a particular language to be included in the history, his evaluation of the goodness of analysis of
any particular language was in terms of its technical relevance to comparative-
method linguistics.
      The second period of translation occurred during occasional evenings, when
the Ojibwa speaker would not be present. At such times, we would survey our
repertoire of inflections for a particular dialect of Ojibwa. Alas, there were
always some paradigmatic forms lacking that were expectable from our knowledge of other Ojibwa dialects and (more generally) from other Algonquian languages. How to obtain the missing forms? Bloomfield avoided the kind of elici-
tation favored by Boas and his students and grandstudents—namely, to make up
the missing form and ask whether one could say that. He preferred to ask tricky
questions (in English rather than in Ojibwa) which would, as it were, trap the
Ojibwa speaker into saying what was wanted. But sometimes to no avail; then
he would turn to me, and with his inexpressibly sad countenance speak in
a defeated voice, giving me permission to elicit 'my way' (= the way I had
inherited from Boas and Boas' students.) So of course I would simply give the
lacking inflectional form, and ask the Ojibwa speaker whether that form was
grammatically possible. The trouble lay in the reply: the query was uniformly
answered in the affirmative. So, I would ask for an 'as though' sentence
including the inflectional form in question; this was harder to obtain, but once
obtained would not allay Bloomfield's apprehension that we might be confusing
the one possible genuine grammar of Ojibwa with many spurious ad-hoc trivia.

      The foregoing description of Bloomfield's 'field work' procedures can with
profit be supplemented by what his friend Roland Grubb Kent did when making an
extended visit to Ann Arbor in 1939, though not a Faculty member as in 1938, for
the sake of the pleasure of the company he found when Bloomfield was working as
described here by Voegelin. Intending to remain for definitely more weeks than
needed for a Summer Meeting of the Linguistic Society, he had brought with him
a sheaf of mimeograph stencils already cut by himself on his favorite typewriter
and had them run off in quantity and cut into half-depth pages and assembled for
use both in Ann Arbor and later in Philadelphia and elsewhere as the title-page
explains.
      In our reprinting, lines of short dashes are used to represent Kent's pages,
and below each such dashed line we reproduce his page-numbers from 2 to 20;
the first page (the title-page) has no such number. The spoofingly serious tone
could be exemplified also by Kent contributions to the irregularly issued items
of printed or bulletin-board-posted lampoonery that flourished in Linguistic
Institutes in most Summer Sessions, even in 1928 to 1931, and occasionally still.

INTRODUCTION TO LINGUISTICS
painless approach

compiled for the
LINGUISTIC SOCIETY OF AMERICA

by
Roland G. Kent

Ann Arbor
July 28–29, 1939

Copies may be secured at 25 cents each from
the Linguistic Society of America, Bennett Hall
University of Pennsylvania, Philadelphia, Pa.

- -

PEDAGOGICAL MOTTO   2

To the goop with the Knott-ed-up brain
Which Kent work without horrible pain,
    All matters linguistical
    Seem highly mystical:
Yet we'll Fries them right down to his plane.

GUARANTEE

No linguistic example in this book has been invented by the
compiler.

ABBREVIATIONS

HMM	Harper's Monthly Magazine	NYr	The New Yorker
Lg	Language	PEB	Philadelphia Evening Bulletin
LP	London Punch	NYT	New York Times
LSp	London Spectator	PI	Philadelphia Inquirer
LST	London Sunday Times	PPL	Philadelphia Public Ledger
Np	Newspaper, unspecified	RB	Radio Broadcaster

All seeming misprints belong to the sources.

- -

I. PHONETICS AND PHONOLOGY   3

Normal sound changes are regular; but when a speaker knows the word only in
its written form, he wil speak it according to his own peculiar notion of the values
by the same letters or groups of letters in other words of the same or of another
language. The following have been heard from RB's at New York stations:

[ˈræ-lai]	in Sir Walter Raleigh.
[i̯aː-ni-ˈkuː-ləm]	in The Pines of the Janiculum.
[po-ˈig-nənt]	in The strains of the music are so poignant ...
[ˈʃkail-kil]	in The Schuylkill River.
[ˈriː-diŋ]	in Reading, Pa.
[diː-ˈbå̄ːtšt]	in Having gone over the pass, the troops debouched on the plain.

Parasitic Consonant

They raised a clambor.—RB.

Consonantal Assimilation

Kept contact with his widely disbursed engineer troops.—NYT 12 vii 31; cf.
                                                        Lg 12.253.

- -

Metathesis   4

"I wouldn't want to be misunderstood," he said, "as defending the actions of some
corporations. I think we have mad bembers there, just as we have in churches."
                                                        —PEB 30 xi 38.

I wanted to get into the movies and went to Hollywood, where my first job was digging concrete hole-posts.— ill Stern, on radio, 10 i 39. ⟦' ill' for 'Bill'?⟧

It's a forward pass! Yes, he has it, he takes it in with one mighty hand, and is down the field like a Chinaman in a bull-shop.—RB.

Exercise: Interpret the metatheses above, and the following:

The orge Minotaurus in Crete.—Berlin dispatch to NYT 4 xii 32.

Accused Reveler: Why, by what you say, one would think I'd been having ogries at my house!

Recapitulation: A parasite is something that lives on something else, and a parasitic consonant is one that grows out of its fore and aft neighbors, getting part of the physiology of each. In assimilation the assimilee merely travels part or all of the way to one assimilant. But metathesis is a downright shifty process, and must be looked out for carefully.

- -

The Word as a Unit   5

The word is a semantic unit, but not a phonetic unit when in a phrase or a sentence. Many persons have little or no idea where words begin and end.

Eliminates All Man Made Static.— RCA advt. sign.

Thief Take Strumpet in Robbery of Home.—Miami Herald (headline), quoted in NYr 21 xii 38.

Members of the diplomatic corps this evening were reported informally discussing a joint de marche. No definite step was taken, however.—New York Herald-Tribune 26 viii 34. [Not a joint of mutton?—Ed.]

My soul is a light housekeeper.—Printed version of Ella Wheeler Wilcox's lighthouse keeper.

- -

Verbal Substitution   6

Writers and speakers often replace an unfamiliar word by a more familiar word or by another word which is also not well understood; note the following, from newspapers:

accused, for caused.

fracas, for fiasco.

expenses minimized, for eliminated or amortized.

an impossible barrier, for impassable.

innocuous, for ineffective.

innovation, for invocation.

Boxing Decreed as Science of Self-Defense, for decried.

A narrow-gouge [gaudž] railroad.—College Professor.

The tripod agreement Russia, France, and Great Britain.—W. L. Shirer, over the radio from Geneva, 28 v 39.

Stenographers often replace unfamiliar words by semi-homophones which seem to them more rational:

Professor E. Meritus.—Kent's stenog.

Degrees taken in abstentia.—Kent's stenog.

I have never studied Avestan, and have entirely forgotten the little old person I once knew.—G. M. Bolling's stenog.

I extend my hearty thanks to all those who dissipated in the examination of the securities.—Letter to bank employees.

- -

Exercise: explain the substitutions in the following: 7

Jersey Waterfall Plentiful

Sportsmen throughout the bays and marshlands of New Jersey report wild geese, wild ducks, coot and jacksnipe aplenty.—NYT 29 x 37.

Lightning Explodes Shotgun

... Both barrels exploded. ... His father was knocked down by the shock, but quickly regained his posture.—Np.

Harry Modernak and Leo Ciro of Merrill, Wis., while tramping through the woods near Land o' Lakes, discovered a dean of several young wolves, and captured the animals alive.—Np.

... The national parks of Canada rebound to her credit and give untold happiness to thousands every year.—PEB.

... So perfect and artistic was the work of the early glassmakers [of Southern New Jersey], done over a wood fire, that it has been irritated in places as far distant as Czechoslovakia.—PEB 20 x 37.

Vatican City, Dec. 25.—Five historic woden boards, said to compromise part part of the "Santa Culla" or cradle of the infant Christ, were displayed today to thousands of children in the crypt of the basilica of St. Mary Major.—PI 26 xii 27.

- -

Popular Etymology   8

Alteration that makes strange words sounds ⟦so in Kent!⟧ as if they meant something, is called Popular Etymology; often the words aren't improved:

    causalty, for casualty.—Lots of people.
    coop, for coupé.—Chauffeur Dialect.
    exhilirator, for accelerator.—Chauffeur Dialect.
    Fels Napkin Soap, for Fels-Naphtha Soap.—Negro Dialect.
    iv'ry, for ivy.—Negro Dialect.

    Popular Etymology may be visual only:
The bell weather of the flock.—NYT 18 iii 39.
The gunwhales of the boat.—NYT 18 iii 39.
Spruce bows provided a Western touch to the decorations.—Raymond Daniell,
    in NYT 27 v 39, describing the trip of the King and the Queen through Canada.

Exercise: Look up Roorback in the Dictionary, and explain the following:
The result was a roarback that stretched from coast to coast. It deafened Mr. Peek, Mr. Exekiel, Mr. Wallace, and Prof. Tugwell.—Paul Mellon's Washington dispatch to PPL 23 ix 33.

- -

II. WORD-FORMATION   9
The Rise of Suffixal Elements

The last part of almost any word may be lopped off and used as a suffix for other words of the same semantic group.

Linoleum, a floor covering of hardened linseed oil with cork and canvas; whence -oleum 'floor covering'.
    congoleum, made of asphalt with cork and canvas (from Congo, a tropical river, because asphalt is from Trinidad, a tropical island).
    tiloleum.

Cafeteria, whence -teria 'self-service shop'. ⟦? apparently a mistake for 'eteria'
    groceteria, shoeteria, dresseteria.   since these are each 4 syllables!⟧
Chandelier, whence -lier 'light-fixture'.
    gasolier, electrolier.

    Exercise: define the following and find the source of the suffix:
motorneer 'trolley-car motorman' (Colorado, about 1895).
electragist 'one who installs or repairs electrical fixtures'.

grapelade	gallonage	flycide	woolware
plumlade	renovizer	youthify	slenderize
profiteer	puzzleteer	dopester	fictioneer
lubritorium	chattersome	bachelorphobia	flowergram

- -

Word-Contamination   10

A mixture of two normal words often results in a new product, which may or may not commend itself:
Eutopia: Greek eu 'well' + utopia '(happy) land of nowhere'.

vindification: vindication + justification.
plentitude (HMM 1920): plenty + plenitude.
anecdotage: anecdote + dotage.
Elyria (Ohio): Elysium + Illyria.
sportfolio (Sp.): sport + portfolio.
bascart 'basket trundled on wheels' (Columbus, Ohio): basket + cart.
ill-kempt (R. Sabatini, Banner of the Bull): ill-kept + unkempt.
Neurope 'new country of Europe, established since 1918'.
Ferrarities 'rare stamps in the collection of the Count Ferrari'.
Pink, parbald J.. W.. S.. .—Time 22 v 39: bald + parboiled + piebald.

- -

Exercise: explain the word-contaminations in the following: 11

Situations are expected within a very short time that will demand a frank and
unequivocable answer.—Turner Catledge, in Washington dispatch to NYT 17 ix 33.

[On a much discussed painting of Susanna, by Tintoretto.] One elderly lady who
drove up in her limousine asked that the painting be removed for a moment so that
she might inspect it more closely. After an inspection she expressed admiration,
saying that she saw no reason why even the proudish should complain.—NYT 25 x 31.

[Of a hurricane in Japan.] The total loss of life is placed at 100. ... Though
nature for almost a week gave suller warnings of the impending onslaughter, the
Japanese Weather Bureau yesterday had merely forecast "cloudy weather with
possible Tokio rain".—Junius Wood, radio dispatch to PEB 15 vi 32.

A strong protest against Polish "repraisals" in Eastern Galicia.—Warsaw
wireless dispatch to NYT 19 xi 38.

He [the orchestra conductor] is now receiving the applaudits of the audience.
                                                                —RB.
- -

Back-Formation   12

A longer word is sometimes shortened to give a supposedly original form from
which the longer is apparently derived.
Given afflicted and affliction,
      we get complected to complexion.
Given cork and corker, speed and speeder,
      we get pep to pepper.
All the minutiae of trivia.—Arthur Krock in NYT 21 v 39. For this, cf. Latin trivium
      'place where three roads meet', whence trivialis 'pertaining to a trivium, com-
      monplace, unimportant', and neuter plural trivialia 'cheap articles peddled on
      the streets'.
Fanatic, shortened to fan 'emotional partisan'.

Ellipsis

Part of a compound word or of a phrase may be omitted, leave a briefer form
to do the whole job.
      interential, for integro-differential.—Mathematical term.
      realtor, for real estate operator.
      unionalls, for union-made overalls.
      Oldsmobile, for Olds automobile.
      drastic prices, for drastically reduced prices.—Advt. sign.

- -

III. MORPHOLOGY   13
Problems of Number

Era was originally a plural, peas and cherries were singular; but now these
are standard in the other number. Working along to standard quality as singu-
lars are plurals data, memoranda, strata.

British sports writers use names of places as plurals: Waterloo Take Their
      Chances; Moseley Batter Away In Vain.—LST 1 i 39.

Exercise: explain the following, stating if standard:
rhinoceri, polypi, octopi, probosces.—Not formed as in Greek!
donkies, monnies, ignorami.—Citations in New English Dictionary. ⟦= OED!⟧

A pence is two cents. — PEB 26 v 39.
Rabies Prove Fatal To Boy. — American Np. headline.
An insignia. — PPL 19 v 31.
Like a candelabra. — NGM 67.781 (June 1935). [['NGM': unlisted; who can say?]]
facsimilies. — NYT 27 viii 33.
apparati. — Louise Closser Hale, HMM Sept. 1930, page 423.
candelabras. — RB 11 ii 39.
ostrakae, pedagogae. — G. Atherton, Immortal Marriage, pp. 155, 278, 352.

- -
Creation of New Forms by Analogy   14
Admiring Lady: Beautiful! And what was it you played?
Musician: Bach's opus 27.
Admiring Lady: Oh, I just dote on opuses!
Taxi Driver (to lady passenger): How's the Mister? I haven't sawn him for a long
The Double Comparative   time.
Supplying cheap electricity through locally owned plants is a more superior
method than the TVA, according to Mr. Baals. — NYT 20 xi 38.

Origin of the Reflexive Passive
Mother: Why is Johnny crying so?
Daughter: Oh, Johnny went and stung himself on a wasp.

- -
                                                                    15
IV. SYNTAX
Ambiguous Usages
Brevity may lead to uncertainty as to parts of speech. Smelt In The Great Lakes
— Np headline. [Sniff, sniff! — Ed.]
Changes in case-usages may also bring embarrassment.
Aunt: When I was younger I could have married anybody I pleased.
Niece: Didn't you please anybody, Auntie? — PEB 11 xii 38.
The Value of the Hyphen
The hyphen is inefficient to show the compounding of a phrase of two or more
words with something else:
The wistful tied-to-New York resident. — NYT 18 xi 37.
A wet spring has started a back-to-the-Dust Bowl migration. — NYT 23 iv 39.

Exercise: explain the following hyphenates:
A large percentage of the beef disposed of in the markets of Honolulu is from
pigeon pea-fed stock raised in the islands. — PI 26 ix 37.
A favorite son-stalking horse. — NYT, of a candidate for the presidential
nomination.

- -
Phrasing   16
The comma is a valuable tool, not to be inserted nor to be deleted without good
and sufficient reason.

Mr. Hamilton, fish magnate of New York. — Np. [Joos says: from all-caps!]]

Vienna, Dec. 10. — Prince Bernhard of Saxe-Meiningen, who has just completed a six-week sentence for Nazi activities, ... has escaped into Benito,
Mussolini's country. — [Oh, that blessed land! — Ed.]

Premier Mackenzie, King of Canada. — NYT. [Better leave it to George. — Ed.]

Like its rivlvaals, the Tiger squad did little more than practice putting on their
uniforms. — PPL 15 xi 30. [Hope it (or they) got them on right. — Ed.]

ALARM CLOCKS
                    real value
                    only 75 cents — Advt. sign. [Accidental truth?
                                                            — Ed.]

- -
[['IV' above with 'SYNTAX' is used again by Kent next with 'SEMANTICS'!]]

IV. SEMANTICS   17

Adjectives Active and Passive

A farmer and his city boarder entered a field, at the far end of which a bull
began to bellow and paw the ground.

City Boarder: Is that bull safe?

Farmer: He's a damned sight safer 'n you are. ⟦Oft-told rural tale!⟧

Idiom

Gossip: I say she used to be no better than she ought to be, but now she is.
—NYr.

Phrasal Contamination

A gold trove. —Np.

Ambiguities

Auto Supply Co.	Central Wrecking Co.
Wrecks a Specialty	Demolishing Engineers

(Signs in Philadelphia)

- -

Mixed Metaphors   18

Marital Rift Still Unbroken. —NYT, headline.

Perhaps a new record will be broken. —RB, at Hialea, Fla., 25 ii 39.

Mr. Speaker, I smell a rat; I see him floating in the air; but mark my words,
I will nip him in the bud. —House of Commons ⟦undated; authorship unknown; but,
according to Miles Hanley, already notorious before 1900 in an extended form,
usually made to end with 'before he inundates the nation' after the words quoted.⟧

I look behind me at the untrodden paths of the future, where I seem to perceive
the footprints of an unseen hand. — U. S. Senate.

Our glorious Republic is now clouded by a greater earthquake than the chain of
Prussian autocracy, in the form of the crouching lion of the East—Bolshevism.
—Memorial Day address in Massachusetts.

Exercise: explain what is the matter with the following phrases, culled from
newspapers: to pull a clever coup

food prices are boundless

- -

V. TEXTUAL CRITICISM   19

The linguistic scholar must be sure that his text is correct before he begins
linguistic analysis. He must therefore first eliminate errors, of whatever sort,
from his materials. The following texts will provide practice.

When the former Prince of ales was the guest of Mr. and Mrs. James A. Burden
at the Syosset (L. I.) estate in 1921 ... —Np.

R. S. Hillyer Chosen Boylston Professor

... He joined the Harvard faculty as an assistant in English in 199. In 926 he became Assistant Professor of English at Trinity College, but returned to Harvard
in 1928. —NYT 14 v 37. [What, no retiring age limit? —Ed.]

Preaches To Movie Queens

Determining that if some of the good people of the town prefer the movies to
church on Sunday evenings, they shall at least hear his sermons, the Rev. Percy
A. Clements, pastor of the Baptist Church of Margate, England, had loud speakers
placed near the picture houses so that the queques awaiting their turn to enter
could listen to his exhortations. —NYT 14 v 38.

- -

TOO LATE TO CLASSIFY   20

The royal carpet again became a center of attraction when a uniformed Sanitation
Department employee emerged from the pier, broom in hand, and began industri-
ally to sweep the rug. —NYT 11 vi 39.

The guns went off in honor of the King and Queen. "There it goes, folks," he
shouted into the microphone, "there goes the 21-son galoot." —NYT 11 vi 39.

The American won and vindicated the seedling committee, which made him sixth choice in the tournament.—Tennis news, NYT 27 vi 39.

My son is at college, in the epidemic course.—Employee, to welfare officer of corporation.

Troops have been ammassed on the frontier.—NYT 1 vii 39.

EPILOGUE

We opine that if mixture gives zest
To the truth, then a mixture is best;
That linguistical science
Sh'd n't glower defiance
If we flavor its abstracts with jest.

So said also the Roman poet Horace:
Quamquam ridentem dicere verum
Quid vetat?
—Serm. 1.1.24–5.

===

Collections are created by collectors: books don't grow on trees. Who collected these items? Internal evidence is unmistakable: Bernard Bloch and Roland G. Kent. Bloch in the summer of 1933, leaving Vermont to join Kurath at Brown University —see the final paragraph of page 53 above—began giving/mailing snippets from local newspapers to Kent, and Kent reciprocated with snippets from Philadelphia papers. The topical area for this particular exchange of bits of paper was what we can now define as significant blunders in print, a counterpart of the derailments in speech which were Sturtevant's source, similarly enriched by items sent/given to Sturtevant by Bloch: see the Preface to the 1947 Sturtevant book An Introduction to Linguistic Science (New Haven: Yale University Press) for his acknowledgements to Bloomfield, Bloch, and [E] Adelaide Hahn, the only ones named among the 'many scholars who have contributed in one way or another to this book' as he says.

It figures in the Sturtevant bibliography prepared by Bloch to accompany Miss Hahn's Obituary (Language 28, 1952) as the second version of his 1917 Linguistic Change: An Introduction to the Historical Study of Language (Chicago: University of Chicago Press) which had been reprinted in 1942. We juxtapose Sturtevant's and Kent's works here in this History without invidious intent, simply to display a neat complementarity of talents and procedures for late-20th-century readers to see. Kent's jeu d'esprit just reproduced above belongs to the 1939 Linguistic Institute, the penultimate one before the Second World War. The 1938 Institute included the very first of the midsummer meetings of the Society, Friday and Saturday, July 29th and 30th, at which unscheduled events occurred with remarkable impacts: two announcements made by reading off a newly arrived telegram each time.

First, that Signer of the Call who was next in line to be nominated as President, Truman Michelson of the Smithsonian Institution, had died July 26th, and now the requisite consultations were taking place and results would be made known soon. (Before the August break-up those results were current gossip: Charles C. Fries as 1939 President, Louise Pound as Vice-President, the first female nominee to a top post; in natural reaction to this, it soon became plain that Miss Hahn would be made President at the earliest opportunity…) Second, on the next day, Saturday July 30th, a cablegram was read off from the podium which confirmed weeks-old rumors: the effects of the invasion of Austria had included the death of Honorary Member Professor Prince Nikolai Sergeevich Trubetzkoy of the University of Vienna on the 25th of June. Before the Annual Meeting of 1938, December 27–29, Martin Joos had begun four years of teaching at the University of Toronto and saw the onset of general hostilities from a Canadian perspective.

In the Business Meeting, Secretary Kent reported 24 formal resignations by name, each effective with the end of the preceding year (1937), and the simple count of persons dropped for two-year non-payment of dues without naming names. Now the list of 24 formally resigning is illuminating when each name is prefixed with the year of joining, called 'election' by constitutional provision:

1936 Samuel Ogden Andrew, retired, at home in Surrey, England; 1930 Edward C. Ehrensperger, Professor of English, University of South Dakota; 1928 Arthur G. Eichelberger, Instructor in Latin, Philadelphia; SC Aurelio M. Espinosa, Professor of Romance Languages, Stanford University; 1931 Eleanor Fleet, Teacher of Shorthand and Typewriting (interest: Latin); 1931 Otto S. Fleissner, Professor of German, Wells College, Aurora, N.Y.; 1928 Charles H. Grandgent, Emeritus Professor (Romance Languages), Harvard; 1935 Clarence Edgar Heffelfinger, Instructor in English, Washington and Jefferson College, Washington, Pennsylvania; 1936 Joseph William Hewitt, Professor of Classics and Dean of Freshmen, Wesleyan University, Middletown, Connecticut; 1931 Dorothy E. Kleinfelter, Teacher of Latin, Palmyra High School, Palmyra, Pennsylvania; FM Arthur Gordon Laird, [retired] Professor of Greek, University of Wisconsin [[Leonard Bloomfield's teacher for Sanskrit and for advanced courses in Greek and Latin in 1906 and 1907]]; 1933 Gerhardt Laves, M.A., Torreón Community Center, Crown Point, New Mexico (Australian and American Indian languages); 1926 John Alden Mason, Ph.D., Curator of the American Section, Museum of the University of Pennsylvania (interest: American Indian Languages) [[from whom Zellig Harris first learned that other language varieties exist than Semitic and Indo-European, preparing him for Sapir and all that]]; 1925 Alois Richard Nykl, Ph. D., Oriental Institute, University of Chicago; FM Wallace W. Perkins, A.M., Woburn, Massachusetts (interest: Romance Linguistics); 1928 Harold Rosen, Ph.D., 1630 Widener Place, Philadelphia (interest: Indo-European); 1931 Shizuka Saitō, Principal of Ōno Chugakkō, Fukui, Japan; FM Harry Fletcher Scott, Emeritus Professor of Classical Languages, Ohio University, Chicago; 1933 George Summey, Jr., Professor of English, Texas A. & M.; FM Helen H. Tanzer, Ph.D., Professor of Classics, Brooklyn College, New York City; 1932 Mrs. Elizabeth Frank Vogel, M.A., New York City (interest: Comparative Linguistics); 1934 Ellen A. Weinberg, M.A., Instructor in Latin, Walton High School, New York City; 1933 Benjamin Weiner, B.A., graduate student at New York University (interest: Indo-European); 1927 Joshua Whatmough, M.A. (Cantab.), Professor of Comparative Philology, Harvard University [[persuaded (by Secretary Cowan) to join again, became President for 1951]]

Note that '1929' does not appear, and that just half of these 24 persons joined later than that; also, that if the category 'Emeritus Member' had existed several of the earlier members could have qualified for the 'EM' label. Obviously no such non-dues-paying membership would have been possible in those earliest years when the Society's finances were precarious, but any time after the first dozen years that innovation would have been reasonable, and we have searched all the evidence to discover how it actually came about. The answer is unexpected: no formal decision was ever taken, and the EM category began and remains entirely informal, extra-legal, and nowhere supported by records of Executive Committee action, let alone alteration of any article in the Constitution of the Society. Thus it would be idle to consider whether this or that person was ever 'entitled' to be an emeritus member, or to appeal to recorded precedents. The starting-point was the Secretary's automatically treating Annual Dues as covered by the same moratorium as applied to a labor-union member upon his being inducted into the Armed Forces, simply because of embarrassed puzzlement: when a member was known to be in uniform, what was an LSA Secretary-Treasurer to do? It appears that the first incumbent of that office, R. G. Kent, had ceased to press members for dues money in both sorts of cases—superannuation and a military-type mail address— and when Cowan as his successor appealed to the Executive Committee for their guidance the subsequent superannuation pattern grew up gradually from numerous single decisions, hardly ever more than two alike on any occasion, over a sequence of years. The sticking point is likely to be whether the member was truly active or can be classed 'EM' simply on grounds of longevity; and when there has been at an Executive Committee sitting a burdensome accumulation of sticky problems, then such a decision is likely to be postponed twice a year for so long that the involved member may wonder whether the rules have been changed. As far as we know, they have not, because there are no rules. Nor can an Annual Meeting properly discuss personalities in the half-day set aside as Business Meeting. Typically, an inquiry is conveyed privately to any member of the Executive Committee; then the decision will follow in more than 30 hours and less than 30 months. Continuing with the December 1938 Annual Meeting, we find other interesting items:

The Director of the 1938 Linguistic Institute, Charles Carpenter Fries, reported that the Linguistic Society of America had contributed $300 for the three invited lecturers from outside of Ann Arbor; but now in December was requesting only $65 total towards such purposes for 1939. The ACLS, he said, had provided ten scholarships for students, plus the cost of bringing the Hidatsa Indian informant onto the scene. ⟦The 1938 Second Circular had made no mention of such a possibility, but the subsequent narrative says that C. F. Voegelin and Zellig S. Harris had worked on that variety of Sioux, while Leonard Bloomfield had conducted the work on 'Chippewa, a variety of Algonkian.' Now that was just the language which Voegelin above (pages 78 and 79) calls 'Ojibwa'—routinely spoken as 'Ojibway' by most of us—presumably to obviate confusion with the unrelated Chipewyan.⟧

Although the 1938 Linguistic Institute offered five fewer courses than in 1937, Fries went on to say, the number of students attending was roughly the same: 329 registrations from 256 persons including 31 holders of the doctorate. In the parallel Sturtevant report we find this '256' replaced by '204'—seemingly by subtracting the 'fringe' students as they are often called, that is to say persons enrolled in just a single 'Institute' course without being registered as Institute students: such were, for example, those registered regularly within the Psychology or the German or the French Department for departmental supervision as Degree Candidates who now casually included an Institute course on advice.

One year later the Society's second Summer Meeting in 1939—see pages 6 and 7 of Bulletin No. 13, issued with a 1940 date—heard 18 papers, among which seven authors and one title are worth listing here: Mary R. Haas, Kenneth L. Pike, Leonard Bloomfield, J Milton Cowan, Murray B. Emeneau, George L. Trager, Bernard Bloch. Bloch's paper titled 'The Theory of a Phonetic Alphabet' was derived from Linguistic Atlas planning and procedures; on this occasion it was so thoroughly discussed that it strongly colored, to say the least, the 1940 'preliminary edition' of Tables for a system of phonetic description which he issued jointly with Trager, New Haven: Chinese Printing Office.

Though recognized as a Meeting of the Society, that week-end gathering could not legislate like an Annual Meeting; but it became the occasion for Resolutions recommending specific actions to the President and the Executive Committee. One such is worth reporting in detail, with some of its consequences, namely, That a small committee be appointed to investigate the problem of the future of the Linguistic Institute and also to study its past record with a view to making clear the nature and value of its contributions to the development of linguistic science. To nobody's surprise, the survey had been started weeks earlier, and it was completed expeditiously and thoroughly because the execution was in the hands of Edgerton and Sturtevant—who were well and truly appointed as that two-man Committee by the President.

Seven sharply defined Questions were mimeographed for distribution before the Summer Meeting members dispersed, or pursued them to whatever was presumed to be their several residences. The 19-page Report printed in Bulletin No. 13, pp. 83-101, was ultimately published with its most fascinating segment relegated to its last few pages: it had arrived after Sturtevant's text for the Report was complete: and because we find it printed without signature, we may gratuitously add that its more than 1200 running words are written in the unmistakable personal style of Kenneth Lee Pike. In the partial text, the labeling numerals come from the questionnaire: no exemplar of that questionnaire is at hand today:

Dear Professor Edgerton, Your questionnaire from the LSA reached me in Arkansas about the first week of October [1939], forwarded from Mexico. There I drafted an answer to the questions, but somehow did not get them copied until my typewriter caught up with me again in this Mixteco town.

1. I favor holding sessions after the session of 1940.

2. They should be held every summer; if that is impossible, every other year.

3. I hope [regularly] at Ann Arbor, so that any interested in an organized program for a degree ... may do so uninterruptedly in cooperation with the University of Michigan.

4. A number of direct personal benefits have come to me ... (a) I had given up entirely the idea of getting any higher education ... when Professor Fries arranged for me to get in residence requirements in the summer time, and do research in connection with my winter employment ... (b) My research in the Mixteco language ... struck serious snags in the way of tone. Professor Sapir gave me ideas during the session of 1937 which proved to be the key to the problem (and not of mine only, but also of various colleagues and pupils of mine working on tonal languages also ...) (c) In my teaching of phonetics in Arkansas, a large part of my course, especially that on phonemics, has been gathered directly from instructors or their publications ...

5. ... At present our investigators who have received direct benefit through your courses, or indirect through our faculty, are in the following tribes in Mexico: Aztec, Mixteco, Mixteco, Maya, Tarasco, Mazateco, Chinanteco, Tsotsil, Tsental, Mazahua, Mixe, Zapateco. Others are in Guatemala, South America, The Philippines, and Africa, and their numbers are increasing rapidly.

6. There is still a tremendous body of tribes and peoples the world over who are illiterate. ... Each of the investigators ... is interested in pure science, it is true, but there is also a social, utilitarian aspect to the work which has actually sent them ... They are interested in Bible translation, the providing of a native literature to each of the hundreds of tribes ...

7. For improvement, we suggest little, unless it be a new course on linguistic aspects of ethnology; methods of getting and classing ethnographical data as grist for the linguistic mill. ... We hope that the courses on descriptive techniques will not be curtailed.

Sturtevant saw that the writer meant to be simply the spokesman for a group and accordingly stated that it was written by 'the head of the Department of Phonetics of the "Summer Institute of Linguistics" at Siloam Springs, Arkansas' and that it testifies to the 'value of the Linguistic Institute in training workers of that (purely practical) school.' In 1976 Joos adds that apparently 'Sulphur Springs' was the usual official name of the local Post Office in the 1930's, though that doesn't mean so very much: the terrain itself has been extensively revised with dams and recreational lakes and pleasure-parks constructed since the Second World War, and the new reliance on Zip Codes discourages uses of local names anyhow.

Returning now to the Sturtevant report presented to the December 1939 Annual Meeting, we quote a few segments, mostly preserving the Sturtevant wording:

In spite of the sharp reduction in the resources made available by the University of Michigan the same number of courses was offered as in 1938. In addition to the promised 23, George L. Trager gave a course in Phonetics and Phonemics: 8 students. Leonard Bloomfield came to Ann Arbor for 5 weekends, giving a series of lectures on Comparative Algonquian and holding conferences, especially for the work in recording living languages. Not including staff members visiting, there were 302 registrations from 152 students, eight of them there on ACLS scholarships. The analysis of a living language included Voegelin's work with a Delaware Indian, Emeneau's with a native speaker of Tamil, and Trager's with a Lithuanian; his regular course in Church Slavonic was a new departure in its thorough use of the more modern methods in descriptive linguistics.

Finally, Sturtevant included a table of staff and student counts from all the Institutes. There he merged the counts of Teachers and visiting Lecturers; we split them for 1936-39, and we guess a '1940' line as best we can: see page 90. Also, Sturtevant reported that 'One subject, Introduction to Linguistic Science, has been treated in each session, but by five different scholars. In this way five widely different points of view regarding the foundations of the science have been presented. Probably the most stimulating of these courses was the one of 1938 〚Bloomfield's〛, which was attended by virtually the entire membership of the Institute.' Joos in 1976 adds that Sturtevant's Obituary on Bloomfield, originally in the 1949 <u>Yearbook of the American Philosophical Society</u> published in 1950, is pages 544-547 of Hockett's 1970 book <u>A Leonard Bloomfield Anthology</u>; that is our source for the paragraph (Hockett's page 546) which adduces the testimony of the wisest scholar who knew Bloomfield regarding his teaching effectiveness:

As far as I know he had but one major triumph as a teacher. In the summer of 1938 his Introduction to Linguistic Science at the Linguistic Institute at Ann Arbor was attended throughout the eight-week session by nearly the entire membership of the Institute. We had always had introductory courses; in the early sessions of the Institute they were conducted by Professor Prokosch, and they always were relatively popular. In the summer of 1937 the introduction was given by Professor Edward Sapir before a regularly enrolled class of about thirty, including at least one member of the staff. This course of Sapir's was so remarkably effective that the director moved the next year's introduction to an evening hour, so that it could be more largely attended. But it was Bloomfield's handling of the course that made it the extraordinary success it was.

Sturtevant's 1939 tabulation of staff- and student-counts of all the Institutes does not separate the [visiting] Lecturers from the full-time or part-time staff teaching throughout the summer; for the first four Ann Arbor years we separate them, and extrapolate a doubtful line for the poorly documented year 1940:

		Session Faculty	(Visiting) Lecturers	Total	Students
1928	Yale			24	45
1929	Yale			23	37
1930	CCNY			27	60
1931	CCNY			23	52

1936	Ann Arbor	16	11	27	122
1937	Ann Arbor	18	13	31	164
1938	Ann Arbor	13	16	29	204
1939	Ann Arbor	16	15	31	152
1940	Ann Arbor	12	8 or 10	20/22	121 including 2/3 Lecturers

For roughly 10,000 running words of contemporary newspaper accounts—the Public Lectures without exception, some of the Luncheon Conferences, and some of the papers presented at the Summer Meetings in each of the years 1938 through 1940—our source is the collectanea of Carleton Hodge, already used above for the Kent 'painless approach' which appears on pages 80–86 here. The collection begins with the Friday, July 1, 1938 report on the June 30th Luncheon Conference, seven column-inches under the irresponsible three-decker headline:

Speech Expert / Calls Language / Historic Key
Prof. Bloomfield, Visiting / Faculty Member Finds / No 'Primitive' Tongues
Lecture Is Third / Of Summer Series

"By looking at man through language we can learn more about man."

This, in brief, constituted the answer given yesterday by Professor Leonard Bloomfield to the question, "Why study the language of primitive peoples?" which was the subject of the first luncheon conference of the 1938 Linguistic Institute.

"More specifically," said Dr. Bloomfield, professor of linguistics at the University of Chicago and visiting member of the Institute faculty, "we can learn not to keep on saying the many wrong things about language that long have been said by people who did not know many languages.

"We find out, for example, that what we had always assumed to be regular and inevitable because it is true of our own language or of European languages in general is, as a matter of fact, distinctly extraordinary and irregular. Of course, we do not know even our own languages very well as yet. There has never been, for instance, a complete descriptive grammar of English that would be satisfactory to the person to whom English was not his native speech."

Admitting that, at least to his audience, the question-topic was chiefly rhetorical since his hearers believed in the value of linguistic study of the languages of
primitive people, [newspaper text has 'people.' at line-end] Dr. Bloomfield nevertheless criticized the wording of the topic because to the linguist there are no
primitive languages or primitive peoples.

"The language of a so-called primitive peoples," he declared, "is looked at by
the linguistic scientist simply as a tool of communication. And since he finds sane,
intelligent speakers in these primitive groups he can only conclude that the language which they speak is not a primitive language." [['a ... peoples' in the text!]]

Joos comments: (a) The sub-head 'Lecture is third of summer series' is mistaken; it seems to have been patched-up by a headline-writer, following the usual
newspaper custom which lifts out high-spots from reporter-written stories against
the plain sense of the story as a whole, and the word 'third' came from some true
statement (never mind whose) that the 1938 Linguistic Institute was the third one at
Ann Arbor. The newspaper's 'morgue' for 1937 used 'second' and the rest is easy.

(b) The 1938 Hodge file names Bloomfield as principal speaker again for 27th
July ('yesterday afternoon' in The Michigan Daily for the 28th) and gives him 16
column-inches under the two-line heading "Dr. Bloomfield Hits 'Liberals,' /
Speech Correctors, In Lecture" which we decipher by reading and for the first
comma. That introduces us to a lucid condensation of a familiar message, and
prepares us to remark that Bloomfield wrote spoken American in the script he
made available to the reporter in his usual self-effacing way, e.g. this bit: "But
unhappily for children in the schools, the speech corrector is not interested in
observing the speech of the standard dialect. He is interested in some kind of
fanciful speech used in a nightmare world where, according to one of the correctors, 95 per cent of us would be constantly making mistakes in our native
language. You see," Dr. Bloomfield concluded, "these speech correctors write
without having made any real observation of the language spoken around them.
They don't know very much about it. My advice to all of you is this. If some
speech corrector comes around and tells you that you must pronounce a word
differently from the way you hear people pronounce it, if, for instance, he wants
you to change your pronunciation of 'route' from 'rowt' to 'root,' or perhaps from
'root' to 'rowt,' treat him gently and kindly, just as if he were quite harmless,
and then he won't get by with it."

(c) The first half of the heading, "Dr. Bloomfield Hits 'Liberals,' ..." speaks
of the reporter's beginning: "I am not liberal about language. You often hear students of language called 'liberal' when they express their views about ideas of
correctness. But that is not being liberal any more than it would have been for a
person to go into a community where witch-hunting was practiced and say to the
people that there were no such thing as witches. I mean that it isn't being liberal
to be against superstition."

With this preface, Dr. Leonard Bloomfield, chairman of the department of
linguistics at the University of Chicago, began his University lecture yesterday
afternoon on the topic, "Linguistic Science and the Problem of 'Correct' Language."

(d) The word liberal in Bloomfield's usage, above and elsewhere, is not to be
misunderstood; to cut a long story short, readers must bear in mind that this time
he was tuning his fiddle to the orchestra: the term liberal was current in that
decade in the context of journalistic or popular discussion of correctness in one
sense especially, namely, the devil-may-care or absolutely latitudinarian view
that 'anything goes' because schools have relaxed the traditional rigidities in the
context of pupil failures to desist from splitting infinitives and the like: that was
what often was said in the 1930's; and this time Leonard Bloomfield was saying in
his clearest familiar-lecture diction, 'Just because I come before you to report a
professional-linguist doctrine which does not include the traditional condemnations,
don't expect me to speak sloppily: after all, I'm a scholar, not a grocery clerk!'
We observe his relaxed dismissal of 'correctors'—and note that in his personal
language, which was a refined Wisconsin speech as explained previously on page 13,
the locution He's harmless is standard for reassuring people that the Village Idiot
doesn't get violent.

Bloomfield's 27th July topic in his Institute Lecture was his counterpart for the Kemp Malone Public Lecture topic in the first Linguistic Institute, 27th July 1928, "The Problem of Standard English"—of which Karl Reuning says (pp. 26 & 27 here) that it drew nation-wide attention for its advocacy of It's me to replace It is I in Standard English, with letters suggesting that he should be dismissed from Johns Hopkins. A decade later, Bloomfield knew better than to speak from the platform in the magisterial tone of a Kemp Malone. For one thing, he had a sensitivity to social nuances that Malone lacked; and where Malone laid down the law, Leonard Bloomfield gently poked fun and deflated the pretentions of a busybody. It is true that he had a complete typescript at the podium on the 27th July, 1936, but his way of public speaking was to follow along with its messages and speech-melodies but sedulously avoid the reading-off drone that comes from exactly holding to the text as a clerk must: his textual wording was all there, yes, but now spoken and freely expanded with repetitions and inserted phrases such as 'you see' used here for its ordinary social value. In a word, Bloomfield communicated, Malone imparted.

The 1938 newspaper reporting of other speaking included notably these names: Kent's July 6th evening lecture, called the 'first formal lecture of the Institute's summer program' from the point of view that newspapers automatically adopt; it was a report on a detailed syllabic analysis of the major works of Vergil and of Horace, and ends, in the newsprint text, 'syllable division does not rest upon the word but upon the phrase, as in ordinary speech. It is recognition of the use of the phrasal pattern of speech that enables the modern scholar to interpret on a purely linguistic basis the peculiar metrical phenomena of the final syllables of Latin verse.' The same column includes 'The Institute program continues today with the regular informal luncheon conference at 12:10 p.m. in the Rackham building, with Prof. Morris Swadesh of the University of Wisconsin speaking on "Complementive and Elliptic Sentences in Modern English." ' From the August 3, 1938, Michigan Daily we could quote a far more informative biography than Who's Who has of Fang-Kwei Li, at the time visiting Professor of Chinese Linguistics at Yale; but Joos can adjust the mention of Morris Swadesh by remarking that his Wisconsin appointment was not a professorship but simply a typing job (on Sapir's Nootka materials) with access to the University's Library stacks and facilities by a card that said he was to be treated as if he were a visiting assistant professor. (He also simultaneously typed his article for Language 11.148—151 [1935] 'The Vowels of Chicago English' during his tenure of that position ...)

From 1939 press stories on the Linguistic Institute and Summer Meeting we take as little as possible. Dr. Leonard Bloomfield is featured in the June 30th headline over the story which quotes Professor O. [sic] C. Fries as announcing that Bloomfield will speak on the subject "Algonkian Sounds," at 7:30 p.m. Friday, in the small amphitheatre of the Rackham building. No other name is misspelled in the eleven column-inches of that write-up, and yet it includes Pillsbury, H. B. Allen of the staff of the Middle English dictionary, Dr. Murray B. Emeneau, Dravidian languages, Charles Voegelin of De Pauw University, Franz Boas of Columbia University. Tuesday, July 18, 1939, is the dating of the 19-column-inch story 'By Harold B. Allen' headed Deleware [sic] Indian Here To Help / Record Tribe's Fading Language—beginning thus: Willie Long Bone, acting head of the historic Indian tribe, the Delawares, has become an enthusiastic admirer of Ann Arbor ... owing to the fact that never before in all his 71 summers spent on the sun-scorched plains of Kansas and Oklahoma, has he enjoyed such a cool summer ... The July 29 paper correctly spells Larynx both on the front page and inside continuation page headlines; the favorite version (used as a pass-word by speaking it with special inside-joke paralanguage) occurs under the sub-head 'Cowan Shows Movies' and also within that story in its first sentence, "Second on the evening program, Prof. J. Milton Cowan of the University of Iowa discus[s]ed his showing of the extraordinary moving pictures of the larnyx recently successfully taken by the Bell Telephone laboratories and loaned to him for exhibiting in Ann Arbor."

For the 1940 Summer Meeting and Linguistic Institute we cannot expect to find any narrative contained in a 1941 Announcement, for Chapel Hill came next. Instead we quote from the letter to Joos from Carleton Hodge dated March 7, 1974, in part:

The titles of the lectures were given in the [year-later issue of the] bulletin listing classes, etc. ... The 1941 bulletin is, of course, from North Carolina and does not list the [Ann Arbor, Michigan] lectures for 1940. I reconstructed what I could from notebooks and the Michigan Daily as follows:

Luncheon Series 1940

Thurs June 27	Albert H. Marckwardt, The Survey of Folk Speech in the Great Lakes Area
Wed July 3	Charles Hockett [Linguistics and Literary Devices] [title not recorded]
Thurs July 11	Harold B. Allen, The Linguistic Dictatorship of Samuel Johnson
Thurs July 18	James N. Tidwell [Dialect in Fiction]
Thurs July 25	Adelaide Hahn, What We Know about the Hittite Subordinating Conjunctions
Thurs Aug 1	Symposium on Semantics (see clipping) *

Summer Lecture Series 1940

Fri June 28	Edgar H. Sturtevant, The Greek K-perfect and the Laryngeal Theory
Thurs July 11	Emil Froeschels [Child Language]
Fri July 12	Leonard Bloomfield, The Phoneme
Wed July 17	Francis M. Rogers, The Relative Frequency of Phonemes and Variphones in the Romance Languages
Fri July 19	Leonard Bloomfield, The Word
Thurs July 25	Roland G. Kent, Varro and his Linguistic Methods
July 26-27	Summer Meeting — see Bulletin 14
July 26	Leonard Bloomfield, The Phrase (part of Institute series)
Wed July 31	Eugene A. Nida, English Syntax
Fri Aug 2	Leonard Bloomfield, The Lexicon
Wed Aug 7	Charles F. Voegelin, Field Work at the Linguistic Institute
Fri Aug 9	Leonard Bloomfield, The Function of Language

* The Michigan Daily report of this as a free-for-all discussion of semantics includes these bits in its total of nearly eleven column-inches beginning on p. 1:

Prof. C. C. Fries, opening the symposium, presented the basic conception that meaning is the sum total of the experience brought into attention by the stimulus of a linguistic form or symbol. ... A dictionary editor gathers as many contextual examples of a word as he can find, and then tries to extract the common core of experience brought into attention ...

Speaking from the point of view of the psychologist, Dean Lloyd Woodburne considered particularly the way in which meaning is learned by the individual. The anthropologist's attitude toward meaning appeared in the contribution of Prof. Charles F. Voegelin, of De Pauw University, who asserted that to him an understanding of meaning must rest upon the basic assumption postulated by Professor Franz Boas of Columbia University, the assumption that mankind has a psychological unity. "Meaning," Professor Voegelin then concluded, "is simply the correlation of a linguistic unit with a cultural unit."

[['Dean Woodburne' [*20 Dec. 1906] is Lloyd Stuart Woodburne who by 1945 was promoted from Assistant Dean to Associate Dean in Ann Arbor and in 1950 became Dean of the College of Arts and Sciences in the University of Washington, Seattle]]

Fairly conspicuous among the courses of instruction in the first five Ann Arbor Linguistic Institutes 1936–1940, the series terminated by moving it to Chapel Hill, were those in Chinese, Japanese, and Russian. The published programs, copied in our pages 57–68, and in part on pages 69 to 72 from a separate document, credit the Chinese teaching's financing to 'the American Council of the Institute of Pacific Relations' and the latter document says it was 'brought into association with the Linguistic Institute primarily through the efforts of Professor Sturtevant.' Well, those statements, true as they are, in 1974 raised more questions in historiography than they answered, causing Joos to write twice to Mortimer Graves. Next, with double-bracketed Joos insertions [[...]] but without maintaining any separation of information from the two answers here drawn upon—yet without putting words into Mortimer's mouth, are his ipsissima verba, which in his usual fashion manage to assign maximum credit to the others involved:

Dear Martin, Ever since I read that piece on Bernard in <u>Language</u> [[43.3-19]]
I have been anxious to write you a letter of congratulation; ... Of course, I was
peripherally and administratively concerned with practically all the 'beginning'
that you describe [[LSA Bulletin, March 1975 (No. 64) pp. 26-28]]: the first
planning of the Linguistic Institutes, the Linguistic Atlas, Boas's Committee
on American Native Languages, and with ACLS activities in oriental studies
which emphasized the need for oriental language competences, especially
Chinese and Japanese. Through my University of Pennsylvania connections,
... I had come to know Roland Kent very well, and through their membership in
ACLS, Edgerton and Sturtevant, who were really responsible for most of my
thinking about linguistics. As War II approached we were very conscious of our
need for people with Japanese, of course. Rather early in 1941 we [[= ACLS]]
had two grants from the Rockefeller Foundation (principally through David H.
Stevens) in the amount of $50,000 each, one for 'Chinese, Japanese, and
Russian' and one more generally for neglected languages [[= languages left
out in usual school and college 'foreign languages' teaching]]. Edgerton and
Sturtevant advised me [[the pronoun, rather than 'us', is honest: languages
as such had long been Mortimer's responsibility within the ACLS]] to use the
money for the production of learning [[pregnant: not 'teaching']] materials
since these were practically non-existent for speakers of English.

But there were also no American authorities on the needed languages, to say
nothing of teachers of them. On the other hand, I knew of quite a flock of younger
linguistic scientists, to whom we had been doling out little study grants for work
in American Indian languages for years. These youngsters had no jobs; to the
head of a department of Romance languages the recommendation that the applicant 'speaks Calusa or Chitimacha like a native' made no appeal at all. So it was
really a pretty natural idea to wonder whether somebody like Mary Haas (master, I think, of Menominee or some such language) could not do the same thing
with Thai (or Siamese as we then called it). She was one of the first (I'd have to
look up the records to remember how the others came in chronologically). She
began by scurrying around the Thai Legation in Washington, and then discovered
that the principal collection of Thai natives was at the University of Michigan;
there she went. She was working away on a description of Thai and the collection
of materials when Pearl Harbor hit us. On that Sunday I was in the living room
of the new house which we were just in the process of building working on repairing and installing an 1830 overmantel around the fireplace, when I heard the
news over the radio. I went up to my study and concocted a letter to Mary saying
that now the time had come to start some real teaching instead of only providing learning materials and suggesting that she start a class in which students
would learning Thai from native speakers under her direction. She took up the
idea enthusiastically. [[See The Linguist as a Teacher of Languages, <u>Language</u>
19.203-208 (1943) by Mary R. Haas, and reprints ever since.]]

It soon became obvious that I could not administer this job and be Administrative Secretary of the ACLS at the same time, so we began to look for somebody to run it. My colleague Waldo Leland thought that Urban Tigner Holmes of
North Carolina would be just the man. In fact, I think he even broached the idea
to Holmes. But, whether right or wrong, I did not think Holmes was the kind of
linguist I was looking for. [[See p. 60 above, under 'French ...']] We finally
settled on Milt who came along in March or April 1942 and we have never
regretted the choice. ...

On the whole I suspect that this idea of learning languages from native
speakers under the control of a linguistic scientist was in the air at the time,
but I am perfectly willing to take the credit for being in a position to initiate
its practical application.

The final paragraph is squeezed in at the foot of the reverse of the single sheet of
typing, and the signature 'Mortimer' slants uphill superimposed on the text.

On 16th October 1974, after reading drafts of both earlier and later pages of the
present History, Graves again wrote to Joos. After the six-year interval without a
copy of his former letter at hand for comparison, he inevitably duplicated a good
deal of what has been copied already above; accordingly, many more omissions
have got to be signalled here; we begin with a 1941 summertime episode:

One day as I was telling one of my contacts in G-2 [[General Staff 2nd =
Intelligence]], a colonel whose name now escapes me, of our new program, he
mentioned that he would very much like to know a couple of Americans who
knew Siamese. ... 'OK,' I says, 'We'll start with Siamese.' The problem was,

that we hadn't any teachers of Siamese. But we did have a lot of these young linguists who had been studying American Indian languages on little bits of grants (doled out by nickel-nurser [Franz] Boas [Chairman of the ACLS Committee on American Native Languages and after 1928 its only active member] since 1927, and we had no jobs for them. It did not take much imagination to realize that these were just the people for the job we had to do. Mary Haas happened to be around [visiting Washington friends in August/September]; I asked her to look for some native Siamese; she found—through their Washington Embassy—studying engineering and such subjects at the University of Michigan. So we sent her to Michigan to exercise her Menominee expertise on them, and produce some learning materials. ... She hadn't been working there more than a couple of months when Pearl Harbor came. ...

For everything I have been able to do in this field and in Oriental Studies and others an awful lot of credit has to go to David Harrison Stevens, Vice-President of the Rockefeller foundation at the time (retired in 1950 at age 65). He supplied practically all the foundation money we had. ... He certainly did as much as anybody in his generation to expand humanistic studies beyond the Mediterranean Atlantic limits to which they were confined forty years ago ... not many linguists know how much he helped them, but nearly every person mentioned in your [LSA History] book has had some benefit from funds which he supplied. He is now living in a retirement home ... C208, 7450 Olivetas Ave, La Jolla, California 92037.

Among those who profited signally from the Stevens efforts without knowing that anyone of that name was involved was Bernard Bloch. In 1963 he was expected to pause in Madison on his way back to New Haven from the West Coast, but then telephoned to beg off: he had just accepted the invitation to come to Lawrence College to be invested with the honorary degree, Doctor of Humane Letters, which (he now said) was the only one worth having—a genuine token of academic merit, while any millionaire or politician could amass LL.D.'s by the dozen—and even though he had heard of Lawrence College as the place that Nathan Pusey got his and so forth, he couldn't guess why they were offering him one: most likely a case of mistaken identity, but, said Bernard to Martin, such a chance was not likely to come a second time so he wasn't about to pass it up.

What Bernard Bloch did not know, and presumably never did find out, was that David H. Stevens was still a Trustee of Lawrence College and was being consulted every time by the Trustees and others planning suitable distribution and choices of their honorary degrees. Mortimer says, 'Dave likes to keep quiet about most such things.'

To finish out this 1936–1940 segment of the Society's history, we quote from Bloch's correspondence with Kent covering relations between an Editor and a Secretary–Treasurer. Bloch as the second Editor had, as remarked elsewhere, factually succeeded Bolling during the 1939 Summer Session in Ann Arbor and was formally elected in the Annual Meeting at the end of that December. (Note also that Kent's successor J Milton Cowan remained in Iowa during his first year as Secretary–Treasurer, 1940, while Kent was President for 1941 and as such was to attend the ACLS Annual Meeting late in January 1941 as our President that year.) Just before leaving Philadelphia, Kent wrote at length to Cowan and Bloch, mostly to Cowan, with copies of certain parts to Bloch,

[no date] Dear Milton: This copy is for you, and contains some useful information here and there. You say that Mrs. C. is interested in stamps. If and when she ever has any leisure time, I'd be glad to know what countries she collects, how large a collection she has, and then we could start exchanges. I have quite a large collection of duplicates.

Feb. 6 1941 / Dear Bernard: / Herewith some sheets of which I gave a copy to Cowan; I have a third copy.
   These sheets include all the various votes of the Society and of the Exec. Com. on procedure, and in conjunction with the Constitution and the rules for Groups include most of what ought to be in a set of By-Laws, something which the Society has never had. ...

15 Feb 1941: Bloch to Kent with copy to Cowan, almost four thousand words:
   ... In general, some of these provisions would be useful in a codification of

procedure ... others appear to me to be not needed. But all of them, so far as
they are adopted for inclusion in such a codification, should be regarded simply
as reminders to the Secretary, to enable him to perform his multifarious duties
as smoothly as possible. Statements which would be more than reminders, and
would in any way circumscribe the Secretary's freedom in executing to the best
of his own judgment the duties of his office, must by all means be kept out of the
list. I don't think I've expressed my meaning very well, but you both no doubt
understand my intention: that what we want, not only for the Secretary but for
every other officer and committee chairman also, is a set of guides rather than
a set of laws or rules. In the present instance there is no question but what Cowan
can profitably take Kent's advice in many matters of procedure (with the understanding that it is advice and not a statement of law); but these helpful hints that
Kent is in a position to give his successor would lose their virtue, I believe, as
soon as they were made into formal by-laws. ... [Joos omits survey of duties
belonging to an Editor, belonging to a Secretary-Treasurer, and those belonging
each other person, group, or category, notably pointing out possibilities of con-
flict between Editor and members of the Executive Committee or Publications
Committee, and finally commenting on one case in which he (much later, and
privately) acknowledged having blundered, with the reference included here:]
So far I have returned unread all contributions received from non-members
(except in one special case where I myself invited the contribution; see Lang.
16.351 fn. 1), and I have considered this to be part of my editorial policy—inherited
from Bolling, but not for that reason only adopted. I still think this is a matter of
editorial policy, to be followed or not at the Editor's discretion. If I am right in
my view, then a vote of the Society is not only uncalled-for but definitely out of
place; but I confess that I am not altogether sure whether I interpret my position
corectly. There are certain general principles which it is clearly within the
editor's province to decide on—thus, whether to accept articles in a language
other than English, whether to accept articles of primarily philological interest,
whether to print replies by aggrieved authors of books unfavorably reviewed, and
so on. In certain other matters the Editor is bound to accept the decision of the
Treasurer—thus in all questions of finance. Now: whether there are any general
principles at all which it is the Society's right to legislate upon, I seriously doubt.
The Society elects an Editor to do a job: to publish a journal and certain other
things, and to make these as good as he can. If the Society feels that the man it
elected is not doing the job as well as it ought to be done, it has an effective
remedy: it can elect somebody else. Beyond that, I don't think the Society can do
anything whatever. Specifically, it has no right to dictate editorial policy, or to
interfere in any way with the Editor's execution of his job. [Theoretically, I suppose I should be within my rights if I got the consent of the Committee on Publications to change the name of our journal from Language to The Linguist's Home
Companion and Repository of Useful Knowledge. But I don't think I'll try to do this.]

- -

⟦Interlude: From 1947/48, and for comparison with the foregoing, the following
Postscript to the letter of acceptance for the Joos Acoustic Phonetics ends with

Do you really think that Acoustic Phonetics is a good title for this book?
I don't. The fifth chapter goes far beyond acoustics, and the implications of
such a title would be misleading. How about this?—Abriss einer kurzen
Einführung in das Studium des Sprachwesens vom akustischen Standpunkte
aus, unter Rücksichtnahme der phonematischen Grundlage der Sprachtheorie.
Something like that, only snappier.

There was no separate signature, of course—not even initials. The proposed
re-titling was not entirely Bernard's invention; it derives from the immensely
long anecdote, said to have been invented in the early 1920's, recounting how a
set of seven men of as many nationalities found themselves agreeing to write up
all that each knew about 'The Elephant' and to meet a 12-month deadline. Bloch's
Beiträge zu einer Einleitung in das Studium des Elephantenwesens, three vol.s
bound as seven, is suspected of having been originally Leonard Bloomfield's.⟧

REPORT
OF THE
FIRST YEAR'S OPERATION
OF THE
INTENSIVE LANGUAGE PROGRAM
OF THE
AMERICAN COUNCIL
OF LEARNED SOCIETIES

1941 - 1942

by

MORTIMER GRAVES, *Chairman*, Committee on the National
School of Modern Oriental Languages and Civilizations;
Secretary, Committee on Intensive Language Instruction

and

J. M. COWAN, *Director*, Intensive Language Program.

December 20, 1942

COMMITTEE ON THE NATIONAL SCHOOL OF MODERN ORIENTAL
LANGUAGES AND CIVILIZATIONS.

Mortimer Graves, American Council of Learned Societies, *Chairman*
Franklin Edgerton, Yale University
G. Howland Shaw, U. S. Department of State

COMMITTEE ON INTENSIVE LANGUAGE INSTRUCTION.

Henry Grattan Doyle, George Washington University, *Chairman*
Mortimer Graves, American Council of Learned Societies, *Secretary*
William Berrien, Rockefeller Foundation
George A. Kennedy, Yale University
Kemp Malone, Johns Hopkins University
Philip E. Mosely, Cornell University

The two committees were composed entirely of men whose names can be found either in the List of Members of our Society, or in Who's Who, or in both, from the 1930's on. Gardiner Howland Shaw, born 1893, was an unmarried Foreign Service Officer in the Department of State, at the time stationed in Washington.

William Berrien, born 1892, was also unmarried. In the 1939 Summer Session, as noted on page 56, he was an Instructor in Portuguese in Ann Arbor; in 1940 he came from Northwestern University to be the ACLS Latin American Studies Specialist, so that he had jurisdiction over the grant noted in Language 17.175:

> The American Council of Learned Societies has been enabled by a grant from the Rockefeller Foundation to offer during the summer of 1941 intensive language courses in Spanish and Portuguese, to be held on the campus of the University of Wyoming at Laramie from June 23 to August 22. Not more than thirty students will be accepted in each course, and each student will be expected to devote his entire attention to the study of one language. No previous training in Spanish or Portuguese is required. For particulars address the Administrative Secretary ⟦ Mortimer Graves ⟧, American Council of Learned Societies, 907 Fifteenth Street, N. W., Washington, D.C.

For 1941-42, Berrien continued as Director of the Institute For Intensive Training in Spanish and Portuguese; then he was taken into the Rockefeller Foundation's central office for the years 1942 to 1944; he went from there to Harvard University as Professor, and there he drops out of our Society's history without ever joining.

The remaining non-member was Philip Edward Mosely, born 1905, at the time Associate Professor of International Relations at Cornell University. He had had field research experience in Moscow (1930-32) and in the Balkans (1935-36) as a Fellow of the Social Science Research Council.

Through all these men, as well as on his routine visits to ILP campuses, Cowan came to know all the dozens of spots where he might settle down after leaving the ACLS, and Mosely's being in Ithaca helped acquaint him with Cornell finally.

INTENSIVE LANGUAGE PROGRAM
1941 - 1942

The Intensive Language Program of the American Council of Learned Societies is supported by two subventions made by the Rockefeller Foundation in 1941 for a two-year period. Under the terms of these grants funds were furnished respectively for "the development of intensive instruction in modern (subsequently interpreted to mean 'unusual', i. e. exclusive of French, German, Spanish and Italian) languages" and for "intensive instruction in Chinese, Japanese, and Russian". Accordingly it is assumed that the success of the Program is to be measured by the amount and quality of intensive instruction in these languages provided through its operation. On this score the Summer Program for 1942 speaks for itself: fifty-six courses, in twenty-six languages, in eighteen universities, involving some seven hundred students is by far the most impressive array of intensive language instruction ever presented in American academic life. It is true that half a dozen of these courses might have been offered without the intervention of the Program, but even these half-dozen have been materially aided by it. The other half-hundred are entirely the creation of the Program itself. It should be added that a dozen of these were, for lack of students or some other cause, not successfully completed. Their claim to enumeration, consequently, is only that they were available if demanded.

The Program is administered by two committees of the Council: the Committee on the National School of Modern Oriental Languages and Civilizations (Mortimer Graves, ACLS, *Chairman*; Franklin Edgerton, Yale University; and G. Howland Shaw, U. S. Department of State) and the Committee on Intensive Language Instruction (Henry Grattan Doyle, George Washington University, *Chairman*; Mortimer Graves, ACLS; *Secretary*; William Berrien, Rockefeller Foundation; George A. Kennedy, Yale University; Kemp Malone, Johns Hopkins University; and Philip E. Mosely).

In 1941 the new Rockefeller money allocated to an Intensive Language Program was made available just at the same time as when the Insurance Building at 907 15th Street was taken over as a whole by a British mission and the displaced ACLS had to be moved northeastward roughly a mile to the only ACLS building known to Martin Joos during the War and again in the 1950's while the ACLS was creating the Spoken English for Speakers of X books. At first that building at 1219 16th Street plus its back-alley garage connected with it on the second-story level by a catwalk was shared uneasily with a medical partnership who could not be displaced from its basement, and thither Cowan came in February of 1942 with minimum files.

Cornell University). Since April 1, 1942 the details of operation have been in the hands of J. M. Cowan, of the University of Iowa, Secretary of the Linguistic Society of America, as Director of the Intensive Language Program. The general division of interest between the two committees is that the first, the Committee on the School, concerns itself more with the scientific features of supplying implementation for instruction in these languages, as will be explained later on in the report, while the operations of the second, the Committee on Instruction, relate more intimately to the provision of courses of instruction. This division, however, has not been rigorously maintained; either Committee retains the right to engage in either type of operation whenever its own ends can thus best be served. The Committees have worked in complete harmony.

The Program operates in the belief that an intensive course in any language can be offered in a college or university whenever there can be assured a sufficient number of tuition-paying students to provide reimbursement to the institution for the expenses involved. The first step, consequently, in encouraging the establishment of a course is the guarantee of such sufficient number of students. Funds are then utilized for the provision of grants to individual students in order that these guarantees may be fulfilled. During the first year of operation, however, the nature of the language under discussion, local conditions, the novelty of the method, and other considerations often prevented the immediate application of this formula, and, because the element of time was considered important, recourse was had to other types of financial aid. Nevertheless, the year's activity has been a gradual approximation to the system of assistance described.

By an intensive course the Committees mean a course which occupies the full time of the student, generally computed at about fifteen hours of classroom instruction, fifteen hours of drill with native speakers, and from twenty to thirty hours of individual preparation per week. Two or three six-weeks sessions of this character separated by short intervals of rest

seem to yield the best results in the shortest time. Here, too, however, accommodation has been sometimes made to suit university schedules and other special circumstances, though the year as a whole exhibits this same progress towards a more nearly uniform procedure.

In some of the languages with which the Committees are concerned, for instance, Chinese, Japanese, Russian, and Portuguese, there was already a modest though improving American tradition of intensive elementary instruction. Some implements—grammars, text-books, phonograph recordings, dictionaries, etc.—were at hand and these were constantly being bettered; there was a small, though quite inadequate, personnel equipped for instruction; and the methods of the intensive approach were beginning to be worked out. But in by far the largest number of the other languages, these desiderata simply did not exist in the English language, and frequently were not available in any language at all. In Malay, for example, the best implements were in Dutch, a fact which makes them all but useless to the American student. In addition they were, on account of difficulties of transport, not obtainable in sufficient quantity. Finally, because they had not been prepared by scholars with sufficient technical linguistic competence and in particular because they had not been prepared for intensive instruction they were, even if they could be secured, in the opinion of the Committee on the School and its advisers, totally inadequate for the work envisaged. Moreover, since all experience with intensive language instruction had already shown a high correlation between good results and good implementation, it became obvious that the first task of the Committees must necessarily be the provision of the implements of instruction before instruction itself. Perusal of the details of the Program will show, consequently, very considerable devotion of funds and effort to the development of grammars and other implementa* of study and teaching. This process, analogous to tooling on the industrial front, was the only firm basis for production later. About half of the funds available have been expended on fellowship awards to Fellows of the National School.

* "implementa" is an unaltered blunder surviving from the Graves typescript, says his letter to Joos in 1974: 'even today my finger frequently confuses "s" with "a" on the typewriter' unless it was somebody's (anybody's!) generation of a plural by analogy with "impedimenta" and left unchallenged by Cowan and his companion for any reason or none. There is apparently one misprint elsewhere: on our page 107, "accommodate[d]" for "...ated."

Mortimer Graves had begun the Intensive Language Program with the help of ACLS staff men—there were no women as long as Leland was still there—and those were only fractionally competent and disinclined to do anything in a hurry. Graves needed a free-wheeling Director of Operations, one who could take off into wild blue yonder on an hour's notice, often to come hundreds of miles back to the Washington office before he was missed. The one person who combined talents and temperament both and could be pried loose from his home base was the only one that was invited: the new LSA Secretary-Treasurer, Assistant Professor Cowan of the State University of Iowa. He easily got 'war-time leave' and came in February.

manuals which would be of general use both to teachers and students. Leonard Bloomfield of Yale University prepared one such entitled *An Outline Guide to the Practical Study of Foreign Languages*. This booklet was published for the Program by the Linguistic Society of America and is now being given wide distribution. Fifteen hundred copies have been sold to the Educational Branch, Special Service Division, Services of Supply, U. S. Army, to be used in the language instruction activities of that Branch within the Armed Forces.

Mention of this fact is made here only to show that the influence of the Program has extended beyond the scope of its own immediate operations. The cooperation of the Program with Governmental agencies will be taken up later in this report. A second manual, *Outline of Linguistic Analysis*, by Bernard Bloch of Brown University and George L. Trager of Yale University, was also published for the Program by the Linguistic Society. It is a more detailed treatment of the descriptive linguistic method as applied to the analysis of the structure of languages. There is reason to believe that this manual will be adopted by the Foreign Language Division of the Office of Strategic Services in New York since this agency has expressed great interest in a preliminary draft which was submitted for examination and criticism. A special edition of the two booklets bound under a single cover was prepared for the Special Service Division. S. O. S. Copies bear the insignia of the Army Institute, and are not available for public distribution.

In the emergency, however, intensive instruction could not wait upon the completion of implementation. The Committee on Intensive Language Instruction, accordingly, had as quickly as possible to set up courses of instruction upon the basis of such implementation as was available. Naturally, every effort was made to provide the best teaching under the conditions prevailing, but it was realized that great improvement would be possible as the improvement in implementation progressed. There resulted during the Summer as will be observed a certain element of duplication in the Program, as instanced by the offering of Turkish at both the American Institute for Iranian*

*The American Institute for Iranian Art and Archæology occupied leased quarters in a Manhattan building; as an organization it lost its identity soon after Second World War, and its holdings of manuscripts and other items that are implied in the Report's wording went to other institutions: Joos has made no effort to pursue them.

informant fees, materials, for the construction of these implements. A list of the first product of this activity is annexed.

Fortunately, one realm of scholarship in which America has been preeminent over the past decade is that of technical linguistics. Nowhere else has the descriptive study of unknown languages as they are used by native speakers been pushed so far forward, and nowhere has there been created such a group of younger scholars equipped with high technical competence in this field. The Committee on the School, consequently, set about the systematic discovery of native speakers (called "informants") of Thai, Korean, Persian, Turkish, Malay, Swahili, Hausa, and the other languages likely to be necessary during the war emergency and the association with them of younger technical linguists who could use descriptive methods to provide the basic materials for the implementation of study. In the process of this operation it was decided to experiment with the actual formulation of a course by this method, in which the control and the presentation of the descriptive features of the instruction would be in the hands of the American technical linguist and the incessant drill-work would be furnished by the native-speaking informant. It was hoped in this way to have the benefit of instruction by native teachers combined with the advantage of instruction in accordance with the most efficient employment of linguistic techniques.

This expectation has been amply fulfilled; several courses have been offered under these conditions, and what was ten months ago a doubtful experiment is now a successful experience. One is chary about speaking of new methods of teaching languages, yet the novel features of this approach promise, when employed by competent scholars with imagination and critical reserve who are not mere adepts at a technique, to yield quite revolutionary dividends, particularly with respect to instruction in those languages not already well studied and well known.

Since the methodology is fundamentally the same regardless of the language being studied, it was desirable to have

Family housing near the ACLS office was hard to find, so that the Cowan family would have to be split temporarily: after all, as he wrote to Joos in 1974 'we naïvely thought it would all be over before too long, and we'd better wait before leaving our house and pulling the kids out of school.' For our LSA History that meant that the better half of its central office, with its massive stock of publications and its files and much of its current letter-writing and all the bookkeeping was centered in Iowa while Cowan shared the bachelor quarters of a friend whose job was in the National Archives. More than a year had passed before a house was found to rent up in Silver Spring, Maryland, and secured by getting its builder-owner a CB commission.

8   American Council of Learned Societies

Art and Archaeology and Indiana University, or by Malay at the University of Michigan and at Yale University; the one took advantage of the best available opportunity to secure intensive instruction, the other, while it presented instruction, devoted its major attention to the provision or improvement of implements. In general these reflect the diverse yet complementary activities of the two committees; to a considerable degree the success of the Program is to be measured by the speed with which the two types of approach coalesce. Persian at Columbia is a case in point. Here a competent teacher and a trained linguist worked hand in hand. The linguist supplied the teacher with his materials and the processes of implementation and instruction were simultaneous.

A detailed survey of the operations of the Program follows:

African Languages. Of the eight hundred or more languages spoken in Africa, half a dozen or so are of immediate practical importance because each is the *lingua franca* by which communication is established over a wide area on the continent. The most important of these are Swahili spoken in the Belgian Congo and East Africa, Fanti spoken on the Gold Coast, Hausa spoken over most of West Africa, Moroccan Arabic, Pidgin English, and in diminishing importance Amharic, Somali, and Afrikaans. An attempt to offer a course during the summer in Swahili at the University of North Carolina, where there was in residence a professor who had learned the language, failed because suitable informants could not be engaged. Work was finally undertaken in this language at the University of Pennsylvania in mid-summer. It was decided that for the time being work in African languages should be confined to the University of Pennsylvania. Under the auspices of the Committee on the School, Zellig S. Harris was already there at work on Moroccan Arabic and had interested himself also in Fanti. Informants were found in this language as well as in Swahili and Hausa, and young linguists were put to work with them. W. E. Welmers in Fanti, Fred Lukoff in Swahili, C. T. Hodge in

Intensive Language Program 1941-42   *9*

Hausa, and Charles Ferguson in Moroccan Arabic. During the summer a course in Fanti (eight students) was held and implementation has proceeded far enough to permit offerings of courses in all these languages in the fall-spring terms of 1942-43. Introductory courses in Moroccan Arabic and Hausa are nearing completion at the present writing. Advanced work will be offered in the next term and a course in Swahili will be organized. Registration in these intensive courses has not been large, but has been decidedly satisfactory considering the fact that these are initial offerings and quite unusual. It happens that the Museum of the University of Pennsylvania has a considerable African collection and a long-standing interest in African cultures. The Director of the Museum, George C. Vaillant, consequently viewed the development of African language instruction at the University with interest and appointed to a post in the Museum a specialist of African studies, Heinz Wieschhoff. This happy collaboration between the Museum and the Department of Oriental Studies, to which Dr. Harris and his associates are assigned for administrative purposes, creates at the University of Pennsylvania the nucleus of an American center of African studies, very much needed in the war emergency (in Germany there were according to latest reports at least sixteen institutions offering instruction in native African languages and civilizations) and of great scientific importance for the future if it can be further developed. Meanwhile, preliminary work in African Pidgin English has been begun at Columbia University by George Herzog; this will be transferred to the University of Pennsylvania as soon as practicable. Tentative discussion has also been held with Mark Hanna Watkins, of Fisk University, and with officials of Howard University, with a view to discovering if work in African languages can be developed at these institutions.

Arabic. Four of the major dialects of Arabic have thus far received the attention of the Program. The implementation by Zellig Harris of Pennsylvania in Moroccan Arabic has already been mentioned. This work is now sufficiently

Asked to explain why the Report has none of the stigmata of commercial type-setting, Cowan almost inadvertently wrote to Joos telling more than what had been asked for, namely, the reason why his dating (20 Dec. 1942) is correct in fact: 'By the way, there's a story about that Report. When it was ready [in Graves typing] we couldn't find a printer who would touch such a small job by the time we needed it. A friend of mine, Henry Edmunds who was working at the War Production Board, had a small hand-operated press. He and I (I had learned printing in the technical high school I went to) set the type and printed it ourselves.' We can guess that the typescript was frozen after the setting was well along, say 20 Nov.

needs or for advanced work, are no substitute for sound implementation to be used in elementary intensive courses. But the cooperation of the Office of Strategic Services must be recorded.

Courses in Syro-Palestinian Arabic were offered at The Johns Hopkins University both in the spring and summer under the direction of W. F. Albright, with the assistance of R. F. Ogden, J. A. Thompson, Habib Kurani, and Nabih A. Faris of Princeton University. The number of students was small, seven in each of the courses, and consequently it was not deemed advisable to attempt an advanced course. Dr. Faris also conducted a semi-intensive course at Princeton during the summer, with seven students enrolled.

A course in the Arabic of Iraq was offered at the American Institute for Iranian Art and Archaeology under the general supervision of Gustav von Grunebaum, with the assistance of Mr. Turabian and Mr. Fouad, with nine students enrolled.

The courses at the American Institute, Johns Hopkins, and Columbia all suffered from the same lack of readily available materials for the proper conduct of an intensive course, but this difficulty was met as best it could be by the preparation of materials as the courses progressed. The only sound implementation which can be shown in this field is that for Moroccan Arabic. In the light of the importance of the Arabic dialects, it would doubtless be desirable to undertake work in the dialects spoken in Libya and Eritrea. Lack of qualified linguists and suitable informants has prevented such an undertaking down to the present time, but the Program has been cooperating with the Special Service Division, S. O. S., in the preparation of phonographically recorded phrase-book materials in these dialects.

Burmese. Paul K. Benedict worked for six months during the spring and summer on an analysis of Burmese with the assistance of a native speaker at Yale University. Progress in implementation in this language has been beset with many complications. The informant was one of two native Burmans known to be in this country. When he was called for induction

advanced so that an analytical grammar, texts, and dictionary are about ready for publication. A preliminary sketch of some of this material is in press and will appear shortly in the *Journal of the American Oriental Society*. Teaching materials have been prepared as the class progressed this fall. This work was coincident with the compilation of an Army phrase book for the War Department under the direction of our workers. Colonel Arthur Vollmer requested Dr. Harris to undertake this work and arrangement was made by which the Army advanced funds to defray part of the expenses for informants. Since the materials requested by the Army could also serve as teaching materials, both ends could be achieved without any additional expenditure of time.

The elementary colloquial Egyptian Arabic offered at Columbia under the direction of Arthur Jeffrey in the spring was so successful and there were so many students who were interested in continuing that it was felt desirable to establish an advanced course. The services of Edwin E. Calverley of Hartford Theological Seminary were secured, together with those of Ibrahim Mansauri and Riad Askar, and both elementary and advanced courses were offered during the summer. It was necessary to limit the registration in the elementary course to twelve and in the advanced course to nine. Because of the large number of applications for these courses, it was possible to get a highly select group of students and these made rapid progress during the summer. Elementary and advanced courses were also offered in the fall. The shortage of dictionaries and text books has compelled the preparation of much of the materials while the courses were in progress. These were manifolded for distribution among the students and will not be published until they have undergone the test of use.

A request was directed to the Department of State and the Office of Strategic Services for assistance in securing foreign materials. Through the latter, several copies of Arabic dictionaries and primers unavailable in the United States have been received. The sponsors of the Program are aware that such importations, valuable as they are to fill temporary

Mortimer Graves was born 1893 in Philadelphia. In the First World War he was an aviator in the Navy. With a 1920 Harvard A.B. he was taken on as a History Master in the William Penn Charter School and also began his graduate student years, 1920-26, in the University of Pennsylvania. 'I'm the world's worst historian,' he says now, 'always more interested in the future than the past.' And, Joos adds, always learning from written and printed items that his professors weren't prepared to decipher, so that they instead read translations or by-passed them. Graves was and remains temperamentally skeptical of all translating, including his own translating work, and has always kept looking for the actual events behind official publications.

George Kennedy of Yale University offered two courses in Chinese at the Linguistic Institute held this summer at the University of North Carolina. The first of these courses was an elementary course designed for students who were primarily interested in structure of colloquial Chinese. The materials for these students were presented entirely in transcription. For those who were interested in the acquisition of written Chinese, concentrated work in reading from characters was offered. The advanced course was likewise divided to meet the needs of students with these different interests.

Upon the conclusion of the courses at Chapel Hill, Dr. Kennedy began an intensive summer course in elementary Chinese at Yale University with forty-three students enrolled.

William Acker offered a course in the spring in Chinese at George Washington University for eleven students. This course was not intensive in nature but was looked upon favorably by the Program because of the fact that many of the people enrolled in it were employed by Governmental agencies which were interested in seeing their people acquire as much knowledge of the language as possible in the time which they were able to devote to it.

Though not formally part of the Program, the intensive Mandarin Chinese of the College of Chinese Studies, moved from Peiping to the University of California (Extension) in Berkeley, should be mentioned. There may quite possibly develop points at which the college and the Program can cooperate.

Modern Greek. Johns Hopkins University has been prepared to offer intensive instruction in modern Greek under Mr. E. Malakis, but to date only sporadic requests for this language have come in.

Hindustani. Murray B. Emeneau of the University of California at Berkeley began work on Hindustani early this spring but was forced to give it up because of the difficulty in securing suitable informants. The Hindustani students on the campus were too busy with their studies to devote a

into the Army, the Director notified officers of Military Intelligence Service in Washington who were interested in the work on Burmese. As a result of their direct appeal to National Selective Service Headquarters the informant was granted occupational deferment. Shortly after this Mr. Benedict accepted a post with the Office of Strategic Services. Mr. R. I. McDavid Jr. replaced him, and work was continued at Yale under the direction of Leonard Bloomfield and with the assistance of William Cornyn. The west coast branch of the Office of War Information then requested the release of the informant so that he could be sent to San Francisco to broadcast directly to Burma. It was necessary to call a conference of all agencies, civilian and military, which were interested in a continuation of work in Burmese. It was decided that the need of the O. W. I. was sufficiently urgent to warrant release of the informant. All parties participating in the conference expressed a desire for a continuation and agreed to assist in locating another informant. The search for native Burmese residing in this country was fruitless, but recently a Burman has arrived from Trinidad and has indicated an interest in assisting the Program. At the present writing it appears likely that an arrangement can be made with the assistance of the Foreign Language Branch of O. W. I. in New York so that the linguistic work in this strategically important language can be carried on from where it left off. Implementation has already progressed sufficiently so that a course could be offered with the aid of a native informant.

Chinese. One of three students in an intensive course in Cantonese given by Yuen-Ren Chao at Harvard University during the summer was aided by the Program. Similar assistance was available in F. W. Cleaves' course in Mandarin but was not necessary because a sufficient number of students enrolled without it.

Fifteen students participated in a course in Sino-Japanese offered by P. A. Boodberg at the University of California in Berkeley. An advanced continuation section as well as a repetition of the elementary course is now in progress.

Trustworthy estimates of Mortimer's scope in understanding archives written or (most usually) printed in languages foreign to our schools run from dozens to twelve or fifteen; the list of alphabets is indicative: Chinese character-text, Japanese read with a Chinese/Japanese dictionary, Armenian, Greek, Russian, Arabic and Hebrew. His personal font of Chinese type supplied inserts into ACLS publications for decades, hand-set by Mortimer when money for printing was scant. His shelves of grammars and dictionaries were famous far and wide and on occasion were appealed to by the Library of Congress—which during the Second World War borrowed his huge collection of maps, very few of which ever came back to him, since most of them had been worn out or lost in the hands of military users.

sufficient amount of time to assure rapid progress, and the other Hindustani residents in the vicinity are apparently employed full-time at good salaries by governmental and private agencies, so that it is impossible to compete for their services.

A course in Hindustani was offered at the American Institute for Iranian Art and Archaeology under the directorship of Bernard Geiger with the assistance of Mr. A. Singh. H. M. Hoenigswald was called from Yale University to assist in the organization of this course after it had started. The preliminary reports from this course show that it suffered from the difficulty which arises whenever an attempt is made to offer an intensive course in a field in which there is inadequate implementation. The formal presentation of structure of the language can only be effective when it is complemented by well organized drill materials exemplifying the structure of the language. In instances where the director's full time is devoted to the structural aspects of the language and the drill is left in the hands of the native informants, experience shows that the informants misunderstand their roles and tend to assume the role of the instructor, repeating the materials which have already been presented instead of devoting their time to painstaking drill. This problem can only be met by profiting from experience and gradually bringing the two aspects of the instruction into their proper relationship.

In September H. M. Hoenigswald began work on Hindustani at Columbia University with an informant. Arrangements have been completed with Hunter College for the offering of an intensive course in Hindustani under Hoenigswald's supervision, beginning in February 1943. According to present plans this course will be continued at Hunter College during the summer as an advanced section and a new elementary course will be started at Columbia University as a part of the coming Summer Program.

Hungarian. Leslie Tihany of Harvard University has prepared a *Modern Hungarian Grammar* together with

exercises which is being used in a semi-intensive course now in progress. An attempt to organize an intensive course this fall failed because of lack of students. Until the present time there have been few applications from students desiring to pursue the intensive study of Hungarian.

Icelandic. Kemp Malone and Stefán Einarsson of Johns Hopkins University were prepared to offer a course in modern Icelandic during the summer but there was not a sufficient number of students to organize this course.

Iranian (Persian). The close cooperation of Stanley Newman and Christie Wilson in the offering of Persian at Columbia University has already been mentioned. Dr. Newman had been preparing texts, phonographic recordings, and a phrase-book under the auspices of the Committee on the School at the time the summer course opened. These materials were all used to good effect in making a successful course in which ten students were enrolled. A sufficient number of the students indicated an interest in continuing the work and an advanced Persian course is now in progress. Dr. Newman's analytical grammar of Persian will be ready for publication in the early spring.

A course in Persian was also offered at the American Institute for Iranian Art and Archaeology during the summer, in which there were four students. This course was under the supervision of Abu Turab Mehra. It did not have the financial guarantee of the Committee on Intensive Language Instruction because it was deemed not wise to support two elementary Persian courses in New York City.

Japanese. Four projects in the implementation of Japanese have been undertaken by the Committee on the School. One of these, being conducted by Morris Swadesh, was cut short when he was called into the armed forces. Bernard Bloch of Brown University has been working on colloquial Japanese with native informants since early spring. His course in spoken Japanese offered this fall had to be limited to fifteen students. Five army officers are taking the course. Dr. Bloch has worked in close cooperation with George Kennedy of Yale University. Dr. Kennedy conducted an experimental course in Japanese at Yale in the spring, with some forty students enrolled. These students are now continuing in an advanced section at Yale which will run throughout the fall and winter. Two informants devote their entire time to the courses at Brown and Yale, alternating in such a manner that the services of an informant are available at all times in both institutions. The most recent project in the implementation of Japanese is the outgrowth of the Second Conference of Japanese Teachers which was held in Ann Arbor, Michigan, September 17-19, 1942. A brief account of the Conference is included here as background. Twenty-six persons attended, including practically every teacher of collegiate Japanese in the country and representatives of government agencies. The earlier discussions of the conference were devoted to the problems of instruction in Japanese. All of the delegates who had been actively engaged in this work reported on the various phases of their experience and contributed much useful information which could be used in improving Japanese instruction throughout the country. The discussion turned to the fundamental problem of how to commence instruction in a language such as Japanese where the system of writing is not phonetic. There was final general agreement that the teaching of spoken Japanese and the Japanese system of writing constitute two distinct and different tasks. It was further agreed that both tasks should not be attempted at the same time and that the early months should be devoted to acquisition of a speaking knowledge of Japanese without burdening instruction with an introduction to the study of writing. It was felt that in the intensive course the introductory period could profitably be devoted to colloquial Japanese in transcription. Those who had already used such an introduction testified that the acquisition of a reading knowledge of Japanese was greatly simplified when the students had a reasonable command of spoken Japanese and that under these conditions progress in mastery of the system of writing was

very greatly accelerated. As a result of these discussions, a committee was appointed consisting of George Kennedy of Yale University, *Chairman*, Bernard Bloch of Brown University, and Ichiro Shirato of Columbia University to organize a sixty-hour basic course in colloquial Japanese. The work of this committee has been going forward since the Ann Arbor Conference and the course apparently will be ready for publication shortly after the first of the year.

Harvard's Japanese course under Serge Elisséeff and E. O. Reischauer showed the largest enrollment [52] of the Japanese courses offered during the summer. A large number of students who completed the elementary Japanese course at Columbia University in the spring continued in the intermediate section under Hugh Borton and H. G. Henderson in the summer. There were twenty-four students in the intermediate section, which was assured by guarantees from the Committee on Intensive Language Instruction. Twenty-five students were enrolled in the elementary Japanese course at Michigan under Joseph Yamagiwa.

There were also sixteen students enrolled in the Japanese course conducted by Mr. Acker at George Washington University in the spring.

It is interesting to note that, although the Japanese courses are always well filled, there is the largest turnover of students in this field. This is due to the fact that courses at Columbia, Harvard, Michigan, and Yale act as feeders for the Signal Corps Japanese course organized by Colonel Eric Svensson, the Navy Japanese School under the supervision of Lt. Commander A. E. Hindmarsh, and the newly organized Army Japanese School. These Government schools take over practically all of the students of Japanese who are eligible for military duty. In some cases the transfer from the courses sponsored by the Program is as high as fifty per cent. If some such working relationship could be set up in other language fields there would be a definite acceleration in the Program with a resulting reduction of the amount of time now devoted to attempts to secure placement for students coming out of courses in governmental and civil agencies where use can be made of their special linguistic training. The activities of the Program in placing students upon completion of courses will be discussed elsewhere in this report.

Korean. A. M. Halpern worked on an analysis of Korean under the guidance of the Committee on the School at the University of Chicago during the summer months. Implementation in this language is far enough along so that a sound course can be offered if the demand arises. Mr. Halpern was called to Washington this fall to offer a semi-intensive course in Japanese at George Washington University for governmental employees. His work in Korean is continuing.

Kurdish. Kurdish was offered at the American Institute for Iranian Art and Archaeology by Dr. Geiger with the assistance of Mr. Turabian for four students.

Malay. Early last fall Isidore Dyen commenced an analysis of Malay at Yale University, where he had been appointed a Research Associate, with view to preparing a systematic grammar and teaching materials in this language. By spring this work had progressed far enough so that an elementary course in Malay could be introduced into the curriculum at that institution. Fortunately Raymond Kennedy of the Department of Anthropology at Yale was prepared to offer work in the cultural background of Malaysia, and the University undertook the establishment of an undergraduate major in Malay studies, open to juniors and seniors. The time is divided equally between the linguistic studies and study of the cultural background in this program. We have here, consequently, the possibility of a development in the Malayo-Philippine field of a center of study not unlike that promised in the African field at the University of Pennsylvania.

Meanwhile, quite without reference to the Program, W. M. Senstius of the University of Michigan had started a course in Malay with a dozen or more students.

Mongol. Ferdinand Lessing at the University of California at Berkeley is offering an intensive course in the Mongolian language with emphasis on the Khalkha dialect. Six highly qualified students having a general background in Asiatic studies entered the course in the fall. At the present time this course appears to be in danger of annihilation because of the operation of Selective Service and activities of enlisting officers of the Army and Navy.

Pashtu. Herbert Penzl of the University of Illinois has been taking advantage of the presence of a considerable number of Pashtu students at that institution to implement the work in this Afghan language. Although Dr. Penzl has been able to devote only part-time to his investigations he has made considerable progress, which was reported at the annual summer meeting of the Linguistic Society of America at the University of North Carolina in Chapel Hill on July 11.

Pidgin English (Melanesian). Both the practical and scientific importance of the "pidgin" varieties of English and French are very definite. For Melanesia particularly, where native speech is mutually unintelligible from island to island, there exists no other language of comparable utility. Robert A. Hall Jr. of Brown University has completed an analytical grammar with texts and vocabulary of Melanesian Pidgin English. This work is now in press and will be published after the first of the year by the Linguistic Society of America. It will constitute a satisfactory working hand-book, should there be call for the establishment of a course in this *lingua franca.* Negotiations are already under way for such a course for both the Navy and the School of Military Government. Hall has also prepared a *Melanesian Pidgin Phrase-Book and Vocabulary* designed for use by the armed forces. Four thousand copies of a special edition of the phrase-book which is now ready for distribution have been ordered by the Army, Navy, and Marine Corps. The copies of the special edition bear an Army Institute cover and are not available for public distribution. The regular edition may be obtained through the Council offices. Work on West African Pidgin English is mentioned above.

Portuguese. Two intensive courses in Portuguese were offered at the Portuguese Institute held at the University of Vermont during the past summer. The work was under the general direction of M. A. Zeitlin of the University of California at Los Angeles, who was assisted by a group of Brazilian scholars and teachers. Forty-four highly selected students were enrolled, and the summer Institute was eminently successful. One course was an elementary course and the other an advanced course for teachers of Portuguese. This course was separately financed and is reported in more detail elsewhere.

Intensive Portuguese was also offered at the University of North Carolina in conjunction with the Linguistic Institute. This elementary intensive Brazilian Portuguese was under the direction of Urban T. Holmes, Jr., who was assisted by P. Pinto, D. W. MacPheeters, and Mr. and Mrs. Peixoto. Nineteen students were enrolled.

Panjabi. After Murray Emeneau was forced to give up the work on Hindustani because of lack of informants, he turned his attention to Panjabi and devoted full time to work on this language with the informants during the summer months. Arrangements were made for a fall course in this language which is of strategic importance because of the fact that it is spoken by a large portion of the Indian army. Unfortunately not enough students applied to make the offering of the course feasible.

Russian. Because of its present political and military significance and possibly because of the wide-spread feeling of closer cultural affinity, Russian has been the most popular language for selection by those universities desiring to participate in the Intensive Language Program. There have been, consequently, more offerings in this language than in any other. During the summer Russian was offered at the American

Institute for Iranian Art and Archeology to nine students. Columbia University was forced to limit its registration to sixteen students; although there were more than forty applicants of first-class, Cornell University offered elementary and advanced courses in Russian to twenty-seven students. The elementary and advanced courses at Harvard enrolled sixty students. Thirty-nine students, most of them regular undergraduates, were in the Yale course, and twelve students registered for the intensive Russian offered at Ohio State University. In the Fall Program advanced intensive courses were given at Cornell and Harvard; elementary courses at Columbia, Cornell, and Yale. Elementary intensive courses were also started at the University of Chicago and the University of Iowa with the support of the Program. These new courses were filled to capacity by selecting the best students from the number of applicants which exceeded the number of students which could be accommodate. *

The Committee on Intensive Language Instruction has received requests for assistance in offering intensive Russian at five other universities. Curtailment of assistance in the development of Russian studies may be necessary in order that there may not be overburdening of the Program in one field.

* See the note on our page 99!

Thai. Mary Haas at the University of Michigan has now been working on an analysis of Thai for more than a year and has made considerable progress toward the preparation of the materials necessary to afford access to this language. During the past summer she offered, with the assistance of resident Thai students, a course for six students. An advanced class is continuing this fall and winter.

Turkish. The Program has supported three separate projects now in the Turkish dialects. Norman McQuown until recently worked on the preparation of texts and other implements at the University of Mexico, where, on account of the presence of a numerous Turkish-speaking colony there was possible an approximation to a sojourn at Ankara or

Istanbul. Charles F. Voegelin was released from his duties in the Department of Anthropology at Indiana University early this spring to work with Turkish students and prepare materials to be offered in an experimental course at that institution this summer. This work went ahead rapidly, and a supplementary seminar in which the students worked along with the instructor learning Turkish and methods of analysis was offered for ten students in the Folk-lore Institute at Indiana University in July and August. Beginning with the fall term an intensive Turkish course was started at Indiana with a capacity enrollment. Mr. McQuown was recalled from Mexico to assist with this work. Turkish was offered in the spring at Columbia University (six students) by Karl Menges, and during the summer at the American Institute of Iranian Art and Archaeology for four students.

In order to determine the extent of intensive language instruction in the unusual languages outside the Program a letter was sent in August to the presidents of one hundred fifty of our major colleges and universities. Supplementary materials consisting of a comprehensive description of the Summer Program, description of the intensive course and an explanation of the sort of assistance available through the Program were also sent. The letter requested a listing with the Program of any courses in the unusual languages which had been offered in these institutions and which in general approximated the intensive course of the Program. Requests for assistance in establishing such courses wherever the facilities of the institution warranted were also solicited.

Responses were received from about two thirds of the institutions addressed. From these replies two facts were immediately clear. All of the intensive language work in unusual languages in the country was being done with the cooperation of the Program. No new courses were listed. Further, many new courses in the unusual languages were being added to the curricula of various institutions. These were practically all three-hour-a-week courses and their

establishment reflected the influence of the Program, though their character did not demand its support. Amusingly enough, a large percentage of the new courses were labeled "intensive".

At that time there seemed to be a general reluctance on the part of university administrators to break the order of the traditional arrangement in offering language courses. On the whole, the feeling seemed to be widespread that such courses are "practical" and "non-academic" and consequently do not rightly belong in a university curriculum. To the extent that this intensive work is designed to provide tool-competence in languages to be used by specialists in disciplines other than language, linguistics, and literature, this criticism, if it be one, is valid. The sponsors of the Program, however, see no mutual exclusiveness in the terms "practical" and "scientific." They believe that 1) a practical tool-command of a language is the best foundation of scientific or academic work in it, 2) that such practical command can be secured most efficiently in the intensive course, and 3) that all instruction which is not based on scientific analysis of the language in question is inefficient. They are willing to contend, consequently, that their operations are not only "practical" and "scientific", but even "academic". Recently there seems to be a swing of attitude in the direction of favoring sound experimentation with intensive language instruction in French, Spanish, German and Italian. The Program has received expression of a desire to undertake such experimentation from four universities.

We should face frankly the difficulties with which the first year of operation has been beset and the deficiencies—some attributable to the difficulties, some not—which that year's activity has exposed. Obviously the most efficient way in which to learn a foreign language is to study under competent teaching in the country of which that language is the native tongue. In the emergency situation this procedure was impossible for almost all of the languages subsumed under the Program. Teachers and implements had to be developed quickly,—and they had to be developed in America. We are far from perfection, but the sponsors of the Program feel very hopeful over the year's experience. Any lingering doubts of American ability to do just this job, and do it completely and well, have been dissipated. The sponsors recognized at the outset that sound linguistic analysis of a language, which is a necessary preliminary to writing a grammar, could advantageously be carried on simultaneously with instruction, and they have worked to achieve a general recognition of this point of view. It cannot be overemphasized that the intensive course which the Program aims to develop is not simply a stepped-up course of the usual sort. Perhaps the unqualified term "intensive course" is not the best usage. For one thing, in the initial stages of the course a native informant is indispensable and emphasis is placed on acquisition of the spoken language. The students are trained to apply the method of analysis which has been developed, chiefly by the Americanists, for recording non-literate languages and to arrive inductively at the structure of the language through the use of speech forms. Work with the informant becomes more a matter of posing and solving problems than one of rote memorization. Study of the system of writing is taken up only after the student has a working knowledge of the structure of the language if the system of writing used for the language in question happens to be non-phonetic and gives no clue to colloquial speech.

University cooperation has been good; the reception of the idea of cooperation has always been friendly, though sometimes local conditions have made impossible the working out of the details. To some extent difficulties of this order are attributable to the fact that the Program has needed the year's experience to crystallize its own ideas, and that consequently proposals made early in the process could not be nearly so specific as those which would be made now. The geographical distribution of the Program's operations is not at present good—confined as these are for the most part to the Eastern States. This state of affairs reflects the accident of the first personal contacts made, and is being corrected as rapidly as possible.

But by far the greatest handicap to the Program's complete success is the lack of good students. Most applicants are—disregarding for the moment the cranks—persons with no particular competence who believe that the mere possession of an unusual language will make them useful, persons with linguistic interests alone—sometimes scientific sometimes not—and polyglots who—unable to make useful employment of some sort of competence in several languages—think to improve their situation by adding a couple more. Applications from persons qualified in a regular discipline who wish to acquire a language competence for use as a tool in that discipline are disappointingly few, yet it is for these that the Program was originally designed. The fact that this factor does not operate quite so thoroughly in Portuguese, Russian, and Japanese—languages for which the need is generally accepted as evident—suggests that the condition may be somewhat alleviated as the American public becomes similarly convinced of the need for the other languages. A major problem of the Program, in any case, is to secure more and better applicants for language training. Very recent developments indicate that this problem may be solved in part by governmental recognition of the Program and assignment of students for this kind of work.

Any program of this sort is naturally handicapped by the operation of Selective Service. In the case of the Intensive Language Program this handicap was reduced to a minimum during the summer by a quite general realization on the part of many Selective Service Boards of the value of deferring induction into the Army until a stage of language competence likely to be useful to the Army had been reached. During the summer the Director made more than a hundred appeals to local boards for postponement of induction until completion of course for students studying under the auspices of the Program. Two students were inducted and one was granted a furlough to complete his course before being called for active duty. At the conclusion of the summer program, it was becoming increasingly apparent that such success in securing deferments could not continue. Most of the students had been drawn from student bodies of colleges and with the lowering of the draft age to include eighteen and nineteen-year-olders it was clear that the operation of Selective Service would diminish the number of available students. The ranks of those qualified to do advanced work in graduate colleges had already been greatly reduced. In an attempt to meet this difficulty and protect those students who were already involved in study of unusual languages, the Director tried to establish an arrangement with military authorities which would enable students taking courses to be included as members of an enlisted reserve in the Army. A conference was called which was attended by officers of those operating divisions of the Army and Navy Air Forces having a need for specialized linguistic personnel. These officers were well aware of the dangers to their needs caused by the operation of Selective Service and expressed a desire for a more closely knit integration of language work being done both by civilian and military agencies. They felt that provision could be made to have such students included in the enlisted reserve. These negotiations were hardly under way when the Secretary of War announced that men in the enlisted reserve would be subject to call for active duty early in 1943. Further attempts to maintain a flow of students under such an arrangement were obviously useless. The efforts of the Program toward securing a unified and integrated plan of operations for all language work being done throughout the country have continued and the cooperation of the various operating branches of the government has been whole-hearted and in many instances enthusiastic.

After having passed through a period of considerable anxiety about the possibility of having the work of the Program disrupted by the operation of Selective Service, its sponsors have become less concerned about such matters because of recent successes of the usual individual appeals to local draft boards in the cases of teachers and research workers who were liable to induction. Since the loss of Morris Swadesh in the early spring, already mentioned above, only one Fellow of the National School has been inducted. Mr. Fred Lukoff, who was working on the African project at Pennsylvania, has been called into the armed forces. This loss can probably be attributed to anomalous procedure; Mr. Lukoff was inducted before the proper appeals could be made. On the other hand, a sufficient number of occupational deferments have been won on the basis of appeals to draft boards so that the danger of our losing key people is at the present time not too serious. Quite possibly the pressure of this handicap will become greater, though we cannot imagine our Axis enemies, excepting in the last throes of desperation, stopping the training of a promising language man in order to turn him into an indifferent soldier,—but they are experts at this total war at which we are as yet neophytes.

The problem of obtaining proper students for the work of the Program and of protecting them from Selective Service until they have acquired a usable competence in an unusual language is intimately tied up with the problem of placing students in the war effort upon successful completion of courses. The function of the Program's Japanese courses as feeders for the various military Japanese schools has already been mentioned. In the face of a complete lack of specification of needs for linguistic personnel—indeed a complete initial unawareness of the linguistic problems in global war, save in the case of Japanese—on the part of the operating units of the armed forces, it was necessary for the Program to anticipate needs and prepare to meet them. Although the sponsors of the Program have never doubted the soundness of such anticipatory training it has frequently been difficult to convince students that they should devote themselves whole-heartedly for from three to six months to some exotic language, the name of which they probably had never heard before the war broke. If it had been possible to give such students some assurance that use would be made of their new competence in the war effort we should have had far more students than we could accommodate for every language dealt with in the Program. Numerous expressions of a desire to establish courses have come in from university administrators with a reservation that the courses would be offered if concrete evidence could be shown that there was a demand for the particular language in the Army or Navy. The lay attitude was summed up in an article which appeared in early summer in one of the national news magazines describing the activities of the Program. The article was sympathetic, but the avowed intention of the Program to develop a stock-pile of strategic language competences was termed "high-sounding". Subsequent developments have shown that the stock-pile could not be created in the sense of a usable reserve to be drawn upon as the occasion arose simply because the students coming out of the courses were, through the efforts of the Program, fed directly into the various civil and military branches of the government. The Program has accepted every opportunity to be useful to government agencies in meeting their emergency needs with respect to all phases of language and linguistic operations, without reference to their direct connection with the Program. This activity has been time and effort consuming and all too frequently has not yielded results commensurate with that expenditure. In general the government agencies do not, possibly cannot, know exactly what they want in language-competencies; in particular they do not forecast their needs sufficiently early to have them supplied, for it is obvious that training in a difficult unstudied language is not something to be accomplished overnight. The problem would be greatly simplified if the government agencies could forecast their needs and in particular if they could hold out some hope that use could be found for qualified persons trained in accordance with such forecast. But probably such efficiency is not to be expected of a democracy.

Cooperation with the Education Branch, Special Service Division, S. O. S., has already been mentioned. The sponsors of the Program believe that this cooperation has resulted in the formulation of a sounder plan of linguistic activity by the Special Service Division than would have been otherwise likely. Besides providing the linguistic handbooks and the *Melanesian Pidgin Phrase-Book* and participating in the production of specially designed phonograph records for teaching foreign languages to enlisted men, they were

instrumental in assuring the appointment of a competent linguist to direct this phase of the Special Service Division's program. The machinery of the Program has been used by the Military Dictionary Project of U. S. Military Intelligence as has been mentioned above and in other ways as opportunity has offered. The Director is constantly called upon for advice on language problems by practically every agency of the Government, which has these problems—Office of Strategic Services, Board of Economic Warfare, Department of Justice, as well as the numerous departments of the Army, Navy, and Marine Corps—and for recommendations of persons with unusual language competences for employment by these rapidly expanding agencies. The Program is not equipped with a staff sufficient to perform these functions adequately, but it does what it can without impairing the performance of its major duty. There seems to be need for 1) an employment service providing a channel of information concerning, and evaluation of, persons with unusual language competences demanded by the Government and 2) of a semi-volunteer translation service through which those with such competences throughout the country might be organized to provide translations for Government agencies. Perhaps the newly created Ethnogeographic Board will assume some of this burden, at any rate there seems no reason why it should be assumed by the Program, unless this is to be considerably expanded. It is hardly necessary to add that the full details of the Program's cooperation with agencies of the Government cannot in all cases at present be divulged, but the record is one which gives the Program a definite and increasing place in the war effort.

As will be seen from the names of one of the Committees in charge of the Program, the sponsors are alive to the need for development in the United States of a National School of Modern Oriental Languages and Civilizations. The activities of the Program have consequently been designed to make such contribution as possible toward this end. At first the conception embraced the creation of a school, presumably though not necessarily in Washington, comparable with the School of

Oriental Studies of the University of London, the École Nationale des Langues Orientales Vivantes of Paris, and similar institutions in Leningrad and Berlin. Recent developments in governmental participation and control in education, the past year's experience, the great size of the United States, and the difference in academic organization, between this and European countries suggest consideration, at least temporarily during the orientation period, of a development of a somewhat different type, not toward a single central school, but toward a central holding agency in Washington, providing relatively elementary intensive instruction in languages and civilizations especially for government personnel and maintaining contact with the departments of the Government concerned with those matters, but carrying on its activities of advanced training and research through and in the universities best equipped in facilities and personnel for such work. The elements of such a pattern are discernible in the development of African studies at the University of Pennsylvania and in the development of Malay-Philippine studies at Yale University, besides the several developments of Chinese, Japanese, and Russian at several other centers. Ultimately a single, centrally located National School would seem to be most desirable, but this does not appear to be an auspicious time to attempt the founding of such a school. No doubt the proper solution will be found at the conclusion of the war, after the American people have gone through a period of becoming aware of the need for such an institution.

The Committees directing the Intensive Language Program look back upon the activities of the year 1941-1942 with considerable satisfaction; they consider it hardly extravagant to claim them as epoch-making,—not only when measured by the considerable number of new courses introduced, but perhaps even more when judged in terms of increased experiment with and advertising of intensive methods, improvement of implementation, and scientific study of linguistic phenomena, much of this last not only for the first time in America but for the first time anywhere in the world.

In addition, almost as a by-product, a considerable number of Americans have been trained to efficient tool-control of unusual languages, and many of them have already been absorbed into governmental activities concerned with the war. By the end of the year well over a thousand students will have completed intensive courses conducted under the auspices of the Program. Study-aids have been awarded to 252 of these and of their number 42 have held grants for two courses. Roughly 42 per cent of available funds have been expended in this manner.

It is proposed to continue operation in the year 1942-1943 along very much the same road, with perhaps somewhat more specific and highly crystallized ideas at the beginning of the year and more attention to the end product, the student. The Program for this year will, it is hoped, accordingly include:

1. The continuation of enterprises of implementation already undertaken, with perhaps modest additions,—for instance in Malagasy, Roumanian, lesser Slavic languages, Pacific Ocean languages (Polynesian particularly), etc.

2. Experiment with semi-intensive instruction in Washington designed primarily for employees of the Federal Government.

3. Stimulation of courses in universities and colleges, as follows:

a) Courses over which the Committees exercise full control similar to the Portuguese Institute at the University of Vermont.

b) Courses offered by the universities and colleges in accordance with guarantees of students by the Committees, and.

c) Courses approved by the Committees, for attendance at which the Committees will make fellowship awards.

These operations will be conducted through the media of conferences, fellowships, and the administrative activities of the Director and his associates.

In addition, the experience of the Program demonstrates
that the time has come for the next step, that is, the
development of the Language Program into a Program of
Regional Studies. For example, instead of developing a centre
for the study of *Turkish*, we should develop a centre for the
study of *Turkey*. In such a development, obviously, language
is the central core, but it should be surrounded by the
disciplines of history, the social and natural sciences, and
those studies which deal with the human being and his
relation to his environment, physical and social. Such a
development suffers from the same disabilities as did the
Language Program,—lack of teachers and of implementation.
Perhaps the year 1943 will see some experimental activity in
the production of both. The idea of regional or areal programs
is a trend in university education, accelerated rather than
originated by the war. It is not at all unlikely that in beginning
some experimental work of the kind suggested now, we can
not only contribute to the war and the peace effort, but can
make some valuable contributions to education for the second
half of the twentieth century.

- -

Annex A, pp. 33–38, is a list of 266 lines in depth on the model of these few which
have been included here because each is otherwise interesting; few members! —

Bender, Ernest	Hindustani	Summer Iranian Inst.
Choseed, Bernard J.	Russian	Sum.-Fall Columbia
Fahs, Ned Carey	Portuguese	Summer Vermont
Rubenstein, Herbert	Fanti	Sum.-Fall Pennsylvania
Sheldon, Esther Keck	Persian	Sum.-Fall Columbia

Annex B, pp. 39 & 40, is printed on the two sides of the same sheet of cover-stock
paper as the outside-front text and inside-front that we reprint both on page 97. Its
title is 'A bibliography of materials produced and in process of production by the
Intensive Language Program of the American Council of Learned Societies'

Benedict, P. K., "Cantonese Phonology", 84 pp., unpublished typescript.

Bloch, Bernard, and Trager, George L., Outline of Linguistic Analysis, 86 pp.,
    Linguistic Society of America, 1942.

Bloomfield, Leonard, Outline Guide for the Practical Study of Foreign Languages,
    16 pp., Linguistic Society of America, 1942.

(The two preceding publications have also been bound together under the title,
Practical Guides for the Study of Languages, Bloomfield, Bloch, and Trager,
for the Army Institute, which has purchased a large number of copies. This is
not available for public distribution.)

Dyen, Isidore, Malay Lessons, mimeographed texts and translations for class-
    room use. Not yet being published for distribution.
    A Malay Grammar, in preparation.

Haas, Mary, "The Phonemic System of Thai", unpublished typescript.
    "Types of Reduplication in Thai", Studies in Linguistics, Vol. 1, No. 4, 1942.
    "The Use of Numeral Classifiers in Thai", Language, Vol. 18, No. 3, 1942.
    Beginning Thai, 86 pp., Dittoed, University of Michigan, copyright 1942, but
    not yet available for public distribution.
    "The Thai System of Writing", unpublished typescript.

Hall, Robert A., Jr., Melanesian Pidgin Phrase-book and Vocabulary, 28 pp.,
    Linguistic Society of America, 1942.

(A special edition of this work has been produced for the Army Institute under
the title, Melanesian Pidgin English, Short Grammar and Vocabulary. The
Armed Services have purchased more than four thousand copies of this edition
but it is not available for public distribution.)
    Melanesian Pidgin English Grammar, Texts, Vocabulary. 160 pp., Linguistic
    Society of America, 1942.

Harris, Zellig, and associates (Ferguson, Glazer, Hodge, Lukoff, Welmers)
    Descriptive Grammars, Texts, Dictionaries of Fanti, Haussa, Moroccan
    Arabic, Swahili. In mimeographed form for class-room use; not yet ready

for public distribution.

Kennedy, George; Bloch, Bernard; and Shirato, I., A Basic Sixty-Hour Course in Colloquial Japanese, in preparation.

Malamuth, Charles, ed., Readings in Modern Russian, Cornell University, 1942, mimeographed. "At the Front and at Home", 78 pp.; "Before the Battle", 4 pp.; "Foreign Policy", 98 pp.; "Modern War Materials", 20 pp.; "National Economy", 124 pp.; "Theory and Practice of War", 91 pp.

McQuown, Norman, Graded Texts and Vocabulary in Turkish, in form for class-room use, not yet ready for public distribution.

Newman, Stanley, A Modern Persian Grammar, in preparation.
Persian Texts, mimeographed texts for class-room use, not yet ready for public distribution.

Penzl, Herbert, "Orthography and Phonemics in Pashto (Afghan)", unpublished typescript.

Swadesh, Morris, "Phonemics and Teaching of Japanese", 72 pp., unpublished typescript.

Tihany, Leslie C., A Modern Hungarian Grammar, 255 pp., mimeographed, Harvard University, 1942.

Trager, George L., Introduction to Russian, 242 pp., mimeographed, Yale University, 1942.

Voegelin, C. F., Colloquial Turkish Grammar, Morphology, Syntax, in preparation. "Turkish Structure", Journal of the American Oriental Society, 1943, in press.
==

Above, just as on the bottom half of page 113, underlining has been used for the original use of italics in the Report's typography; otherwise we match precisely. This 'Annex B' contains so much information of permanent historical value that we omit nothing: our Index (at the end of the present volume) should be consulted for the particulars of (a) other mentions of the same persons in this LSA History, or (b) other treatments of the same language by the same persons or by others.

Some items listed in Annex B are easy to find in the Fifty-Year Index, some projected items never were completed, some typescripts were taken over later by the post-war Program in Oriental Languages of the ACLS as narrated here on later pages. Mary Haas, "The Thai System of Writing," was completed late in 1955 and issued by the ACLS as a paperback volume of pp. xiv & 115, 6 by 9 inches, and copyright 1956, uniformly with her 1954 Thai Reader of 223 pages and 1955 Thai Vocabulary which has xiv pages in its front matter and continues as pp. 217–589, so that the pagination which twice uses the numerals 217 through 223 is a result of some miscalculation in Berkeley not worth pursuing any more now in 1976. The Kennedy–Bloch–Shirato item, here said to be 'in preparation', was abandoned. The Newman Persian grammar was never completed. The Penzl item eventually was expanded and published in 1955 as A Grammar of Pashto, pp. vi & 170, photo-offset printed from page-copy typed on this same typewriter by a typist trained by Joos. Having perfected page 169, she asked Joos what to ask Penzl for to fill out the vi + 170 = 176 pages, a total which, being 11 times 16, makes a snug fit in print-shops. 'The book needs a map,' said Joos, 'and if he can't provide one, then a picture or two.' The result of her letter was disconcerting: instead of the expected Afghan scenes, a studio portrait made in Ann Arbor came to her, and she turned that over to the Washington Planograph Company, which manufactured in due course that unique volume, the only one issued by the Program in Oriental Languages with an author's likeness in it. The Swadesh item seems to have vanished. Trager's book presumably exists in other exemplars than the one presented to Joos, which has served as a side-light to the Bloomfield works which are dealt with later on here.

In the year following the foregoing Report's issuance in December, 1942, public reactions were numerous and immensely varied. Graves in Washington, and his Director of Operations who travelled everywhere and was exposed to them all, presently composed a standard answer to be given out as a press-release; with the normal result that newspapers quoted mutilated versions—and reprinted them from each other, of course. Finally the scholarly journal Hispania printed the text which follows next; since its Editor, Dean Henry Grattan Doyle of George Washington University, was Chairman of the Committee (see p. 97) this is definitive:

A STATEMENT ON INTENSIVE LANGUAGE INSTRUCTION

J. Milton Cowan and Mortimer Graves
Intensive Language Program, American Council of Learned Societies,
Washington, D.C.

Inasmuch as there is bound to be—in fact has already appeared—a certain amount of criticism of "extravagant claims" alleged to be made by the advocates of modern intensive language teaching, it seems wise to set down the rather modest "claims" which these advocates really do present. They follow:

(1) The "dribble method" of learning languages (three hours a week for years) has failed to give students practical command of any language. It may, of course, have had other educational values, but the need now is for practical speaking command.

(2) Better results are to be obtained by more concentrated use of the students' time (a minimum of ten hours per week). Only continued experiment will give us exact knowledge as to when, in the increase in concentration, a period of diminishing returns sets in. Our present guess is that, if the study is to occupy three months or more, about twenty-five hours a week of class-room contact and supervised study is the optimum, though there are varying opinions among the advocates with respect to this.

(3) Major emphasis at first should be placed upon the acquisition of spoken language. There is a variety of opinion as to exactly when study of the written language should begin, but this difference does not affect the general principle.

(4) Language instruction should be controlled by a trained technical linguist. In the ideal case he would be completely bilingual and an inspired and inspiring teacher. Unfortunately these qualities are not combined in one person sufficiently frequently to meet present demands. Moreover, whenever they are so combined we have a person so valuable that his time should not be inefficiently used in doing the incessant drill-work necessary for proper control of spoken language. This drill-work should be carried on by native speakers who need only good intelligence, good ears, an acceptable dialect, some small training and tight control. Since the optimum condition is too infrequently met to supply the language needs of the present moment, recourse has to be had to such approximations to it as are possible under the existent local circumstances.

(5) There is probably no new method of language training. It is most likely that the successful features of the alleged new method have been implicit in all good language teaching. Since, however, there have been hitherto practically no materials planned for intensive study of spoken language, there are now appearing some new materials. These are in varying stages of experiment and trial and will doubtless be greatly improved with experience. Intelligent and thoughtful criticism of them will be welcomed.

(6) Language is not to be taught "without grammar," nor "as a child learns his native tongue." A student should learn all the grammar useful to him, but he should learn it scientifically, not as a kind of theology, and he should learn it only when and as it becomes useful to him. Moreover, he should not learn language as a child, but with all the tools that maturity, intelligence, and education have given him.

(7) Within the limits of agreement on the need for intensive instruction in spoken language by scientifically-trained personnel, there is room for wide divergence as to detail and even for the personal eccentricities of teachers.

(8) The expression "intensive language" is sometimes used in a context which implies the exclusion of area study. This is not a necessary, though it is sometimes a useful, extension of the term. We all—even the alleged "mechanists"—acknowledge that a language does not operate in a vacuum.

[Reprinted in Newmark's Twentieth Century Modern Language Teaching, with publication date May 5, 1948, we find the title distorted to read 'A Statement of Intensive Language Instruction' instead of 'on'; further, the calendar-year 1943 for Hispania XXVII is illusory: Doyle had taken on the editorship of a moribund journal, had fought a paper war to get out the first number with ACLS help, and

had agreed to print any condensed statement describing the ILP that Graves
could furnish; Cowan thereupon prepared a typescript of a perfected version,
got Graves's endorsement, and had it delivered to Doyle's office in October
or so—the distance is less than two miles or three kilometers—to appear in
the earliest possible issue, which turned out to be the year-late one named.]]

The final sentence, 'We all—even the alleged "mechanists"—acknowledge
that a language does not operate in a vacuum,' is said to have been added late by
Cowan. It is a pointed allusion to the nowadays only rarely mentioned Bloomfield
article, 'Secondary and Tertiary Responses to Language' Language 20.45−55,
which was mailed to members in early June, 1944, and which, with its antecedents
and consequences for many subsequent years, constituted a sizeable chapter of
our Society's actual history: see the Index. That final sentence couldn't have been
composed by Graves; we understand that when the galley proof came to him in
the ACLS office he said 'Boys will be boys!' and let it stand.

Later references to the Intensive Language Program, after the 1943 experience,
almost uniformly use the acronym A.S.T.P. (within weeks condensed to ASTP) and
writers employing it often betray confusion or total ignorance as to the meaning of
each of the four letters. The 'S' originally abbreviated 'Specialist' in the military
sense of a non-commissioned officer whose duties were ancillary in some special
way, e.g., confined to communications; but since TP meant Training Program, the
normal military language, instead of using 'Specialist's' or 'Specialists", cut the
knot by shifting to the derivative adjective 'Specialized' [parallel to Naval Officer]
and making it Army Specialized Training Program, early A.S.T. Program. Only
rarely do we encounter hints that ASTP work was designed for and normally confined to enlisted-men classes, and never any recognition of its origin in foundation
funding or ACLS planning, not at all in Government money:

> The first ASTP language course began in April, 1943. At the end of the year
> there were approximately 15,000 trainees studying languages under this system
> in fifty-five colleges and universities throughout the country. ... The beginners
> were given frequent tests, as a result of which they were shifted into fast or
> slow sections. Frequent promotions and demotions were made to allow trainees
> to progress according to ability. ... In general the men selected had definite
> linguistic aptitude and, in the opinion of the supervisors, were superior on the
> average to the students at representative universities and colleges. Most of the
> trainees displayed greater enthusiasm than is seen in regular classes. Only
> rarely did the trainee view his assignment as just another job to be done. In
> almost all units, observers agreed, the esprit de corps existing among both
> teachers and trainees has rarely been equalled.

Hispania 27.402 f, 1944, quoted the foregoing from A Survey of Language Classes
in the Army Specialized Training Program, the Report of a Special Committee,
prepared for the Commission on Trends in Education of the Modern Language
Association, New York, 1944. Under Rockefeller Foundation financing, the survey
staff—the six foreign-language specialists called 'observers' above—spent six
weeks visiting 44 institutions chosen to represent all sorts (large, small, public,
private, southern, etc.) and situated almost everywhere apart from the hardly
accessible Far West. Besides visiting the enlisted-men's ASTP groups, they took
in on certain campuses some of the Civil Affairs Training Schools, familiarly
CATS, where post-war dealings with defeated populations were being prepared
for: relatively mature professional people—economists, lawyers, anthropologists,
cultural geographers, political scientists, orientalists, and even Germanists like
Joos and other Ph.D. holders—were invested with 'direct commissions' without
having had military training and issued uniforms bearing insignia of 'assimilated
ranks' according to academic rank attained or the like and additionally civilian
passports before leaving United States territory.

Eventually we can dismiss such acronyms as ILP, ASTP, and CATS, purely
war-time epiphenomina easily forgotten in a handful of years. One acronym, however, retained permanent significance to each of roughly a million uniformed persons. This one is USAFI, far oftener so written or spoken than its full name, the
successor to the Army Institute, the United States Armed Forces Institute, and

pronounced either 'you-sáf-fee' or 'you-sáh-fee' by everybody. Until its demise, the USAFI was, just as it was at its start in 1941, another one of those 'correspondence schools' which have been familiar in American education since late in the 19th century and in the various States are most usually conducted by the State's University Extension system or equivalent. Army Institute or USAFI began as a marginal office in or near the University of Wisconsin in Madison, expanded and in consequence moved its central office eastward along State Street in steps and, well after the fighting was over, paused for many years in a commercial structure at the northern corner of the Capitol Square roughly a mile from its start; finally, while its services to uniformed persons (technically called 'personnel') taught principally those born long after its founding, the world-wide USAFI operation was centrally guided by a staff of 197 Federal Civil Service employees located at 2318 South Park Street (about 2.5 miles or 4 km from the first locations) with a Madison budget exceeding $6,000,000 [as we used to say, 'six megabucks'] apart from the costs for postage, telephones, and the like, charged directly to the Department of Defense in Washington. The total destruction of USAFI was one of the triumphs of the national presidency following its 1972 re-election. It was not instantaneous, being valiantly contested by Wisconsin people in Congress. From our LSA point of view, the process ended when the Madison USAFI management, under orders to terminate all operations forthwith and destroy unused lesson materials, followed the recommendation of Harry T. Charly who had been dealing with Milt Cowan about such matters for quite a long term of years, that one full set of materials for each of the two dozen languages (both paper and recordings, which were on tapes for the most popular languages but on disks for the others) should be sent to the Madison-residing Historian for such areas, Martin Joos, who was listed in the local telephone book. [[At the moment of writing, everything is on shelves within 10 feet (3 meters) of the typewriter in use today, 25th July, 1976]]

These Spoken Language Series latterly made up a minor fraction of USAFI's services to the Armed Forces, just as languages had been a minor fraction of what the 1941 inventors had proposed; and when in 1944 the Spoken Language books and disc-records came into the picture they came as hitch-hikers on the supervision and implementation/distribution facilities of a USAFI which had foreseen nothing of the eventual language needs of men in uniform. They had an idea natural to us and to the allies we best understand, such as the Scots and the Scandinavians, but incomprehensible to our adversaries, namely, that a civilian Army is most effective when its morale is maintained by bringing civilian amenities along into the theatre of war; and specifically, when it is composed mostly of young men whose schooling has been interrupted by effects of the Selective Service and its alternate entry via volunteering before one's Number was called, then the cure for dismay or boredom is simply to continue their education no matter what their personal interest, whether vocational or academic. We condense from USAFI archives:

Colonel (then Lt. Col.) William R. Young on 2nd October, 1941, submitted to Brigadier General F. H. Osborn, Chief of the Morale Branch (later Office of Armed Forces Information and Education) a Memorandum for the General's signature, Subject: A Correspondence Course Program for the Army.

On 25th November, 1941, a Memorandum for the Chief of the Morale Branch came down from the General Staff which said (among other things) 'The Chief of Staff approves the organization of a correspondence school course as outlined in the accompanying memorandum for the Chief of Staff dated Oct. 2, 1941, and directs that not to exceed $390,000.00 be allotted from the Chief of Staff's Contingent Fund to finance this program during the remainder of the present fiscal year [ending with 30th September 1942].'

In Madison, March 27, 1942, General Orders No. 1 issued by the Army Institute was signed by the second-in-command of the University ROTC, who had been chosen to get his promotion from Major by the document he cites: 'Under the provisions of paragraph 4, AR 600-20, the undersigned hereby assumes command of the Army Institute, The Special Services Branch, Madison, Wis.' Signed: William R. Young, Lt. Col., F[ield] A[rtillery], Commandant.

One language whose inclusion in the Spoken Language Series was maximal will serve to illuminate more details than any other. Its military title is Spoken Russian, [Army] Education Manual 524, by I. M. Lesnin and Luba Petrova. Competent directories of scholars list Miss Luba Petrova, Lesnin's assistant, but ignore her principal, the mysterious man who was Lesnin. Well then, who wás Lesnin, hunh? He was, Joos eventually learned a dozen years or so later, a pseudonym for the only person competent to do all the deeds required to create not only the Basic and the Advanced Spoken Russian books but additionally the theoretical frame for the pronunciation key and the grammatical key to the Russian-to-English part of the War Department Technical Manual TM 30-944, Dictionary of Spoken Russian, dated 9 November 1945, which is printed without naming any author anywhere in its 579 pages of two columns each, trim size 20x26.2 cm or 7.85 inches wide by 10.25 deep. It is only by stylistic analysis that the unmistakable expository style of Leonard Bloomfield emerges from pages 215-234, where we see him laying out the known facts in complete independence and unsurpassable succinctness—only slightly disturbed by a couple of sets of misprints in the pages (218, 219) on 'Alternation of Sounds' which confuse students: (a) p. 219, 2nd column, line 5, 'unstressed' a mistake for 'stressed' which strayed upward two lines from correct 'unstressed' in line 7; (b) p. 218, last 6 lines, a cluster of errors introduced by some busybody who understood so little of the Bloomfield message that he contradicted it inside the [ ] brackets, namely by changing these two—[brad zabíl], [djed zabíl]—to the false [brat zabíl] and [djet zabíl], perhaps not realizing that these are governed by the first words of the same paragraph 'But when words belong together in a phrase' or else not realizing that Odessa speech differs from Bloomfield's in not following the same sandhi rule. More than once, groups of Joos students have protested that the [boh dast] against citation-form [box] can't be right: after all, they said, [h] is not a voiced symbol! We simply remark Bloomfield's choice in this book as a neat pedagogical device which is very likely to fail because a teacher misunderstands it or can't defend it against half-knowledge politically. In other books he makes other choices, and one of those is another thing worth commenting on.

Readers who are not among Leonard Bloomfield's closest friends could hardly be expected to make anything of his alter ego I. M. Lesnin; the insiders, increasingly rare now in 1976, still include Cowan and Graves, and Cowan considers the Joos explanation unduly simplistic. One root source is the enigma of unknown age which is created out of reciting slightly distorted or dialectally spoken English letter-names, or writing them down in majuscule letters with interspersed marks of punctuation and challenging a victim to interpret the result as a social colloquy: FUNEM? YSIFM. FUNEX? XOEFX. OKMNX! (Joos and Bloch constructed this at the time we were interchanging cryptographic challenges; that's why there are five groups of five letters each. The marks of punctuation here do not include the commas which would have clarified the text notably; they are used, one explains, only to mark off the groups ...) Now this example, recited in Bloomfield or Bloch style for reporting something said to have been overheard in a quick-lunch place, goes: Have you any ham? Why, yes, I have ham. Have you any eggs? Eggs? Oh, we have eggs. OK, ham and eggs! — And I. M. Lesnin in the context of Spoken Russian must be 'I am listening' when spoken in such English and imitated by a Russian who has not learned how to listen to English by English listening-habits but instead ... And this still supplies only one source for the choice of 'I. M. Lesnin' for its service as a pseudonym, leaving the question 'What was the specific stimulus causing this pawky scholar to assert that he was listening?' Well, the printed Spoken Russian book was not properly harmonized with the disc-recordings which pre-date both our use of tapes and our long-playing discs—78 r.p.m. recording on wax was all, and when it was discovered that every page had errors or wrong dialect forms— what to do? Answer: Bloomfield single-handed listened and revised all the print (partly by textual change, partly by inserting notes and uses of the asterisk*) to meet an urgent deadline for fulfilling a schedule for delivery to the Field; for five weeks, we have been told, he filled solitary post-midnight hours with that.

Letters from J Milton Cowan to Joos in 1973 explain the fraudulent Copyright:

The Linguistic Society of America was the original applicant for registration in the Copyright Office of the Library of Congress, as the assignee of the author's rights—nearly all book copyright applications do come from an assignee of the author's property-rights, and usually that assignee is the 'publisher' identified by filling in the line provided for the publisher's name on the printed form provided. For Spoken Russian the author's name was entered as I. M. Lesnin, his/her citizenship as USSR, his/her domicile as USA, his mail address only c/o ACLS at the current address on 16th Street N.W., Washington, D.C. The Copyright Office shot back a form-letter asking for further biographical particulars which came to the desk of Mortimer Graves and, says Cowan, 'was conveniently side-tracked.' And Copyright Certificate No. AA 492378 was issued to LSA with nothing further on it.

The Copyright Gazette goes to all libraries and to others who subscribe; thus it came to the notice of Russian watchers fairly soon, and they started inquiring after the whereabouts of Lesnin I. M., obviously a native of the Soviet Union with an ascertainable place of birth and presumably relatives still resident where they could be sought out by agents of the Government and ... Mortimer Graves was an old hand at that game, as earlier LSA History pages have made clear, and Cowan in the same building (when not a thousand miles away for a couple of days) was a delighted pupil; and so for a number of months they played cat-and-mouse with dead-pan letters that nowhere mentioned Cowan but did mention known persons, a different one each time, until the civilian-edition publisher, Henry Holt and Company, requested details for use in textbook publicity; a fake biography was then efficiently assembled in a small committee including Bloch and Bloomfield contacts, and sent (with a covering-note in code) to everybody's old friend in the Holt office, New York City, Archie Shields. Joos has seen only leaked excerpts from that biography, and Cowan has not supplied a complete version; but Joos has been given to understand that it placed Prof. Dr. Ignatius Mendeleeff Lesnin very close to each fine line from his 19th-century student days at unidentified borderline institutions down through the decades when he taught Russian in Turkey (or was it Greece or Rumania?) and dropped out of sight until he came to the United States with a Mexican passport of unknown date or number and so to New Haven. All so plausible that for a good many years the ACLS incoming mail included bits of Lesnin froth designed to identify claimants for what he had coming to him. The Cowan letter to Joos dated 10 December 1973 supplies specifically requested dates:

Two dates are significant. May 4, 1944, the ACLS and Henry Holt and Company signed a contract for public editions of those works, the first editions of which we re published for the War Department. August 17, 1945, is the date of copyright registration for Spoken Russian, Book I. Now, none of these books were printed by the Government Printing Office! For a hectic period there, JMC-ILP was one of the largest book publishers in the nation. Not only did I style all of the books and read page proof (we were in too big a hurry to bother with galleys) on everything except the foreign language material, but I also found printers who could guarantee delivery on short deadlines, got them paper allocations from the War Production Board, and handled the paperwork on overseas shipment of several hundred thousand books for the Government.

Since I controlled the printing, after the Holt-ACLS contract was drawn I could tell Archie which printer was producing that book and could authorize the printer to do the number of copies Archie wanted as overruns, costing HH&Co. only the extra paper, presswork and binding.

For those overruns, which were comparatively small (guessed at about 5% as a usual thing) but sufficient for test-marketing Book I (those 12 'Lessons' which were to be used with one set of disc-recording per teacher: Book II of 18 more Lessons was designed for use without recordings in a second High School semester or College quarter or whatever experience imposed) after which later school sales would be supplied from reprinting, 'Archie supplied his own paper, but not literally,' for the printers had the stock and used it up under orders from customers who transferred to them the allocations that they had wrested from the WPB. In the Russian case the manufacturer was the Edward Stern Press in Philadelphia, 'which firm,' Cowan wrote, 'did many of our jobs. I drove poor Mr. Wm. Hamburger prematurely into his grave by browbeating him with threats of imprisonment if he didn't deliver on time.'

Earliest to be printed of all the Spoken Language items was Book I of Spoken Chinese, E[ducation] M[anual] 506, 2 January 1944, with a far shorter Introduction than the other Spoken X books were provided with. With the second and subsequent ones, we find each Book I of an EM introduced by a sequence of pages, iii–vi, in which the section-titles are adapted to the particular language, e.g.:

1. What We Are Trying to Do. This course in spoken Hungarian ...

2. The Hungarian Language is spoken by about thirteen million ...

3. How to Use This Manual. ... a native speaker and this book. The two must be used together, and neither one is of any use without the other. ...

4. A Native Speaker is the only good source of first-hand knowledge ... The method used in this manual requires a native speaker ... or next best, the voice or a native speaker recorded on phonograph records ... The native speaker ... is referred to as the Guide. He will give you the Hungarian to imitate, and will check your work; but he is not the teacher and should not be asked to explain ...

5. The Book is divided into parts ...

6. The Basic Sentences in each unit are arranged so as to give you a number of new words and a number of new ways of saying things; first broken up into words or short phrases, and then combined in complete sentences. ...

7. The Aids to Listening represent the sounds of Hungarian in the letters of our alphabet ...

8. The Hints on Pronunciation are to help you to speak as nearly as possible like a native Hungarian. No language has sounds exactly like any other; and ...

9. Pronouncing to be Understood. Of course the better you can pronounce ...

10. The Native Speaker is Always Right. If the manual or the records ... different from that of your Guide, follow the Guide. ...

11. The Word Study gives you new uses and new combinations ... You are taught how words are built up, ... [[i.e., this is the stuff we call 'grammar']]

12. The Listening In gives you a number of conversations, anecdotes, ...

13. Conversation ... the principal aim of the course. You should know ...

14. In Speaking Hungarian do not think out what you want to say in English and try to translate it into Hungarian. Instead, think in terms of the expressions you have memorized that apply to the situation. Keep the conversation going by asking questions ...

The General Foreword composed by Mortimer Graves (anonymously: that is to say he names himself only in the third person) was used unchanged throughout the Holt printings of civilian editions throughout the years of interest to us. We print a skeletonized version to remind readers what ground it covers; the complete text will not be printed anywhere in this History. [[On 'more than thirty' see later!]]

This is one of a series of self-teaching textbooks in more than thirty languages initially prepared and published for the Armed Forces and now offered to the general public. ... the product of team-work between numerous collaborators. A brief review of the origin and growth ... Early in 1942, within a month of Pearl Harbor, the Joint Army and Navy Committee on Welfare and Recreation began ... A survey of materials ... confirmed their suspected inadequacy. Many of the pertinent languages had never been taught ... few of them had ever been studied or described by competent linguists. ... The form of the materials had to be such that they could be used for self-instruction ... But the Army and Navy fortunately did not have to start completely from scratch, for several months previously the American Council of Learned Societies had organized its Intensive Language Program ... The Joint Army-Navy Committee drew the Intensive Language Program into its deliberations and planned a development of language instruction for the Armed Forces. Responsibility for the prosecution of this development was entrusted to the Education Branch of what is now the Information and Education Division, A[rmy] S[ervice] F[orces], functioning through its subsidiaries, the Language Section and the Editorial Staff of the United States Armed Forces Institutes. These in turn called upon the Intensive Language Program of the Council for coöperation in the production of materials, a coöperation which has since been so intimate that it is impossible to tell what proportion of any single operation is the responsibility of each. The series of more than thirty language textbooks is one result ... not only has every listed author coöperated in the production of elements of the series other than his own, but also many of our most valued collaborators do not appear as authors at all. ... it would seem almost invidious to cite the names of those collaborators, in addition to authors, whose contributions are more readily identifiable than those of others. Yet for the sake of the record, perhaps this should be done. The Intensive Language Program of the American Council of Learned Societies, without which this series would not have been possible or would been of completely different character, owes its existence to Mortimer Graves, Administrative Secretary of the Council. Colonel Francis T. Spaulding, Chief of the Education Branch above referred to, saw the implications of teaching language to American troops and assumed the responsibility for developing a program to this end. The detailed planning and construction of the series now presented owes more to Dr. Henry Smith, Jr., (then Major and Chief of the Language Section in the Education Branch) than to anyone else. Constant liaison with the Intensive Language Program was maintained through J. Milton Cowan, its director during the preparation of the series. William E. Spaulding directed the Editorial Staff of the United States Armed Forces Institute. The dean of American linguistic scientists, Leonard Bloomfield of Yale University, gave unstintingly in many ways—ways as difficult to appreciate too highly as they are to describe succinctly. Almost the same may be said of Lt. Morris Swadesh, Lt. Charles Hockett, Robert A. Hall, Jr., Norman A. McQuown, Doris Goss, José Padín, and others who served from time to time on a special advisory and editorial board. ⟦Joos omits a dozen lines at end⟧

That 'more than thirty languages initially prepared and published' was Mortimer's promise to all parties concerned at his time of writing, early in 1944; over thirty were under contract, each person by contract with the ACLS at least, and the ACLS had contracted with the War Department for a certain specified list of books-and-records implementations named by language without naming persons, of course: that is always the military theory: persons are interchangeable, since persons of the same military rank must step into the shoes of casualties without loss of time ...

Well, with the cessation of hostilities late in 1945 the military procurement system (in which our books were in the Service Of Supply area that controlled the procurement of e.g. telecommunications equipments and their Service Manuals, all manufactured to meet Government Specifications by any available makers!) abruptly shifted into reverse-gear. Those 'more than thirty languages' began to shrink, to dwindle towards a roughly half-size list whose membership naturally seemed to depend on such things as whether the disc-records had been or already were being pressed: without the modern use of tape, the speakers did their work in the Library of Congress installation adopted in the 1930's for recording voices of historical interest, where the immediate result was a disc of rather soft wax which (if not junked because its content was fatally flawed) would presently be dusted with graphite and sent on its way for further steps toward final pressing of relatively fragile 'shellac compound' disks for The Field: 78 r.p.m. of course. Shock-waves from that abrupt termination more or less violently made their way downward to the authors of record. Mortimer Graves was one of the buffers. As one who had flown in the First World War for the Navy, he was prepared to feel the shock vicariously for each person down to the perhaps reluctantly liberated author and the author's paid staffers. Ultimate effects upon the Courses varied; one of the slowest and most thorough workers was Merrill Y. Van Wagoner, who never could be hurried: his Spoken Arabic (Iraqi of Baghdad) was the only Arabic item completed, and when it was issued in 1949 [signed M.Y.V.W., New York City, 1948] it would have been too fat in the page-size used otherwise (8 inches wide by 5.25 deep = 224x137 mm) with its roughly 500 pages that could not be accommodated in the buttoned side-pocket of the military tunic as in the 1943 plan. With a separate grant that ultimately derived from oil revenues, they say, it was printed with the exceptional page-format, 7 inches wide and 9 inches deep trim-size, that only this one book has in all Holt Spoken Language Series, and with its title-page noting that it was 'Originally prepared for publication by The United States Armed Forces Institute' and overleaf page reading 'This material was prepared under the direction of the Linguistic Society of America and the Intensive Language Program of the American Council of Learned Societies. / Copyright, 1949, by the Linguistic Society of America'

Thus we cannot be surprised that, e.g., no other Scandinavian book ever came along to match the Danish of Jeannette Dearden and the stunning Spoken Norwegian of Einar Ingvald Haugen and his wife and her mother. The Graves list of 'more than thirty' was roughly one third published when the abandonment order came down; he fought ingeniously to get them all published, and had to give up when the War Department cut him off at the pockets with five (here asterisked with *) sunk without a trace from the publicity-sheet he issued in 1944 and called Language Courses Prepared Under This Operation which prefaces 'Spoken' to each name except for one book named 'Colloquial Dutch' which was issued without records:

Iraqui [sic] Arabic, *Moroccan Arabic, *Bengali, Burmese, Chinese, Danish, Colloquial Dutch, (Spoken) Dutch, Finnish, French, German, Greek, Hindustani, Hungarian, Italian, Japanese, Korean, Malay, Norwegian, *Persian, *Polish, Portuguese, Russian, Serbo-Croatian, Spanish, *Swedish, Thai, Turkish.

We note that everybody knew that Icelandic was urgently needed and Swedish too, but cannot spare the space for speculating on their absence. Readers can guess at other absences; we can assure them that whatever language they think of was thought of first by Mortimer Graves, but this is not the place for details.

The publicity-sheet originally was page-numbered to fill 4 2-column pages next after the Copyright page of the civilian-edition books, by calling them pages iia, iib, iic, iid (but with small-capital letters preceded by a short dash each) and incorporated by tipping-in that extra insert before the Introduction beginning p. iii. Its first employment was when those inserts were separately sent in bundles to every target imaginable from Pentagon to local School Boards for distribution, and also in the Spoken German book by Jenni Karding Moulton and William G. Moulton, where the extras are still more with numbering iie, iif, and iig, plus an unnumbered half-title in extra-large italics saying "Book One" before page iii. We quote that Authors' Preface (no other book of the series has any!) only as to its long footnote attached to its first clause by asterisk, thus: 'When the authors were asked to write the present book,* and were told the general plan ...

*The original request was made to me, and the book started out as a one-man job. I worked out the material, put it into as final a form as I could, and then submitted it to J. K. M. for corrections and improvements. Units 1—10 were largely written in this way. Beginning with Unit 11, however, the work became definitely a coöperative venture. I continued to do the grammatical parts and the exercises, but the remainder of the material was written jointly. Usually I would set the subject of a unit and the grammatical topics to be covered, J. K. M. would write a first draft of the Basic Sentences and the Listening In conversations, I would pare them down to keep them within necessary limits, and then we would work out the final version together. As a result, the units from 11 on are probably better than the earlier ones, certainly more interesting. Those who know J. K. M. will recognize her light touch on nearly every page. If this book had a dedication, it would be to her. As it is, I can only express my gratitude, quite inadequately, in this little footnote.—W. G. M.'

Dated September 3, 1944, the place named is Providence and Washington, and the two sets of initials are both printed with the date, hers first!

The Spoken Dutch and Colloquial Dutch books, both constructed by Bloomfield, bore a relation to each other and to the other parties concerned which was so extraordinary as to deserve a considerable section of this History. Here it will be necessary to draw upon private files and memories; since the official documents say nothing about the most revealing details the narrative will be mostly Joos's.

Cowan was based in Washington, in the ACLS office, and had been doing work which I suspected was the sort of thing I ought to be doing myself; I was wrong; then in August, 1942, I received a telephone call at home in Toronto inviting me to report as soon as possible to Arlington Hall in Virginia to do 'translating'—which turned out to be cryptanalysis and kept me occupied for slightly more than 48 months. From that work, however, I had several kinds of escapes, such as the Library of Congress and the second-hand book-shops; or, when my wife was free to come along, as she was only on Sunday, we had bicycle excursions all around the region—even up into the Appalachian Trail area via Snicker's Gap. Always I worked 7 days and then got a day off, making an 8-day cycle with a creeping off-day—Monday one week, Tuesday next week, and so on until Saturday-plus-Sunday gave me days-off counted as the end of one week and the start of the next week: two days free! Around 11:20, then, on a marginal day of November in 1943, when I had visited only one or two Washington bookstores and picked up one hefty tome from a bargain counter, a chilling drizzle drove me to the ACLS office for warmth. There I was told that Cowan wanted to see me that same day: eight days' delay would be too long. When he came in from who knows where, there was a hasty conference in which Cowan explained the contents of an awkwardly shaped bundle which, he said, was a job of the sort I had been hoping for and could I tackle it immediately and telephone to say whether I could do it at all? And by the way, he supposed I must be fluent in Dutch. I wasn't; but the chance to get my teeth into something substantial in a language area—after the war, cryptanalysts would be a dime a dozen, and the chance to impress Leonard Bloomfield, if only indirectly, was not to be lost, so I said that within 48 hours I would learn enough Dutch to tell whether I could do the job at all and report the fact by telephone. Altogether I spent something like an hour at 1219 16th Street N.W. Then, the drizzle having ceased, I wrapped those irreplaceable marked-up page-proofs in my slicker along with a Dutch grammar from Mortimer Graves's shelves and (leaving my second-hand purchase behind) set out in chill sunshine for the Joos apartment six miles beyond the Potomac and close behind the Arlington Hall grounds newly occupied by four-story brick buildings since 1942. I arrived soaked through and chilled, the rain having begun again, and went to bed alone—my wife was on night-duty that month—prepared to fight off a cold. (Failure of the expected fever to come on schedule is unexplained to this day.) Studying my collectanea the next day, I found I had been pitchforked into that remarkable Bloomfield transaction with barely sufficient information to enable me to do what was called for—formulate detailed procedures for undoing what had been wrongly done to Bloomfield's work by busybody meddling, so that those page-proof sheets could be cleaned up by a printer's staff—but far from enough to understand why. It was not until 1974 that ad-hoc Cowan letters came to clarify the mystery.

Bloomfield's procedure for covering the total military requirement for Dutch can be described as comprising two or more steps of research and composition. First he constructed a complete college-classroom textbook for use by experts— who were expected to have a native Dutch drill-master continuously available— so that the expert could draw upon its strongest feature, the topical vocabularies, to create his own lesson-plans week by week. Second, treating that first book as a source of information, he wrote a derived Spoken Dutch typescript conforming to the settled schema for the Spoken Language course-writing teams, the template or matrix into which things were to be fitted, which the largest group of them had begun quite early to call 'the mould' (chosen as a more professorial spelling than 'mold' with special intent) with derivatives that included ambiguous mouldy, mouldier, mouldiest and phrases which kept the house dialect light, even fluffy.

Finally, Bloomfield's way of obviating the 'Query to Author' nuisance was to ship both typescripts together to Cowan at the ACLS, so that they could go along through the process as companions, intending the college-classroom version to supply answers in cases of editorial doubt. Under the established rules, so far adhered to precisely under an agreement between the ACLS and the Language Section, namely that the Language Section was to treat all Spoken Language type-scripts as authoritative and simply rubber-stamp them and send them direct to the printer, that ought to have worked. Cowan's corresponding procedure, which saved always at least six weeks of publishing time and often about ten weeks, was a routine planned to be automatic. First, each completed Author's MS was regis-tered in the ACLS office, so that thereafter all inquiries as to the book's progress could be answered clerically. Second, the MS was sent to the War Department's Language Section for a pro-forma treatment called 'review and adopt.' Third, the Language Section sent the MS to the designated Printer; that Printer/Press put it into type and put the whole into pages and made the required number of page-proof copies. Fourth, that Press sent those page-proofs variously as agreed: (a) the MS with a set of proofs to Cowan, the MS multiply marked-up and barely decipherable and rather tattered, (b) page-proofs to the Author ... (c) information copies to ...

Cowan in 1964 wrote again to Joos: 'I gave you only copy of the original Spoken
Dutch typescript and the page proofs together with the altered typescript from
which they had been set; I explained the dilemma to you and asked you to determine what the minimum proof changes would be to restore the integrity of Bloomfield's original formulation; you never saw the Colloquial Dutch typescript.'

When the page-proofs for Spoken Dutch had come to him a few days earlier,
Cowan had discovered, to his amazement and consternation, that the copy had
been extensively (and unsystematically and irregularly) altered by War Department functionaries under a superior officer who had undertaken to enforce the
right to 'review and adopt' as stipulated in publication contracts for items still to
be written under contract. Now that phrase could mean anything from the simple
rubber-stamping initially promised all the way to total revision to suit the latest
official notions; cautiously tested by telephone, this particular Author adamantly
refused to permit publication of anything like the page-proofs he had received: it
has been said that Graves, no stranger to harsh language, was impressed and said
there was nothing to be done.

The Dutch language at this season, the Winter of 1943/1944, was far more important than the public could be allowed to suspect. In staging areas of three or
more quarters of the globe, preparations were being made for incursions into at
least Dutch Guiana (or Surinam) in whose estuaries enemy bases could hide and
support submarines and otherwise threaten our security, in the Netherlands East
Indies and all that huge region now called Indonesia the Dutch language was the
dominant European language, and of course in the Dutch-Belgian homeland a single
language was spoken in two slightly different varieties: 'Dutch' in the Netherlands,
'Flemish/Vlaamsch' in Belgium; and finally, the Afrikaans of South Africa began as
a variety of Dutch and is still mutually intelligible with Dutch. And now all these
enterprises were at the mercy of one cloistered academic in New Haven, Connecticut. What to do? Admirals joked about blowing him out of the water, colonels
about dropping paratroopers to take him alive; but then it turned out that he had
never been personally under contract for Dutch work and still owned the rights.
How about a rush job by somebody else? No, all competent 'personnel' were busy.
It would have to be a political solution.

Archives tell us nothing; they are empty; all the negotiations were by telephone
or face to face without written memoranda: nothing resulted other than cryptic
instructions to printers. The ACLS had money to make promises with, yet money
seemed to mean nothing to Leonard Bloomfield personally; what he cared about,
apparently, was something said to be named 'academic honesty' or the like, and on
that basis he drove a hard bargain, to judge from his demands that were met.

First off, he required the 'classroom book' to be scheduled for immediate
printing and binding (instead of the originally intended post-war scheduling) and
distributed (without recordings, of course!) to the same military units that got
Spoken Dutch and its records. Assured by the ACLS that that was being done, he
forbore to stipulate quantities, but gave his simple consent. What would those
first books be called? Well, let's just ask him! Cowan passed the word along, and
the result that EM 550 was issued as Colloquial Dutch, 29 February 1944, copyright
entry effective 15 May 1944, Cowan certifying that the Army, Navy, and USAFI had
promised to give those tons of paperbacks the same 'distributions' as the forthcoming Spoken Dutch books-and-records from the Army Language Section. Spoken
Dutch was ultimately issued 1 November 1944 (Copyright certificate date 23 Nov.
1944) and sent out in all directions in somewhat less than ship-load lots but not so
very much less: its final designation in 1974 appears on its front cover, printed
first as EM 529 and later re-numbered as USAFI textbook A 629: accompanying
disc-records have latterly been long-playing ones on vinyl, but the huge stock
of paperbacks was re-numbered with a rubber stamp after blotting out 'EM 529'.
〚See our Index for the gruesome tale of the ultimate 1974 termination of USAFI〛

We return to our page 121, lines 7 and thereafter: Francis Trow Spaulding was
a noted educator when given his direct commission. Later he was New York State
Commissioner of Education, truly a hardship post; he died 25 March 1950. His

brother William Ellsworth Spaulding (1898—19   ) in 1974 was nominally retired but
still active and influential in Houghton Mifflin. During the Second World War he was
the single book-printing boss that Graves and Cowan and others in the ACLS office
most often spoke of in Joos's hearing, usually simply by his initials WES; and, on
occasion, by shortening his usual written **signature** WESpaulding by cutting it off
just after the 'p' and leaving the 'p' unexploded, thus: /wesp]/ or spoken 'Wesp' to
the bafflement of non-insiders in the Spoken Language game or otherwise involved
in the Battle of the Potomac said to be fought in such bewildered confusion that we
spoke of its locale as Foggy Bottom.

While Cowan was winding up his regular work in Cornell University in anticipation of his 1972 retirement, he drafted a narrative 'USAFI and the Spoken Language
Series' and circulated it for criticism both in Ithaca and elsewhere. To WES he
sent four firm pages plus a fifth sheet which in rough outline covered the period
1946—1971. That went by mail to Boston automatically, and remained unanswered
until Spaulding's return from a visit of a number of months to the African field;
then under date 22 March 1972 he wrote Cowan a letter beginning 'Just back from
the land of Swahili and Geez. Great country but my God how it needs good linguistic guidance for the 3—8 year-olds! Without it they're never going to make a no-
ticeable dent in the problem of illiteracy. On the other hand, maybe ... ' and along
with it sent a marked-up copy of Cowan's missive which his letter speaks of thus:

> Enclosed is one copy of your USAFI statement with a few marginal com-
> ments. Shouldn't the "Useful words and phrases" records for shipboard use
> be mentioned and the cooperation of John Langenegger (?), engineer in the
> recording lab in the Library of Congress? Also I think the assembling of
> guides for so long a list of languages was interesting and something of an
> accomplishment.

The guides he spoke of were the Guide's Manual for Spoken X; the bulkiest of
them is EM 563 for Japanese, 528 pages prepared under the direction of Mikiso
Hane, an Edwards Brothers lithoprint job issued 1 December 1945. The items for
shipboard use were at the time called First Level Implementation: those pairs of
discs were stamped from 78 r.p.m. masters: for Cowan and Smith samples used
unexpectedly, see LSA Monograph No. 23, pages 129, 130, and the plates.

The 'USAFI statement' is printed here next almost complete and inflated by
inserting WES marginalia in simple square brackets [...] and Joos remarks in
doubled ones [[...]]. Fully redundant WES pencillings have been ignored.

> Shortly after Pearl Harbor, the War Department (via Army Service Forces,
> Moral Services Division) entered into a contract (No. W-2181-55-144) with the
> American Council on Education (ACE) for the establishment of an Editorial
> Staff for the United States Armed Forces Institute (USAFI). Among other things,
> the Editorial Staff was charged with the production of self-teaching foreign
> language courses. ACE set up the physical facility at American University.
> [[Joos: That campus, on the very edge of the District of Columbia beyond
> everything else out to the northwestward, had suspended its peacetime tasks
> as far as we could casually observe. Language trainees and other uniformed
> persons slept in its buildings now called 'barracks' and exercised on its
> playing fields, so that admission through its gates into its 90 acres (37 ha.)
> of total area immersed one in the atmosphere of a military 'facility' and a
> non-uniformed visitor felt lost. Officers were billeted in faculty residences;
> CATS and ILP trainees were everywhere; and when I finally discovered that
> Hockett had returned to the continental United States from his slow boat to
> China and was there too with Chinese informant(s) I armed myself with a
> letter from the Commandant at Arlington Hall introducing me and requesting
> all courtesies,— in particular a look-see at the Language Development shop
> where Hockett ought to be: no such person was locatable by telephone, so I
> never did see him that month, but I was welcomed in the Spanish & Portu-
> guese crew, found acquaintances after their evening meal, and finally just
> went off home via Chain Bridge to a late supper.]]

> Policy determination on such matters as which languages were to be imple-
> mented rested with the Joint Army-Navy Committee (JA-NC). These were in
> turn carried out by the Army Education Branch, whose chief was William E.
> Spaulding, who had previously been engaged professionally in educational
> publishing with the Houghton Mifflin Company. The professional linguist on

Col. Spaulding's staff as Officer in Charge of the Language Section was the well-known Dr. Henry Lee Smith, Jr. [WES: He served in this capacity with the rank of Major and was known to his friends and associates as "God"]

The American Council of Learned Societies (ACLS) under the guidance of Mortimer Graves had become active in the preparation of language materials for out-of-the-way languages as early as 1939. At the time of Pearl Harbor, the ACLS set up its Intensive Language Program (ILP) and J M. Cowan, then Secretary-Treasurer of the Linguistic Society of America (LSA), became its Director. The JA–NC drew the ILP into its deliberations from the very beginning.

Feeling the need for specialized competence in editorial problems of language publishing, Director Spaulding engaged the services of José Padín, who had been the foreign language editor of D. C. Heath and Co.; Padín in turn arranged to have three Heath authors assigned to the project: François Denoeu (French), Vincenzo Cioffari (Italian), S. N. Treviño (Spanish). The Language Section assigned Dr. Morris Swadesh as a linguistic consultant. Professor Robert A. Hall, Jr., who had produced a <u>Melanesian Pidgin English Grammar</u> for the ILP, was added on the recommendation of the <u>ACLS</u> in February, 1943.

Because an attempt was to be made in these new courses to break with the old familiar college classroom texts and incorporate the ideas of descriptive linguists, both about the arrangement of the grammatical material and pedagogical practice, for these essentially self-teaching texts desired by the JA–NC, an experimental class in Spanish was set up at the American University under the direction of Treviño and Swadesh. A Spanish course was evolved as a rough model to be followed in the preparation of the other courses. As it finally worked out, Denoeu and Hall became the authors of <u>Spoken French</u> with Denoeu supplying the basic conversations and Hall the grammatical analysis. When it came to publication, <u>Spoken Spanish</u> bore only Treviño's name, probably because it was considered improper for a person in uniform assigned to a task to receive public credit (and royalties). Cioffari managed <u>Spoken Italian</u> without too much guidance other than conforming to the general format, which had come to be relatively fixed (30 Units [12 with phonographic recordings plus 18 without], five blocks with each block made up of 5 Learning Units and one Test Unit—a pattern of remarkable persistence even a quarter of a century later; such is the inertia of educational innovation). <u>Spoken Portuguese</u> was a sort of committee production. Padín had been unable to engage the Portuguese author he wanted and chose Margarida Reno to supply the language content; Cioffari did the grammar and Hall the transcription. All three are listed as joint authors.

[Joos: Swadesh of course regarded himself as a civilian preposterously drafted and required to be grateful for escaping some guard-duty and kitchen police; this exacerbated his outrage on being denied access to royalties—which he spurned as a Capitalist sequestering of The People's Property. And Hall retained his doubts about the grammar-theory notions of all three Heath authors.]

Readers who wish to pursue this fascinating chapter of history further will find the rest of it neatly laid out in the 'Golden Reminiscences' paper by J Milton Cowan in the LSA Bulletin issued for March, 1975; I correct the third line from the end of the first column on page 34: Bill Smith was William S. B. Smith. And on page 33, seventh line from its end, Tigner Holmes is a casual-mention form for Urban T. Holmes; finally, just after that, the 'Assistant Professor of German' was Penzl.

Returning to the Society's Proceedings and the like for our sources, we pick up the narrative from Bulletin No. 16, issued with the April–June 1943 issue of our quarterly <u>Language</u>. It begins with three pages of Proceedings...Summer Meeting / Chapel Hill and Durham, July 10–11, 1942. Only 40 'members and members-elect' registered; absences included both the President and the Vice-President; others who attended although non-members were not recorded and could at best turn up on later lists of members but would not deserve mention, unless otherwise in this History for later deeds: in case of doubt, see the Index.

Nor did the reported 40 include either of the two Directors of the imminent 1943 Linguistic Institute at the University of Wisconsin at Madison. Memorable members present included: Cowan, Franklin Edgerton, W. J. Gedney, E. Adelaide Hahn, R. A. Hall Jr., H. M. Hoenigswald, Harry Hoijer, George A. Kennedy, R. G.

Kent, Hans Kurath, George S. Lane, Winfred P. Lehmann, Herbert Penzl, Thomas A. Sebeok, and E. H. Sturtevant. That Bulletin ends, as usual, with the current List of Members 1942, each normally listed with the current address if known: only a few of permanent interest are listed here:

Jack Autrey Dabbs, M.A., Captain, 141st Infantry, Personnel Adjutant, U.S.A. (1938); William J. Gedney, A.B., Pvt., Linguistic Service Unit, Special Service Div., U.S.A., Room 1917, 165 Broadway, 215 W. 23d St., New York City (1940); Charles Francis Hockett, Ph.D., Lt., Education Branch, Special Service Div., A.S.F. ⟦= Army Service Forces⟧, Hurst Hall, American University, Washington, D.C. (1939); Heinrich M. Hoenigswald, Fellow of the National School of Modern Oriental Languages and Civilizations ⟦of the ACLS⟧, 503 W. 121st St., New York City (1939); Urban T. Holmes, Jr., Ph.D., Principal Research Technician, Office of Strategic Services, 1445 Spring Rd., N.W., Washington, D.C. (FM); Martin Joos, Ph.D., War Department, 1201 N. Cleveland St., Arlington, Va. (1936); John Kepke, M.A., War Department, Box 1135 Central Station, Arlington, Va., 1 Grace Court, Brooklyn, N. Y. (1930; Life Member, 1935); Winfred Philipp Lehmann, Ph.D., Cpl., Signal Corps, 1233 N. Utah St., Arlington, Va. (1938); and finally ACLS President Fred Norris Robinson, Ph.D., Professor of English, Harvard University (1926): total personal members: 586.

Immediately thereafter follow the 47 names of Members of the Group for American Indian Linguistics alphabetically from Leonard Bloomfield to C. F. Voegelin, and the Bulletin ends by listing the 150 Subscribing Libraries: total text pages: 48.

Page 6 was filled solid with italic type narrating the vicissitudes of compensating for the impossibility of holding a constitutionally valid Annual Meeting when the Government has banned the requisite massive travel; it ends: 'In the following pages are presented the reports of the officers and committees of the Society, such as in previous years have been included in the Proceedings of the annual meeting.' The Report of the Secretary includes details of the 3.3% drop in net personal members, with a list of 31 who had resigned in good standing effective with the end of 1941. That was the time of the ultimate resignation of SC member John L. Gerig; the Secretary being swamped with war work, nobody pursued him. The Report of the Director of the 1942 Linguistic Institute at Chapel Hill, Urban T. Holmes, Jr., tells us that 20 students were enrolled for the full fee but we do not learn what that fee was, and the 12 others paid the $10 fee as holders of doctorates. The Thursday Luncheons were well attended; the five speakers were Miss Hahn and Messrs. Edgerton, Kent, Hoijer, and Sebeok. The Sunday evening Public Lectures were given by Alfred Senn, Franklin Edgerton, George Kennedy, and finally a joint lecture was given by Albrecht Goetze and Myles Dillon on the common features shared by Hittite and Old Irish within the Indo-European framework.

Hans Kurath conducted the Introduction to Linguistics. Simultaneously with the Institute there was an intensive course in Portuguese directed by Urban T. Holmes, Jr., supported by the ACLS rather than being under our Society's auspices; student attendance from each group at many classes of the other group was free; that was what made it possible for the Luncheons and Sunday Evening Public Lectures to be 'well attended' when then were only 32 students enrolled in the Linguistic Institute.

These Reports record the successful invitation from the University of Wisconsin to hold the 1943 Linguistic Institute in Madison. (Eventually the 1944 Institute also was held in Madison, but that was the last Institute in Wisconsin: the vanishing of a great many rare books from the collection assembled to serve the visiting members of the Institute Faculty, some of them at extraordinary expense, was spoken of in every Administration discussion of subsequent proposals, and that was that.)

From the 1942 personal membership to the 1943 figure there was again a notable shrinkage, 22 losses or 3.9% of the net. Resignations tendered by 32 members lost us Professor Norman L. Willey, a 1935 joiner, who had taught in Ann Arbor Linguistic Institutes 1936–1940 and been one of the five-man Administrative Committee, and also lost us the other such man, Professor William H. Worrell: see p. 56! Others worth mentioning among those resigning in good standing—nobody dropped for non-payment of Dues is ever named by our Secretaries in print—include these four: Charles J. Donahue, Ph.D., Capt., Signal Corps, U.S.A. (1933), who was in a precarious state of health when Joos first saw him in the Fall of 1942, the keenest cryptanalyst in the room presided over by John Norman Seaman, J.D. ('Cap'm John'), Captain, Signal Corps, U.S.A. (1940), where Joos learned professional deciphering tricks: he had been put in charge of our tiny odd-languages crew (unknown or so-far unclassified languages, plus Finnish, Swedish, and whatever we volunteered for) when the higher-ups learned that his several expertises included Tibetan and Old French: Donahue had been sent to this room to work because it was quiet there and his special language field was Old Irish and he spoke Modern Irish: simple logic of the military sort grouped us for that short while before he vanished in November, 'invalided out' we heard; second, Louise Pound (FM); third, Edwin Carl Roedder (1929 member, born 8 April 1873) who directed the 1930 and 1931 Linguistic Institutes at C.C.N.Y.: he died three years later, 1945; and fourth, Harry A. Rositzke, Ph.D., Cpl., 405 TTG:PP, Basic Training Center No. 4, Miami, Fla., 1936 member.

The 1943 Summer Meeting (Friday/Saturday, 16/17 July) was the first of the two held in Madison in successive years, and it was the one that Joos attended: with his wife coming along to renew old acquaintance and establish her status as an RN so she could work professionally in the District of Columbia, both came and went by day-coach, and the records show that Joos was a discussant of only two of the 16 papers read in the three sessions, a reticence which after three decades can be explained only by assuming he heard very few papers and made his intended impact only by announcing that the Trager-Joos publishing of Studies in Linguistics had not been terminated as rumors had said but had merely become irregular: Trager was involved in a complicated move from Yale to Washington, D.C.

Both at home and overseas, the 18 months from that 1943 Madison meeting to the December 1944 Annual Meeting in New York City was a crescendo of hurried work for all active linguists, cryptanalysts, and military people. Besides what Joos participated in and otherwise witnessed (partly narrated already pp. 118-126) from his successive offices in the secrecy-of-communications complex in Virginia and when visiting the ACLS complex and otherwise prowling the region including the naval counterpart where A.A.Hill worked even more secretively, we enrich this History's pages, whenever that would clarify the career of our Society itself, from all available sources. If the result seems to emphasize either cryptography or the Intensive Language Program unduly, the answer will have to be that there was in fact very little LSA work apart from those personal involvements in war-controlled activities, and that further information is fully accessible in reprinted volumes of Language and needs no duplication here: finally, please once more note that the Joos historiography speaks by request for J Milton Cowan as well as for Roland Grubb Kent and even for certain pre-LSA voices.

Resignations effective with the end of 1943 were 16, among which six are worth listing for reasons easily findable by use of the indexes, the LSA Fifty-Year index plus the Index of this present History:

Harry A. Deferrari, Ph.D., Associate Professor of Romance Languages, Catholic University of America (1934); Joseph H. Greenberg, Ph.D., Sgt., 2nd Signal Service Batl., A.U.S., Washington, D.C. (1941); Harry M. Hubbell, Ph.D., Talcott Professor of Greek, Yale University, New Haven (FM); Frank G. Ryder, M.A., address unknown (1939) who promptly resigned in good standing; John Reed Swanton, Ph.D., Ethnologist, Smithsonian Institution, Washington (SC); and Leslie C. Tihany, Ph.D., Office of Strategic Services, Washington (1940).

Instead of resigning, for which there were the same reasons as for Tihany, if one considers only the externals, we find by looking at three successive Lists of Members that Archibald A. Hill, Ph.D., Lt. Cmdr., U.S.N[aval] R[eserve], Apt. B-200, 3731 39th St. N.W., Washington 16, D.C. (1928), who for 1941 was listed as in Charlottesville as in 1928 and for 1942 was listed as at a less convenient Washington address, was in a very convenient apartment at the end of the War: there he told us, during the evening festivities which he called his mustering-out party, that his LSA publications had been accumulating in their wrappers and that he gravely doubted whether he would ever be able to write for publication again at all!

There was an Annual Meeting (called '19th') in New York City, December 29/30 1944, under the rule that 'scholarly' conventions were allowable while sales and other commercial gatherings could not be allowed to overload travel and hotels.

Accordingly, we had the Biltmore Hotel convention facilities to ourselves. 'Guests' registered to the number of 28; no such name appears in our printed records apart from those who converted that status to regular membership by payment of $5.00 Dues for the ensuing year 1945; in addition there were an unguessable number of casual visitors (one recalls a few in French and in a few in British uniforms) who did not include themselves in those 28 but did stay, perhaps for lack of anything else to do with their half-hours: traces of that phenomenon could be found, it is said, but we haven't looked for them.

Asterisks below signify that Baugh was at the same post in the 1944 and the 1943 Lists of Members; that Austin's posts were different on the record while his work was the same; and that Barnhart moved from the Chicago post to a higher-level one in New York; these *** are samples of possibilities; other, parallel cases are left unmarked but can be detected, often, by recognizing that the 1945 posts are also stated in the listing below, simply flagged by the underlined 'next' for that:

William Mandeville Austin,* Ph.D., Language Technician, Language Section, Information and Education Div., War Department, 165 Broadway, New York City, next Fellow, Intensive Language Program, ACLS, Hunter College (1937); Clarence L. Barnhart,* Ph.B., Dictionary Editor, Scott Foresman & Co., Chicago, next Dictionary Editor, Random House, New York (1935); Albert Croll Baugh,* Professor of English, University of Pennsylvania (1936); Ernest Bender, B.A., Fellow of Intensive Language Program, ACLS, University of Pennsylvania (1940); Bernard Bloch, Assistant Professor of Linguistics, Yale University, next Associate Professor (1931); Yuen-Ren Chao, Ph.D., Visiting Professor of Chinese, Harvard University (1939); Edith Frances Claflin, Ph.D., Lecturer in Greek and Latin, Barnard College, New York City (FM); Emory Ellsworth Cochran, Ph.D., Acting Chairman, Dept. of Foreign Languages, Fort Hamilton High School, New York City (1943); William Stewart Cornyn, Ph.D., Instructor in Linguistics, Yale University, next Assistant Professor (1941); Cornelia Catlin Coulter, Ph.D., Professor of Greek and Latin, Mount Holyoke College, South Hadley, Mass. (1927); J M. Cowan, Ph.D., Director, Intensive Language Program, American Council of Learned Societies, Washington, D.C. (1937); Ephraim Cross, Ph.D., Assistant Professor of Romance Languages, City College, New York City (1927); Jack Autrey Dabbs, M.A., Captain, 141st Infantry, Personnel Adjutant, A.U.S., Austin, Texas (1938); E. Jeannette Dearden, Ph.D., Language Section, Information and Education Div., War Department, Room 1917, 165 Broadway, New York City, next Somerset Center, Mass. (1939); Isidore Dyen, Ph.D., Assistant Professor of Malayan Languages, Hall of Graduate Studies, Yale University, New Haven, Conn. (1934); Helen S. Eaton, Linguistic Research Assistant of the International Auxiliary Language Association, New York City, next 148 Hollis Ave., Braintree, Mass. (1927); Franklin Edgerton, Ph.D., Salisbury Professor of Sanskrit and Comparative Philology, Yale University, next Sterling Professor (SC); Charles Albert Ferguson, M.A., Fellow of Intensive Language Program, ACLS, Upper Darby, Pennsylvania, next Dept. of Linguistic Analysis, University of Pennsylvania, Philadelphia (1942); J. William Frey, Ph.D., Assistant Professor of German and Mathematics, Franklin and Marshall College, Lancaster, Pennsylvania, next Head of Department of German (1941); Charles C. Fries, Ph.D., Professor of English, University of Michigan, Director, English Language Institute, Angell Hall, Ann Arbor (FM); Allan Harrison Fry, Ph.D., Radio Program Officer, Co-ordinator of Inter-American Affairs, 3084 Dept. of Commerce Building, Washington, D.C., next 39 Green Ave., Lawrenceville, New Jersey (1939); Elizabeth F. Gardner, M.A., Assistant in Instruction in Japanese, Yale University, next Instructor (1935); William J. Gedney, A.B., S/Sgt., Language Section, Information and Education Div., A.S.F., 165 Broadway, 86 Bedford, Apt. H-2, New York City, next with residential address only (1940); Louis H. Gray, Ph.D., Professor of Comparative Linguistics, Columbia University, New York City, next Emeritus (SC); Yakira Hagalili, A.B., Assistant in Instruction of Hindustani, University of Pennsylvania, next a non-member (1943); Sivert N. Hagen, Ph.D., Professor of English, Franklin and Marshall College (1936); E. Adelaide Hahn, Ph.D., Professor of Latin and Greek and Head of Department, Hunter College, New York City (FM, Life Member 1935); Robert A. Hall, Jr., Litt.D. (Rome), Assistant Professor of Italian, Brown University, Providence, Rhode Island (1935; Life Member 1943); Miles L. Hanley, M.A., Professor of English, University of Wisconsin, Madison (1929); Zellig S. Harris, Ph.D., Associate Professor of Hamito-Semitic Linguistics, University of Pennsylvania (1929; Life Member 1945); Einar Haugen, Ph.D., Thompson Professor of Scandinavian Languages, University of Wisconsin, Madison (1937); George Herzog, Ph.D., Assistant Professor of Anthropology, Columbia University, New York City (1931); Charles Francis Hockett, Ph.D., Lt., Language Section, Information and Education Div., A.S.F., 165 Broadway, New York City, next Capt. (1939); Carleton Taylor Hodge, Ph.D., Fellow of the

Intensive Language Program, ACLS, 33 Kent Road, Upper Darby, Pennsylvania, next 7860 Beverly Blvd., Highland Park, Pennsylvania (1938); Heinrich (next Henry) M. Hoenigswald, Litt.D., Instructor, Department of Oriental Studies, University of Pennsylvania, Philadelphia, next Instructor in Japanese, Hall of Graduate Studies, Yale University (1939); Fred Walter Householder, Jr., Ph.D., Greek and Latin, University Extension, Columbia University, New York City (1944); Lee S. Hultzén, Ph.D., Auburn, New York, next Assistant Professor of Speech, University of Illinois, Urbana (1937); Roman Jakobson, Ph.D., Professor of General and Slavic Linguistics, École Libre des Hautes Études, 205 W. 88th St., New York City (1941); Martin Joos, Ph.D., War Department, 205 N. Trenton St., Arlington, Virginia (1936); Henry R. Kahane, Ph.D., Assistant (next Associate) Professor of Spanish and Italian, University of Illinois, Urbana (1940); Renée Kahane-Toole, Ph.D., University of Illinois, Urbana (1940) (Mrs. Henry R. Kahane); Allen B. Kellog, Ph.D., Instructor in English, Indiana University, Bloomington, next Professor of English, Indiana Central College, Indianapolis (1939); George A. Kennedy, Ph.D., Associate Professor of Chinese Language and Literature, Hall of Graduate Studies, Yale University, New Haven, Connecticut (1937); Roland G. Kent, Ph.D., Professor of Indo-European Linguistics, University of Pennsylvania, Philadelphia (SC; Life Member 1927); John Kepke, M.A., Language Technician, Language Section, Information and Education Div., War Department, 165 Broadway, New York City, 1 Grace Court, Brooklyn 2, N.Y. (1930; Life Member 1935); J. Alexander Kerns, Ph.D., Assistant Professor of Classics, Washington Square College, New York University, New York City (FM); Harold V. King, M.A., Instructor in Latin and French, Culver Military Academy, Culver, Indiana (1943); Alice E. Kober, Ph.D., Assistant Professor of Classics, Brooklyn College, Brooklyn, N.Y. (1933); Helge K. A. Kökeritz, Ph.D., Professor of English, Hall of Graduate Studies, Yale University, New Haven, Connecticut (1941); Hans Kurath, Ph.D., Director of the Linguistic Atlas of the United States and Canada, Professor of Germanic and General Linguistics, and Chairman of the Division of Modern Languages, Brown University, Providence, R.I., next Professor of English and Editor of the Middle English Dictionary, University of Michigan, Ann Arbor (FM); William Rockwell Leete, M.A., Professor, Nanking Theological Seminary, 7th Floor, 150 5th Ave., New York City; 144 Brattle St., Cambridge, Mass., next 175 Lawrence St., New Haven, Connecticut (1938); Wolf Leslau, Licencié-ès-Lettres (University of Paris), Professor of Semitic Languages, École Libre des Hautes Études, New York City (1943); Juan Lopez-Morillas, Ph.D., Assistant Professor of Romance Languages, Brown University, Providence, R.I. (1941); Kemp Malone, Ph.D., Professor of English, Johns Hopkins University, Baltimore, Maryland (FM); Clarence Augustus Manning, Ph.D., Assistant Professor of East European Languages, Columbia University, New York City (FM); Raven Ioor McDavid, Jr., Ph.D., Language Technician, Language Section, Information and Education Div., War Department, 165 Broadway, New York City, next Fellow, Linguistic Atlas of the United States and Canada, Box 628, Greenville, South Carolina (1937); Norman Anton (next Anthony) McQuown, Ph.D., Language Technician, Language Section, Information and Education Div., War Department, 165 Broadway, New York City, next Lecturer in Linguistics, Hunter College (1937); Karl Heinrich Menges, Ph.D., Visiting Professor of East European Languages, Columbia University, New York City (1938); William Gamwell Moulton, Ph.D., Assistant Professor of German, Yale University, Language Section, Military Gov't Div., P.M.G.O., War Department, Washington, D.C., next Captain, A.U.S., Special Project Center, Fort Eustis, Virginia, 1 Everitt St., New Haven, Connecticut (1940);

Moulton's entry illustrates so many possibilities, most of them cloaked in military secrecy, that its abbreviations can be usefully spelled out here and in part explicated for the sake of the light they throw on the Society's involvements in The War Effort: he had completed (with his wife Jenni Karding Moulton) both little volumes of Spoken German four months before the Annual Meeting (December 1944) whose attendance-list is here being accounted for; he had acquired his Direct Commission while that work was in progress at Brown University, and had been moved to Washington to finish it and supervise the printing and the making of the records at the Library of Congress: that is why the dating of the whole complex is printed as Providence and Washington, September 3, 1944, as already remarked. The work was officially then a duty-assignment in the Military Government Division of the Provost Marshal General's Office and executed under that office which had the greatest flexibility possible in choosing duty-assignments for its officers and men; then when that job was finished, Moulton became, logically enough, a Prisoners-of-War expert in the governance of such POW compounds as the Fort Eustis one ...

Mary Munch, M.A., War Department, 4602 Wilson Blvd., Arlington, Virginia,
next 301 Prospect St., New Haven, Connecticut (1943); Stanley S. Newman, Ph.D.,
Language Technician, Information and Education Div., War Department, 165
Broadway, New York City, next c/o Embassy of the United States, Mexico D.F.,
Mexico (1933); Eugene A. Nida, Ph.D., Professor of General Linguistics,
Summer Institute of Linguistics, 506 Commonwealth Bldg., Philadelphia, Penn-
sylvania, next Professor of Linguistics, Summer Institute of Linguistics, 450
Park Avenue, New York City (1939); Charles J. Ogden, Ph.D., 435 Riverside
Drive, New York City (FM); John B. Olli, Ph.D., Instructor in German, City
College, New York City (1931); Carmelita L. Ortiz (non-member 1943 & 1944);
Leo Pap, A.M., Lecturer in Spanish, College of the City of New York (1941);
Herbert Penzl, Ph.D., Pvt., Language Section, Information and Education Div.,
A.S.F., 165 Broadway, New York City, next Assistant Professor of German,
University of Illinois, Urbana (1938); Luba Petrova, Instructor in Russian,
Information and Education Div., O[fficers] C[andidate] S[chool], Florence,
Italy (1944); John Phelps, Attorney, Baltimore, Maryland (1929); Ernst Alfred
Philippson, Ph.D., Assistant Professor of German, University of Michigan,
Ann Arbor (1936); Gladys A. Reichard, Ph.D., Associate Professor of Anthro-
pology, Barnard College, Columbia University, New York City (1943); Ernst
Riess, Ph.D., Emeritus Professor of Greek and Latin, Hunter College (1925);
Kimberley Sidney Roberts, Allentown, Pennsylvania, next Haverford, Penn-
sylvania (1939); Fred Norris Robinson, Ph.D., Professor Emeritus of English,
Harvard University (1926); Philip Scherer, Ph.D., Teacher of German, Stuy-
vesant High School, Brooklyn, N.Y. (1936); John Norman Seaman, J.D., Captain,
Signal Corps, A.U.S., Arlington, Virginia (1940); Thomas Albert Sebeok, B.A.,
Instructor in ASTP, Indiana University, Bloomington, Indiana, next Instructor
in English (1941); Edward Henry Sehrt, Ph.D., Professor of German, George
Washington University, Washington, D.C. (1926); Alfred Senn, Ph.D., Professor
of Germanic Philology, University of Pennsylvania (1931); Ichiro Shirato, M.A.,
Instructor in Japanese, Columbia University, New York City (1943); Jane
Shwitzer, M.A., Madison, Wisconsin (1944); Frank T. Siebert, Jr., M.D.,
Merion, Pennsylvania (1934); Muhammed (next Mehmed) Ahmed Simsar, Ph.D.,
1 University Place, New York City (1936); Taylor Starck, Ph.D., Professor of
German, Harvard University (FM); Edgar Howard Sturtevant, Ph.D., Lecturer
in Linguistics, Yale University, next Professor Emeritus of Linguistics (SC;
Life Member 1936); Donald C. E. Swanson, Ph.D., University of Minnesota
(1939); Paul Tedesco, Ph.D., Institute for Advanced Study, Honorary Fellow,
Yale University, New Haven, Connecticut (1938); George L. Trager, Ph.D.,
Chief, Linguistics and History Section, Board on Geographical Names, U.S.
Dept. of Interior, Washington, D.C. (1931); R. Whitney Tucker, Ph.D., Profes-
sor of Foreign Languages, Pennsylvania Military College, Chester, Pennsyl-
vania, next Swarthmore, Pennsylvania (1929); W. Freeman Twaddell, Ph.D.,
Professor of German and Head of Department, University of Wisconsin, Madi-
son (1930); Charles Frederick Voegelin, Ph.D., Associate Professor of Anthro-
pology, Indiana University, Bloomington, Indiana (1934); James Roland Ware,
Assistant Professor of Chinese, Harvard University (FM); Ralph W. Weiman,
M.S., Chief, Language Section, Information and Education Div., A.S.F., 165
Broadway, New York City (1942); Rulon Seymour Wells, III, Ph.D., Instructor in
Japanese, Yale University (1944); William E. Welmers, Th.B., Fellow of Intensive Language Program, ACLS, Oreland, Pennsylvania (1942); T'ung Yiu, M.A.,
c/o Gest Oriental Library, Princeton, New Jersey (1943).

These 96 persons recorded as present in the Annual Meeting, Friday/Saturday,
December 29/30, in New York City, amounted to 17% of the personal membership.
No greater fraction of the total current membership has ever been assembled at
any subsequent time.

In assembling all the listed personal information with each name above the plan
was to create a cinematic display, a moving picture presenting the whole war-time
span of our Society's personal involvements. Expanded treatment of the Moulton
case, and that one alone, is conspicuous here; that, however, should not be allowed
to distort the totality. Relatively few of the 96 lacked personal tasks which were
categorially war-effort work. Only casual significance attaches to the uniforms
worn by some and the civilian garb of others, for the military persons were most
likely under orders to attend this meeting in mufti if at all. What is significant in
this particular Christmas Week gathering is not in every case apparent in the list
but is instead an absence, a lacuna in the list of Members resident within reach of
New York City; some of us, for example Archibald A. Hill, were too firmly tied to
some urgent task to leave the Washington area on either of the two days.

Whereas in the ordinary way those attending an Annual Meeting of our Society
find themselves conversing exclusively about civilian matters, so that anybody in
uniform is definitely out of it, the 1944 congregation in the Biltmore was almost
all composed of 'civilian soldiers' who were more comfortable in 'mufti' and in
conversation about language than about the exciting events overseas in that crucial
season: see any chronology of events in the Second World War—to which few of us
gave the journalist's name 'World War II' because that sounded illiterate: that was
still long before illiteracy became fashionable among American linguists, you see.
We generally didn't know about the military status of our acquaintances, and most
of them were commissioned (like Hockett) and thus able to conceal the fact as the
Privates, Corporals, and Sergeants were not permitted to. Exact counting thus is
impossible, but an expert estimate can be given: 80 of the 96, give or take two,
were being paid by the Government or by the ACLS for militarily crucial work.

Both typical and idiosyncratic was John Kepke, around whom vivid memories
of that 1944 Annual Meeting mostly cluster. Born in 1891, he served in uniform on
the Mexican border before 1917 as a member of the National Guard under Pershing
and then got into the Plattsburg (upstate New York) Officers Candidate School and
got a commission in the Artillery and was sent to France as a 'balloon observer'
sent aloft behind our lines in the 'basket' of a tethered balloon to report by phone
on the accuracy of our artillery's aiming by spotting shell-bursts on the maps of
the terrain that our American Expeditionary Force got from the French; always a
swift learner, he was returned to the United States to serve as an instructor: see
the Obituary by Raven McDavid in Language 43.825−26, 1967. For this Annual
Meeting he was able to register from both his home and his job; he had gone to
that from his first war-effort job (February to August 1943) in Arlington Hall (alias
4602 Wilson Blvd [the address given by e.g. Mary Munch, who was by rule required
to conceal its existence: Kepke, as in duty bound, gave a local post-office box as
his address when Joos first knew him for those six months)], the job that he held
from the day of his Arlington Hall arrival in response to distress signals from
Joos, who was overloaded with Finnish translating that Kepke first handled and then
trained others to do: work combining cryptography and awareness of idiom in five
languages (he spoke German from childhood, and had learned Russian as well as
learning both Swedish and Finnish from the Mechanical Engineering crews he met
in the SKF plant [Svenska Kullager Fabrik] where he gained the basis for his first
advanced degree, M[echanical] E[ngineer]: Engineers did not in that era earn the
Ph.D. degree, and the ME degree had the same ranking and was conferred only on
the author of a published Thesis: his dealt with improved ball-bearing journals to
replace the Timken roller-bearings which had been the best heavy-duty bearings
previously. In no need of ready cash, he took his SKF fee in the form of shares of
SKF stock, which helped make him a millionaire in the 1920's, after which he only
worked or studied for fun. (That ME thesis is not listed by McDavid; it was published in Sweden, of course, and most likely was written in German.)

Whatever Spoken Language enterprise we start out from, if we continue toward
completing a survey we very soon encounter the denizens of Bascom Hall, at that
time the principal humanities building of the University of Wisconsin in Madison;
and if we in the 1930's sought out the personal leadership we were told to look for
them between classes in the University Club at the foot of Bascom Hill a quarter
of a mile away towards the State Capitol building one mile further to the east. A
letter to Joos from Twaddell dated 24 December 1973, and a slightly later postcard
together say: 'I was uncommonly many-hatted: a technical linguist, a classroom
language teacher, administrator [[as Chairman of German and of ad-hoc commit-
tees]], diplomat with the local military hierarchy, channel via Uncle Milt [[Cowan]]
to and from the Provost Marshal [[General]]'s office and some other War Dept (as
we called it then) agencies. That, God wot, was enough ... at least USAFI was not
one of the important contributors to the burdens. ... I was not in charge at USAFI
on the occasion of the LSA Annual Meeting of 1944. It is quite possible that I was
pressured into attending because of that uncommon combination of linguist-
teacher-administrator-curriculum designer. Not to speak of my wanting to use

such travel-authority as I had for the purpose of getting together with the brethren.'
⟦In twaddellian language, 'brethren' is a technical term, belonging to the same
semantic field as 'uncle' (e.g. 'Uncle Milt' = J Milton Cowan) and 'cousin' (e.g.
'Cousin Martin'), for various stable placements among fellow academics. Here
we may usefully adduce these names from the 1944 Annual Meeting: Twaddell
had written his Ph.D. Dissertation under Taylor Starck in Germanics at Harvard and still today is glad to acknowledge a relation of devotion toward him.
Marginally, E. H. Sehrt of George Washington University was involved in ways
gratefully remembered four decades later.⟧

Einar Haugen, Thompson Professor of Scandinavian, had come to Madison two
years later than Twaddell, at the beginning of the 1930's, and remained until 1964
before moving on to Harvard, 18 years after Twaddell's 1946 move to Brown University, Providence, Rhode Island, his home base nowadays in 1976. We'll return
presently to this pair of close friends, after saying more about two others who
also used Bascom Hall, Alfred Senn and Miles Lawrence Hanley.

Senn was born in France of Swiss parents in 1899, and was naturally in school
in Switzerland at the outbreak of the War; he eventually got his Ph.D. there in
1921, and went to Lithuania to continue his studies in the Baltic languages. After
nine years in Lithuania, he came on a study grant to the 1930 Linguistic Institute
at CCNY, arriving a little late because of being detained a few miles away at
Ellis Island by deeply puzzled Immigration functionaries who debated whether he
ought to be deported because he filled in both the 'Professor' box and the 'Student'
box on the landing form; moreover, was he a French or a Swiss or a Lithuanian
citizen, or even a stateless refugee who ought to be carrying a Nansen passport?
When Institute Director Sturtevant at last got word of this, he sent a two-man
task force to Ellis Island, Karl Reuning and Franklin Edgerton, who untied or cut
the Gordian Knot in less than an hour: a few minutes to interview Senn, and then
a telephone consultation with the Commissioner of Immigration, who happened to
be a boyhood chum of Edgerton's—they wore same Old School Tie!

After the Institute, Sturtevant took Senn to Yale for an interim year as Sterling
Fellow; and there the negotiations were centered during 1930-31 while Senn made
up his mind to stay on our side of the Atlantic and bring his wife and children to
America. Sturtevant, Prokosch, and others sifted the qualifications of campuses
which both had good libraries and could provide a teaching position for a scholar
who, no matter what academic title was given him, intended in any case to keep on
compiling Lithuanian materials towards a modern dictionary of the standard language with the coöperation of Europeans. Now the University of Wisconsin had so
many of the requisites that a visit to Madison took place within the Fall Semester.
Notably, the Library had been building up steadily since about 1868 and had never
suffered damagingly from political storms or even Depression scanting and was
now found to be outstanding in just those fields which interested Alfred Senn. Professor Julius Olson, Head of Scandinavian Studies, who appointed Haugen after an
interview in 1930, had taken Wisconsin's considerable Finnish population under
his wing as geographically and culturally Scandinavian and automatically Baltic
languages too, steps in which he had the warm support of A. R. Hohlfeld of the
Department of German. Senn had come with his own check-list in hand, and now
found (to his surprise: he had not really credited the fame of Madison as The
Athens of the Midwest) that a lot of his listed books were shelved in Madison, in
the Library of Congress, and nowhere else in all North America—not even Yale.
At the end of the Spring season, in 1931, Alfred Senn was appointed Professor of
Germanic and Indo-European Philology, so far within the Department of German;
one year later, when Arthur Gordon Laird retired, Senn moved a little way along
the corridor to become Laird's successor as Chairman of the Department of
Comparative Philology, still with the major part of his salary retained as an item
on the German budget—so that Hohlfeld called upon him to teach a fairly long list
of advanced courses and seminars.

The six years 1931 to 1938, ending with Alfred Senn's departure for the University of Pennsylvania, included midway the development of Twaddell's Monograph
No. 16, On Defining the Phoneme. Towards perfecting that, Senn's puzzlement was

crucial: paragraph by paragraph, it showed Twaddell which arguments would have
to be spelled out more thoroughly to be intelligible to European readers; and one
positive contribution has been certified to Joos: 'Guess what! Alfredo has just
seen the light: Phonemes, he said to me yesterday, were what makes it possible
to write a language alphabetically, and was that a fair statement? Nothing could
be fairer, I said, and thanked him for the formulation.'

Twaddell and Haugen recognized each other as natural allies within half a year
of first meeting in Madison. Both were born in that remarkable year of 1906 which
gave us a group of three Presidents of the Linguistic Society of America within a
single lunar month: Twaddell and Trager were both born on the 22nd of March and
Haugen 28 days later. They met, Twaddell recently told Joos, in the University
Club on a day that was extremely cold and dry, so that friction of shoe-soles on
the carpet electrified the one to come second and caused a startling shock when
their hands touched; that means that they met in a month when Bloch and Joos both
were in Massachusetts in the first winter of Linguistic Atlas field-work. Haugen
has reacted characteristically to a draft for the present page, protesting that he
profited a great deal more from what he got from Twaddell than Twaddell could
have learned from him. 'The influence was all the other way around,' says his
letter to Joos in March, 1974, 'since I owe my introduction to general linguistics
to him, after having been trained by George T. Flom at the University of Illinois
in Old Norse and historical linguistics.' However, what the draft specifically had
in view was such lessons as can be learned in field interviews and in no other way.
Haugen had begun taking systematic notes from voices of Scandinavian immigrants
and their descendants, born anywhere from the middle of the 19th century to a few
years previous to his visits to the 1930's farmsteads (or villages) where they lived.
Twaddell, in contrast, did his researches on campuses, in classrooms, or at home
with wife, children, and perhaps visitors; hence he was fascinated by experiences
on farms that he could now learn about from experts.

Subsequent language publication by either Haugen or Twaddell was normally
somewhat colored, usually enriched, by slants derived from the other. For the
academic year 1933–34, Twaddell had been made a member of the Program Committee of the campus Language and Literature Club, and had been requested to
spice the year's half-dozen monthly meetings with 'something about the Phoneme'
now that Bloomfield's 1933 book Language had appeared and was disturbing the
peace in language departments including English. Bloomfield came for a lecture
visit early in 1934; the writing of On Defining the Phoneme got started promptly,
beginning with a letter from Twaddell to Bloomfield requesting criticism of one
or two restatements of the book's and the lecture's messages, and ended when
the Twaddell typescript was mailed off to Editor Bolling. Its footnotes were placed
by design so that the dead-pan rejection of a note frivolously inserted from a Joos
letter could be cut out editorially; it can be read today as the last footnote of the
Introduction, page 7, and more conveniently in the reprint in Readings in Linguist-
tics I, where it ends page 56 as fn 9. When that vulnerable footnote survived into
the printed Monograph No. 16, March, 1935, Twaddell took that as an example of
Bolling's well-known pawky humor, not realizing that in the crucial year 1934 the
mechanics of his editing had to be delegated because of cataract trouble. ⟦That
must also have been the mysterious reason why the Joos review of Zipf's book,
The Psycho-Biology of Language, was preposterously altered from the approved
page-proof by adding a terminal 'e' to the first word of Godfrey Dewey's title,
Relativ Frequency of English Speech Sounds, stolen from midway in the Joos
spelling of judgement in the same review—a misspelling which still today keeps
turning up in all references to Dewey's book by title and likely will persist.⟧

The Haugen-Twaddell coöperation just once generated a jointly signed item,
their 'Facts and phonemics' in Language 18.228–237, 1942. Otherwise there are
acknowledgements such as that in fn 1 of the first page of Monograph 16, 'In the
preparation of this study I have drawn heavily upon several of my friends. ...
My colleagues Professor A. Senn, Professor E. I. Haugen, and Mr. David Sheldon
have been most helpful. I am indebted to Professor Leonard Bloomfield ...'

When Twaddell in 1946 left Madison to go to Brown University the uprooting left traces behind in the Department of German in Bascom Hall; one was a handful of pristine copies of Monograph 16, and another trace was something that came to the surface accidentally in the Summer of 1967: in the Department's dead storage area called the Rumpelkammer which sometimes was unvisited for two years straight, we found more than seven issues of Language from the years 1942 and 1943, among them Trager & Bloch, The Syllabic Phonemes of English, 17.223-246, with notes in Twaddell's hand red-pencilled in its margin, e.g., p. 235, fn 21, opposite the 7 lines that run 'The total pattern is best revealed ... while /w/ is lowered' we find:

Consider woo = wuw. Phonetic resemblance!

and twice we find, in "..." which evidently flag the word as a quotation from one or another Trubetzkoyan disciple or from the Master himself, actualized opposite red-underlined 'the element heard as a lengthening of the vowel ... may be some kind of semivowel' on p. 239, late in section 11, and again on p. 240, opposite lines 10-14, wherein there are scattered red underlinings, single or doubled, thus:

What is the phonemic interpretation of the lengthening element which we have been writing with a raised dot? It cannot be any of the vowels, not even /ə/ (in spite of the phonetic resemblance), since there is no example anywhere else in the total pattern for two vowels in succession. It functions like the two semivowels /j/ and /w/, and like these must be reckoned a consonant ...

Joos guesses that this is one of the two personal copies of Language, either that of Twaddell or (conceivably) that of Haugen, which served to assemble their ideas by being passed between them and between conferences held by Twaddell while he drafted the text of their 'Facts and phonemics' article; it also bears black-pencil markings ascribable to either man, not numerous, and always simply down along a margin or placed as a short underlining; once a black arrow points to fn 12, to agree, seemingly, with the Trager & Bloch wording 'admittedly subjective ...'

In strong contrast to this holograph evidence of a known collaboration, Joos remarks in 1976 that the Haugen-Twaddell interaction produced, normally, not a salad of separately discernible ingredients but instead: an omelette which we could never undertake to unscramble, yet salted with personal wit and flavored with a peculiarly Scandinavian grim-seriousness that friends can both detect.

Now instead of giving two personal names to such ingredients, we can equally account for this interaction, plus dozens of other interactions as well, by pointing to the peculiarly Madisonian milieu in which this and indeed the whole development of the USAFI complex burgeoned; and, spreading out from Madison, we encounter the home of George Tobias Flom, Haugen's teacher in the University of Illinois, still within the confines of the same fairly small County of Dane (!) less than 20 miles (or 30 km) to the southward of the State Capitol and the University campus. Closer to the campus and to Capitol Square a mile east of it, we immediately see on the map that the ground-space is squeezed, confined, between Lake Mendota to the north and Lake Monona to the south of the mile-long State Street linking one to the other, so that that street is the axis of a slender area between the lakes; also, taking a broader view, we see the Capitol situated centrally on a mile-wide isthmus between the western University moiety and the northeastern factory area that is richly served with railroads and is the locale for Madison's light industry and generally highly-skilled workers' residences, while the hotels were originally all around Capitol Square and the department stores too, leaving State Street as the core of the Student Quarter and the place for light lunches and other conveniences. The terrain has of course always fostered an automatic symbiosis of Students and Faculty, especially on the fringes of the Campus area to the westward of Bascom Hall where both Haugen and Twaddell dwelt for many years in the 1930's, and the continual infiltration of new Faculty members, half them naturally staying for only two years and up to six years before that crucial Promotion to Associate Professor or Moving On to a job on another campus, and the details of the symbiosis viewed as an economic interdependence profiting both the job-holding students and the households of young professorial staff where the students tended furnaces, mowed

lawns, shoveled snow or raked leaves, did odd jobs and even carpentry according
to individual talents, or equally well tutored children in algebra or Spanish or sat
them while parents were out for an evening, or did the same for neighbors, the
physicians, or lawyers, and some who were hardly distinguishable from members
of the State Legislature or actually were members or judges; the police mostly
lived on the other side of Capitol Square. The typical young-faculty house, or as
a case of equal probability the typical Professor's Widow's house, had two floors
plus a convertible Attic aloft, and below the front-porch level an almost totally
convertible Basement, making four levels of occupancy in all. It was in the home
of the Widow Terry that the Haugens and the Twaddells dwelt, in layer-cake relation of the two households (the Attic having been first converted elaborately with
built-ins for the Twaddells) from the Summer of 1932 onward for three or four
years until the Twaddells moved to a house they rented totally for themselves a
scant ten-minute walk from the Terry house where the Haugens stayed on in the
Attic plus the floor below it.

    ⟦Terry was always in the Physics Department and his specialty was vacuum-
tube oscillators, in the initial and continuing development of which he was one of
world's pioneers though not a patentee as far as Joos knows. In the biennial City
Directory, Earle M. Terry and his wife Sadie (once Sarah in the 1909 edition)
can be found in successive houses with successively more room for students to
live there too and be listed by name, until his demise during the year 1928–1929
while Joos was working for the Western Electric Company in its Hawthorne
communications-equipment factory employing over 50,000 of us at times; today,
there is an endowed chair in Madison, the 'E. M. Terry Professorship', whose
incumbent maintains the Physics Museum where visitors can see successively
bigger and better functioning Oscillator tubes which Terry made by hand from
the departmental stockroom's supply of varieties of glass, of platinum, and of
tungsten metal (nowadays 'wolfram' metal, symbol W), apart from those totally
destroyed behind Terry's wired-glass screening by explosion instead of simple
burn-out. Terry's personal traits—extreme shyness, dedication to students in
small groups or singly, tenacity in decades-long programs, sweetness towards
serious students asking for help—were taken for granted among Electrical
Engineering students who were assigned to him for High Voltage Laboratory.
We never said he was Jewish. We had heard or read the word anti-semitism
and wondered whether we would recognize it if it turned up in Madison! And
that is the background reason why Martin Joos, on first seeing Bloomfield, felt
he belonged in a Physics laboratory, a reason only recognized four decades
later: Earle Terry and Leonard Bloomfield, say the long-buried memories,
were alike enough to have been brothers.⟧

    From his cellar-level private laboratory in Sterling Hall Professor Terry sent
out his wireless news and music, as 'Experimental Madison Station [XM] in the
ninth territorial district of the United States' which gives his official call 9XM,
beginning in 1916 as a specially licensed exception to the universal black-out of
Amateur Radio for the duration of the War. Eventually he used an antenna wire
strung about 100 meters uphill to a steel-tubing flag-pole planted just outside the
southwest corner of Bascom Hall, thus a scant 3 meters (10 feet) distant from the
window of the German Department's basement-level office occupied by Chairman
A. R. Hohlfeld in the 1920's and eventually by his successor as Chairman, W. F.
Twaddell. Haugen's office-space was less stable in size and in location, always
in Bascom Hall and usually fairly close to the German area; Hanley's, two floors
higher in the English Department's core-area in the northern wing of Bascom.

    In the context of the 1944 Annual Meeting of the LSA in New York, these notes
can serve to characterize the Madison frame within which Haugen and Twaddell
spent an almost random assortment of relaxed hours and fractions together, the
matrix of their informal collaboration in research-based language pedagogy.
Haugen's two-volume formal report, perfected March 10, 1952, is The Norwegian
Language in America, published jointly by the American Institute at the University
of Oslo and the Department of American Civilization, Graduate School of Arts and
Sciences, University of Pennsylvania, and printed and bound in Norway, subsidized
by the Norwegian National Research Council 'Norges Almenvitenskapelige Forsk-
ningsråd' and the Ministry of Church and Education, xiv + 317 + vii + 377 pages.

That is Haugen's formal post-war report on his American Norwegian research in a third of a century (during which he published numerous articles and reviews on the nature of personal bilingualism and bilingual regions in general) and counts as the core of his scholarly work; meanwhile, and beginning with his Madison arrival, he was developing practical books for college teaching of Norwegian in regions of its retreat as a cradle and community language. Antecedent to the USAFI books is the mimeographed Beginning Norwegian whose construction towards issuance in 1934/1935 took place in the Terry house; its 1937 letterpress form (New York: F.S. Crofts & Co.) was followed in 1940 by Reading Norwegian to constitute a new basis for college teaching of the language in modern spelling and contemporary idiom. One base for them was built up by his students counting word-forms in the oldest, the 19th-century, and the contemporary forms of literary Norwegian, the latest of them being the text of 15 volumes of Sigrid Undset with well over a million running words: see the review, Language 18.302—304, 1942.

To finish the list of Madison people to be accounted for in reporting the 1944 Annual Meeting, we turn to Miles Hanley as the remaining Faculty member of the group. On returning to Madison in 1934 from Linguistic Atlas work since 1931, he was assigned (apart from his office in Bascom) a capacious space that had been condemned as totally unusable, namely the unwanted fractions of the condemned building on the former Engineering grounds on lower Bascom Hill, anciently the first 'central heating plant' still standing with its moderately tall chimney and a quantity of 19th-century coal-dust. In 1930 it had been re-named Radio Hall; for better than three decades it was the home of the nation's pioneer Educational Radio Station, renamed from 9XM to WHA. That was where about two dozen of us impecunious students made the Index Verborum to Joyce's Ulysses, duly included in Haugen's Norwegian Word Studies (reviewed as mentioned above in Language) as an item in the 32-item Bibliography early in the first volume of the 2 volumes.
- -
The foregoing accounting, beginning on page 132 with John Kepke, deals with the personalities best known to Joos among the 96 known to have attended the Annual Meeting of the LSA in December, 1944, in New York City. At the inevitable cost of over-emphasizing each event in which Joos was a participant a single point of view has been used to illuminate the central years of the Society's career; and within the years of most rapid flux, 1940–1945, the 1944 Annual Meeting serves best for gathering together bundles of personal careers where they intersected just then, and following some of the most illuminating of them backwards from there and to a useful extent forwards beyond 1950. There can be no question but what several other personal viewpoints than this single one could have served, but that can't be helped: no other single person has been found to undertake the present task.

There is also a built-in bias in naming only those 96 persons who attracted the historiographer's attention but leaving unmentioned certain others who were too young to have become visible. In partial correction, we take from Language 18.306 & 307, 1942, thirteen names under the rubric 'The following have been elected to membership in the Linguistic Society' with information still of interest in 1976:

Ainsley M. Carlton, Ph.D., 315 Georgetown Ave., San Mateo, California; Indo-European and Germanic linguistics.

Robert T. Clark, Ph.D., Professor and Head, Department of Germanic Languages, Louisiana State University; New Haven, Connecticut; Germanic and general linguistics.

A. Ferdinand Engel, 1143 New Hampshire St. N.W., Washington, D.C.; Italian.

Charles A. Ferguson, A.B., Graduate Student, University of Pennsylvania.

Edna E. Fritsch, M.A., Instructor in Phonetics, Moody Bible Institute of Chicago.

Kenneth H. Jackson, M.A., Associate Professor of Celtic, Harvard University.

Fred Lukoff, Graduate Student, University of Pennsylvania; African and Semitic linguistics.

Anne Milliken, Navy Department Civil Service; 2912 Dumbarton Ave., N.W., D.C.

Jacob Ornstein, Ph.D., Instructor in Spanish and Portuguese, Washington University, St. Louis, Missouri; 423 Randolph St., N.W., Washington, D.C.; Romance and Slavic philology.

Richard Saunders Pittman, A.B., Apartado 20, Cuautla, Mor., Mexico; American
   Indian languages.
G. Raymond Shipman, M.A., Editor, Bureau of the Census, Dept. of Commerce;
   1821 P St., S.E., Washington, D.C.; Indo-European and Romance linguistics.
Earl E. Tidrow, Jr., A.M.; Instructor in French, Brown University, Providence,
   Rhode Island; Old French.
William E. Welmers, Th.B.; Graduate Student, University of Pennsylvania; Semitics.
Of these, Ferguson and Welmers were the only two to attend the 1944 Annual LSA
Meeting, two years later than this listing.

Twelve months later, the Government's ban on 'conventions' was again imposed
for the 1945 Holidays, and with good reason. With the official cessation of the War,
first in Europe and then in and near Japan, the families and friends of Service-men
inundated Washington with letters and telegrams and personal visitations to insist
on bringing The Boys home from overseas without delay. With the next national
election, not of a President but of 435 members of the House of Representatives
plus 3̶2̶ Senators out of the total of 96, constitutionally fixed in the first days of
November, 1946, so that the whole of 1946 was under political-campaign pressure,
the result was inevitable: Demobilization, the voters were told, was in safe hands.
In fair weather and foul, winter or spring or summer, North America's railroads
and airlines were overloaded until late in 1946. Civilians either traveled daringly
by Greyhound bus or by personal automobile on much-patched tires, or hitch-hiked
or arranged, many weeks in advance, to travel by train with a bottle-baby, or got
a reservation for one person, the mother alone, on train or plane, optimistically
resolved to insist on holding the seat when threatened with loss of it by being displaced ('bumped') at some way-station by a ticket-holder who held a higher Prior-
ity, a thing that could occur a dozen times during the journey from D.C. to Madison.

The 1946 Summer Meeting was more satisfactory. Deprived of the hoped-for
1945 Annual Meeting, Members received a Bulletin reporting Executive Committee
informal consultations during October/November which also promised further
progress and reports early in 1946; finally, there was confirmation of what had
been rumored, that the Executive Committee's authority to act in the name of the
Society in any matter whatever (except amending the Constitution) had been used
to make E. Adelaide Hahn the 1946 President.

The weeks leading up to the Summer meeting of the Executive Committee late
in the Summer Session at the Linguistic Institute in Ann Arbor were rife with talk
about plans for the 1946 Annual Meeting to be held in Chicago on days overlapping
the conventions of five 'affiliated' societies, old and recently founded ones both,
namely the American Anthropological Association, the American Association of
Physical Anthropologists, the American Folklore Society, the Society for American Anthropology ⟦meaning the anthropology of indigenous peoples of the Americas
from Alaska to Patagonia, especially 'cultural anthropology'⟧, and the Society for
Applied Anthropology ⟦which Philleo Nash had just invented⟧. Those others had
their own paper-reading sessions planned to begin with Saturday 27th December
and to end with Monday the 29th; the LSA sessions according were to begin with
that Monday and continue as long as necessary, conceivably including New Year's
Eve but in any case ending early enough for escape from the festivities predicted
for that very first such evening in seven years without war-clouds over it.

President Hahn had a scheme for splitting the 1946 Annual Meeting into an
Eastern and a Western moiety, explaining that that had been done before (in some
circumstances which have become obscure to historiographers now) by splitting
into Northern and Southern sessions. That started a wrangle which could be given
space on this page but will not—since both Cowan and Twaddell refuse to state its
details and no other first-hand report is possible any longer now. To Adelaide,
the APA always was the Senior Society, the LSA the junior one. The discussions
revolved around the very real danger of allowing fragmentation to characterize
the future forevermore if allowed to commence just then, the year for rebirth. A
title, Rump Session, was finally settled upon for the Rochester APA/LSA one, and
in the closing days of the Summer Meeting, when Joos presented his acoustic
phonetics lecture she presided—and asked whoever could to come to Rochester.

Since there was no person charged with a duty to sign up the LSA members present in the joint session with the APA, the only names we can be sure of were the three who presented papers in a late-afternoon gathering after the American Archaelogical group's meeting: Edith Claflin, Robert A. Hall, Jr., and Henry M. Hoenigswald. All three remained in the East; but President Hahn came to Chicago by overnight train so that she was there to preside over the Executive Committee's sessions in the Palmer House, 22 years to the minute after she had been on hand to count the house when the Society held its initiating Meeting.

On the Monday, and again on the Tuesday, our Annual Meeting was visited by all sorts of persons, probably over twice as many as are listed as 'members and members-elect' in the subsequently printed Proceedings; there we find 57, but two of them—M. S. Coxe and G. R. Herner—must have neglected to pay any Dues, for both are absent from all membership lists. Deleting them, we list 55:

Bennett, Berg, Bloch, Bobrinskoy, Buck, Cowan, Edith Crowell, A. L. Davis, Dillon, Dunkel, W. F. Edgerton, Gelb, Georgacas, Gerstung, Goodwin, Jean Griffith, E. Adelaide Hahn, Haugen, Heffner, Joos, Kepke, Kerns, H. V. King, Kurath, Lane, Leopold, Levy, Lounsbury, McDavid, McGailliard, McQuown, Messing, Metcalf, Mutziger, Nida, Paper, Penzl, Petit, Pike, Scherer, Sebeok, Seifert, Sherman, H[elen] Hide Shohara, Aasta Stene, Swadesh, Swanson, Trager, Twaddell, Voegelin, von Grunebaum, Wise, Wolff, Wonderly, Yamagiwa.

Certainly at least 45 of these 55 persons—better than 4 out of 5—indelibly mark the permanent history of the Linguistic Society of America and so of linguistics. Readers may profit from comparing this with another statistical fact, p. 131.

VI: RECONVERTING: 1946 — 1950

The Chapter ending with Page 139 carried the external history of the Society to the end of December 1946. Now we step back to the end of 1945 and further back to the first week of October just before that. The Japanese surrender had just taken place; we are about to narrate events which Joos could see only dimly, and yet the Joos point of view is the only one that can be kept under control in the narrating.

In the last days of September, that is to say during the last few days of FY 1945 (= Fiscal Year 1945, after which FY 1946 would extend for 12 months to 1 October 1946), there came to the Joos desk in Arlington Hall, where routine work was now continuing on improvements in deciphering equipments, an official letter from a high-level Foreign Service Officer in the Department of State which offered Joos an advancement in Civil Service rank and 'permanent' appointment (in contrast to early release from the current emergency appointment which was likely to vanish with the official end of hostilities) if he would undertake to develop, beginning as soon as the transfer could be managed and in any case 'prior to' 15th December, a language teaching 'facility' within the Department of State's Diplomatic and Consular Service for which the outline of planning had already progressed during the months beginning 1 July 1945 to the point where one 'highly qualified' boss was to be found and offered the job, and was Joos a Citizen of the United States cleared for sensitive employment? Yes? Good; and here is the Job Description, and would Dr. Joos just take it home and prepare, during the next few days, a Table of Organization with job descriptions and requisite capabilities of each slot within it, plus the budget for salaries and supplies needed during an initial fiscal year; then in a final interview the agreement would be firmed up and prepared for top-level signatures which would make it a Contract of Employment.

The papers Joos carried off home (was his wife a native-born citizen and fully discreet—that is, would she keep mum, making sure of never finding out what her husband was doing to earn that handsome projected salary?) were too utterly goofy to be taken seriously; and yet ... The basic idea was to teach each extra language, beyond the normal French that every FSO called home for refresher courses was to study to the extent needed, filling the remainder of his 35-hour week principally devoted to International Law and the Rule Books, entirely in after-hours Evening Voluntary Laboratory work, 5 or ten such hours a week, or in extreme cases 12 or 15 hours; the Facility was to be equipped with all the Linguaphone disc-records in the world, and work-books and examinations to match; and if perchance those were not quite adequate, the Facility could procure, on Joos's requisition which could presumably be countersigned and put through in a month or so each time, a set of those phonograph records which had been rumored to eventually be used in a school called USAFI way out in the Midwest some place so that we could get them free of cost through channels if Joos thought they could possibly be used for supplementary study; and now Dr. Joos must forgive him for rushing off but Jester —was that really his name? yes, the framed document above his desk was issued to O. Jester—was already 10 minutes late for a Very Important Interview and thank you very much.

It took until the next day at 10 o'clock to find out how to reach Haxie Smith on the telephone, and another 24 hours before hearing his voice. Thereafter, Joos and Smith kept each other (and Milt Cowan) informed while each separately did detective work on his own grounds and elsewhere. Joos repeatedly sent written reports; Cowan's voice was heard occasionally; Henry Lee Smith, Jr., never wrote to Joos, who was not sure of having extricated himself from a precarious position until the word came through, late in January, that Dr. Smith was actually on the ground in Washington and had lined up some warm bodies from 165 Broadway.

Besides the work which the military men in that establishment expected those lamentably un-disciplined men to execute, there was of course other activity with languages that would have been hard to explain to the Inspector General. Part of that was something which the experts believed necessary, namely, construction, at least sketchily complete, of at least one _inverse_ spoken-language course, which was to deal with e.g. the English/Spanish problem as one of learning English when the learner's native language is Spanish. Somehow the 'inverse' came to be so often replaced by 'inverted' and 'reversed' that eventually, when a standard word had to be adopted for letter-writing and the like, it turned out to be 'reverse' and the first of them, a miniature mimeographed one for learning English in Mexico, was privately circulated with the title El inglés hablado and usually called/cited as 'the Reverse Spanish' book. Rewritten repeatedly amid considerable discussion for more than two years, worn out and ultimately destroyed each time except for souvenir sheets, it was ultimately mimeographed afresh before an ample supply was transported to Washington in January, 1946, and there used up in various ways that need no further discussion here. Year by year thereafter, both in the State Department's Foreign Service Institute and in the Division of Modern Languages of Cornell University, the two ends of what was referred to as 'The Washington-Ithaca Axis' rather privately, there came to be more of those things for various languages; and presently they acquired a model with an official title: Structural Notes and Corpus was multilith-manufactured in a very large number of copies containing ten Groups of five Lessons each, intended to constitute the first half of a Volume One, while development went on, to a second volume of comparable size, which was to complete the project as a whole as it developed coöperatively in the Ithaca-Washington axis. That second volume was never converted into field-service books as it stood; its multilith form followed along just 3/4 of the way in the basic format, and then was temporarily closed and manufactured with plastic-spiral 'binding' in a hundred or so copies ending with a single sheet of 'Group 15: Lesson 75' that was soon supplemented with unbound sheets to the number of 28, bearing 56 pages, which read:

Note to teams:
The material for the remaining five groups will be given in a skeleton form, in order to get the most important parts of it into the hands of the two teams concerned in a hurry. ...
The two teams immediately concerned are welcome to add their own reading lessons, additional ... If there is demand and time, the General Form staff will prepare such materials during the summer (July-August). [... of 1952]

The Joos home study in Madison, Wisconsin, has a perfect set of those 28 sheets as well as a copy, Copyright 1954, published by The Committee on the Language Program, American Council of Learned Societies, Washington, D.C., of Book II (Preliminary Edition) of the whole as already described, ending with Page 434.

In January of 1946, however, the 'Reverse Spanish' was carried by Dr. Smith to Washington in the form of a freshly cut set of mimeograph stencils and quite a number of souvenir pages of the penultimate 165 Broadway form. Clearly there would have to be something of the sort, but this one had issued from its cradle in rather primitive condition and was regarded as a make-shift: 'Haxie was definitely unhappy with it,' says a Cowan letter to Joos in 1974; but it remains unclear just what epoch this remark would best fit, and we needn't say any more about it.

The first letter-press book entitled El inglés hablado, Copyright 1952, was published by Henry Holt and Company. Its tone and a good many of its details are best clarified by the record of who was where in the 1948 and later Membership Lists. By 1948 the staff in the Cornell Division of Modern Languages included Agard, Cowan, Fairbanks, Hall, Hockett, Moulton, Olmsted, Paratore, Partridge. The 1949 recruits, Clarity, Frith, Goodison, and Charles Cleland Harris, rounded out the earliest dozen of Cornell names; and Cowan by letter tells Joos that in the course of 1950 he 'had a staff (Welmers, McDavid, Seeler, with Hockett giving general supervision and Agard doing the Reverse Spanish) working on the development of Structural Notes and Corpus as well as some students working on the various other reverse courses.'

Parallel to those 16 Cornell names, we find on the LSA List of Members this partial roster of persons who state that they are members of the Foreign Service Institute, Department of State, in most instances adding illuminating information on their status there: John M. Echols, Ph.D., Language Instructor (1934 Member); Charles A. Ferguson, M.A., Language Instructor (1942); Carleton T. Hodge, Ph.D., Language Instructor (1942); Edward A. Kennard, Ph.D., Foreign Service Institute, Dept. of State (1947) without statement on placement; Naomi Pekmezian, M.A., Language Instructor (1946); Henry Lee Smith, Jr., Ph.D., Assistant Director for Language Training, Foreign Service Institute, Dept. of State (1936); George L. Trager, Ph.D., Language Instructor, School of Language Training, Foreign Service Institute (1931). Then we may add, to those seven FSI staff members for 1947, two added beginning with 1948 or 1949: Fritz Frauchiger, Ph.D., Associate Professor of Linguistics (1941); Lili Rabel, A.M., School of Language Training, Foreign Service Institute, Dept. of State (1949). Now nine names make a strikingly short list compared to the 16 Cornell names. But there are plenty of obvious reasons for that illusory disparity. In Cornell, those scholars filled the peak of a school which students entered from high schools with very high rankings in humanistic studies; in the FSI, everything was inevitably dominated by the general philosophy of a hive of budding diplomats: 'Don't make waves; strive to match the French in urbanity and Culture, the Arabs in subtlety, the British in probity (marry into a good family, of course) and Keep Your Nose Clean—and you may make Ambassador in thirty or forty years if you choose the Right Languages Right Now—or be left waiting in Limbo: it's mostly blind luck anyhow, so why worry about it at all!' Also, and crucially, the State Department's permanent book of rules forbade FSI people to maintain active participation in such entangling alliances as, e.g., the academic affiliations with one's College Professors and Alumni Associations if not specifically directed and authorized to do so for Foreign Service reasons. In those circumstances, it was tantamount to a near-reversal of Policy when Dean Smith delicately introduced the FSI titling of individuals with standard Academic Ranking, apparently beginning when Fritz Frauchiger was taken on with the rank and salary offered him that corresponded to his civilian achievements. The LSA List of Members, however, is not a safe authority for a historiographer to rely on in individual instances, since many of our Members don't bother to correct it but let the entry stand unaltered despite academic promotions. - - - - - - - - - - - - -

The foregoing pairs of rosters of involved LSA members certainly are far from exhausting the totality of members who in December of 1948 were active enough in the missions of the Society to merit listing just here; but we must not attempt too much in the present Chapter. There will be very little real loss to readers, since the desiderated names, or pairs or small clusters of names, will come in along the way, and together will add up to an impressive list. (See our Index for others!)

During the late summer weeks of 1950, Mortimer Graves prepared a little brochure of 3 sheets of paper folded and saddle-stitched into a 12-page self-cover pamphlet; its front cover, not numbered as a page, reads

A NEGLECTED FACET OF THE NATIONAL SECURITY PROBLEM
By Mortimer Graves
American Council of Learned Societies
1219 Sixteenth Street, N. W.
Washington 6, D.C.

The first verso page, overleaf from that cover, is called '1' and the facing recto is '2' and so on through the final, verso, page reading

Washington, D.C.   Mortimer Graves
October 15, 1950

⟦The text inside follows next, all omissions signalled by ... as usual⟧

⟪Readers are presumed able to date the invasion of South Korea...⟫

The product of American industry spreads all over the world. Wherever there is a paved road there is an American automobile ... Half of the world's trains run on American rails. No region is too remote to be the concern of American diplomacy. And all too frequently American armed forces must ply their trade in lands and among peoples whose very names would have been unknown to an earlier generation.

One would suppose accordingly that many Americans would be equipped with scientific and detailed understanding of these multifarious cultures, that the United States would lead the world in the study of foreign lands no matter how distant, that no society could be named for which there was not an American expert, and that the American academic structure would reflect this world-perspective. Unfortunately a true picture is almost the reverse of this.

〖In continuing we reprint rather less than a quarter of the remainder:〗

Those of us who participated at the beginning of the second World War in the frenzied search for Americans having even a nodding acquaintance with those civilizations and areas suddenly made pressingly important, remember how ridiculously unprepared the United States was for participation, to say nothing of leadership. We improvised, some might say, magnificently, but our pride in this improvisation should not blind us to the fact that it should not have been necessary. And even the improvisation was the child of crisis; as the crisis subsided, almost pari passu the newly won academic interest in the remoter continents ebbed, until now the candid observer finds little hope for improvement until the onset of another crisis ... a schedule of what seems to be our minimum needs, dividing the world into about forty areas of cultures and civilizations and indicating the number of Americans trained in each of these areas and readily available below which it would be dangerous for us to fall, viz.:

Australia—New Zealand	20	Mexico	50
Balkans	30	Moslem World	30
Brazil	30	Netherlands	10
Central Africa	20	Northern South America	30
Central America	50	Philippines	20
Central Asia	15	Polynesia	10
China	100	Portugal	20
Eastern Mediterranean	30	Russia	100
Eire	10	Scandinavia	20
France—Belgium	50	Siberia	10
Germany	50	South Africa	10
Great Britain	50	Southeast Asia	30
India	50	Southern South America	50
Iran	10	Spain	30
Italy	50	Turkey	15
Japan	30	West and North Slavs	30
Korea	20	West Coast of South America	40
Malaysia	20	Western Mediterranean	20
Melanesia	10	TOTAL	1,070

Within each of these areas, in addition, one would wish further distribution by disciplines—economics, literature, philosophy, the sciences, etc.

These figures are to a very considerable degree arbitrary ... and yet there is no argument by which any one of them can be deemed extravagant when we consider that we are talking about the facilities of a nation of one hundred and fifty million people, the richest and most powerful the world has ever known. Rather would it seem that the figures represent an absolute and almost trivial minimum. Nevertheless, after all the forced draft of a total global war and a decade of world-wide activity, we are not equipped with even an approximation to this minimum.

〖Seven of the eleven text pages are omitted at this point!〗

... No contribution to the preservation of peace can be so great as that which could be made by greater American fundamental knowledge of that three quarters of the world which lies outside of the West European North Atlantic zone. And even the successful prosecution of a war is impossible without this knowledge. Pearl Harbor and its consequences were the ghastly price of American ignorance of the

Far East. Twenty-five thousand American casualties and billions of dollars are
down payment on American ignorance of Korea; the instalments have not yet begun.
And unless we do something about it soon, American ignorance of Turkey, Iran,
Uzbekistan, Indo-China and twenty other areas promises even less attractive
dividends.

Washington, D. C.   Mortimer Graves
October 15, 1950

- -

Ten months earlier, Graves had visited the Society's Annual Meeting of 1949 and
heard certain papers presented which obviously could not have been written at all
but for the war-time experiences of their authors. Publications representing two of
the new lines of thought are Hoenigswald's 'The principal step in comparative
grammar' in Language 26.357-364, 1950, and then not much over a year later the
powerfully seminal paper by Zellig Harris, 'Discourse Analysis' at 28.1-30.
(Others could equally well be mentioned here, but this is not the place for full
inventories.) Together, those two papers show that after three years of post-war
recovery, the membership's research and publications were proliferating anew,
displaying startling phenomena for which no Line of Descent is evident other than
derivations from the forced inventiveness of the War years which involved linguists
in cryptography situations that stimulated hitherto unknown applications of literary
categories to utterly non-literary puzzles of desperate urgency; that was what we
learned to call a 'spin-off' like the new technologies emerging from Space twenty
years later or so in response to the Life Support problems of airlessness aloft.

In LSA Bulletin No. 19, dated October-December 1946, we find the reports that
enable us to decipher the records that are almost visible in successive Lists of
Members: The extraordinary Executive Committee meeting held in February,
1946, of course included the formal reports of Editor Bloch and Secretary-Treasurer Cowan:

Following Mr. Bloch's report, Mr. Cowan reported that the stock of certain
of the publications undertaken jointly by the Society and the Intensive Language
Program of the American Council of Learned Societies had been turned over to
the Society for future distribution. This action was reported in the minutes of
the Executive Committee of the ACLS for June 16, 1944, as follows:

The [ACLS] Administrative Secretary [Mortimer Graves] reported that
several of the earlier publications issued by the Intensive Language Program
of the American Council of Learned Societies had recouped to the Council
from sales their full cost of production, and he recommended that the re-
mainders of the editions and the rights and interests of the Council in the
publications be transferred to the Linguistic Society.

Voted, To authorize the transfer to the Linguistic Society of America of
all rights and interests of the Council in the following publications, together
with such stocks of them as remain unsold on June 30, 1944: Outline Guide
for the Practical Study of Foreign Languages, Bloomfield; Outline of Linguistic Analysis, Bloch and Trager; Melanesian Pidgin English: Grammar,
Texts, Vocabulary, Hall; Melanesian Pidgin English Phrase Book, Hall; with
the reservation, however, that the proceeds from any single sale of more
than one hundred copies of ... Phrase Book ... shall accrue to the Council.

Next in the same LSA Executive Committee meeting, February, 1946, we find
that Cowan quoted an ACLS Executive Committee's Minutes of its meeting of the
previous December 13th, 1945:

The Director [Hans Kurath] reported on the progress of the Linguistic Atlas
of the United States, and submitted estimates for the completion of the field
work in the South Atlantic States during the next eighteen months. Mr. Cowan
reported that a fellow of the Intensive Language Program, Mr. McDavid, had
been allowed to devote two months of his tenure to field work for the Atlas in
South Carolina, when it developed that the Intensive Language Program's
project on which he had been working was impossible of completion at this
time. The Director [Kurath], with the approval of Mr. Graves and Mr. Cowan,
recommended an appropriation of $6,000, chargeable to the Linguistics*
Research Fund, for the completion of the field work on the Atlantic Seaboard,
pending the organization of the new* Committee on the Language Program.
It was agreed that an appropriation of $6,000 for this purpose, chargeable to

the Linguistic* Research Fund, should be included in the vote of appropriation [which the ACLS Executive Committee was planning to recommend to the annual meeting* of the American Council of Learned Societies scheduled for January 24th and 25th at the Westchester Country Club, Rye, New York].

**** As the First World War came to its end of hostilities in Western Europe, the several national Academies set about preparing for their future, and sent delegates to the Versailles conference to do in concert whatever they could get agreements for. Waldo Gifford Leland (born 1879 in Newton, Massachusetts) in 1901 got an A.M. in History at Harvard and then embarked on what was probably a sort of Grand Tour in Europe, acquainting himself especially with museums and languages with special emphasis on French. In 1903 he became a staff member in the Carnegie Institute of Washington, a status maintained continuously to 1927, eight years after the ACLS was formed with Leland as its 'organizing secretary' and evidently with the simple purpose of qualifying the United States for membership in the International Union of Academies: alone among the nations of Europe and the Atlantic regions, we had no national academy, and that was impossible to explain in French to any of Leland's compeers, so (with the approval of the Carnegie Institute and of others, no doubt) he gave out that we had something equivalent and native, a self-organized Council of learned societies devoted to humanistic studies of which he was the organizing secretary. Thenceforth and until he retired in 1946, Leland was by title the ACLS Permanent Secretary, functionally its actual Director; the title 'Permanent Secretary' is disused since Leland's retirement and the concomitant reconstruction of the ACLS total structure and the functions of its Committees.

LSA Bulletin No. 23 says that LSA Delegate to the ACLS W. F. Twaddell, at the December 1949 Annual Meeting, reported to the Business Meeting there that

> The Council's activities during the past year have been chiefly aimed at reorganization of its own structure and a new Executive Director's familiarizing himself with his work. 〚That was not Mortimer Graves: we know him as Executive Secretary, a seemingly minor shift from his Assistant status but in fact involving a total overload of added functional burdens〛 This is promising for the future; but it has involved a certain slowing down of Council activities in some fields, including linguistics. 〚Joos omits a good deal here〛

> The funds available to the Committee on the Language Program (J M. Cowan, H. G. Doyle, S. A. Freeman, H. L. Smith jr., W. F. Twaddell; Mortimer Graves ex officio) have decreased, and no new grants have been made available as yet. The Language Program of the Council has thus consisted chiefly in terminating the Intensive Language Program; a modest program of scholarships and fellowships to the Linguistic Institute has been continued, on a slightly reduced scale.

That Language Program always was just whatever the ACLS was doing that was classed as a language-program item; and that can be here editorially defined as excluding the translation program which began much earlier and flourished in the 1930's and helped publish especially translations from Arabic, especially since grants (from whatever source, and often the ACLS was not involved) for translating typically came with a proviso that none of the grant money was available for book-printing, and also as excluding translation from Classical languages; in other words, the ACLS language program in the 1940's and 1950's dealt with fresh research projects in modern languages, usually neglected or non-school languages.

Half a year later Twaddell's Committee on the Language Program was dropped from the roster of ACLS working committees during June of 1950, and a 'new' one with partly retained membership was appointed; in the LSA Annual Meeting of 1950 in Chicago, he reported (as LSA Delegate to the ACLS) officially that

> The Council's Committee on the Language Program met twice. In June, the old committee prepared a docket of agenda for the new committee, which was to come into existence on July 1. In November, the new committee considered the needs of the immediate future, in particular the program of cooperation with the linguistic activities of the Department of State. The Committee on the Language Program consists at present of the following members: J M. Cowan (chairman), S. A. Freeman, M. Joos, A. H. Marckwardt, H. L. Smith jr., and N. A. McQuown (secretary).

We of the New CLP ⟦Joos remarks⟧ in our first meeting felt that six of us alone, even with Mortimer Graves sitting in (which he could not do in every half-day, worse luck) would be somewhat deficient in dealing with the enormous range of proposals that might be referred to us for study and recommendation, and what if one of us were to be forced to skip a meeting? Then Marckwardt agreed to ask Graves about that, and brought in a totally satisfactory answer. There would be no objection to our co-opting additional persons on particular problems; or in case we anticipated an accumulation of problems calling for a particular expertise we could ask for the CLP to be enlarged. In consequence, Bernard Bloch and A. A. Hill were immediately added; and before the first twelvemonth had passed, Stephen Freeman had missed two successive meetings and then resigned: attendance at two or three meetings each year in Washington had become unhandy for him, now that his other obligations had increased.

Meanwhile Smith had begun to bring in one deputy or another of his from the Foreign Service Institute, Department of State, e.g. his fiscal expert Howard Sollenberger or his tape-recording expert Robert Stockwell, so that the membership in the CLP seemed to become diffuse, hard to define even on a single occasion; and again, when the Joos Book Construction shop got started in 1953–1956 and the ACLS focal office soon thereafter abandoned Washington in favor of a floor or two in a New York City building conveniently close to United Nations Plaza, we come to the 18-year segment of LSA History which Archibald A. Hill is to write starting with Chapter VII.

Index

Read, Allen Walker (*1906; as of 1939, said to be 'then of Missouri, now of Chicago' and lately [1974] at New York City's Columbia University): 44

Reading Norwegian, by Einar Haugen, New York: F. S. Crofts & Co.: 1940: 137

Recording and Analysis of a Living Language (Ann Arbor Linguistic Institutes of 1939 and 1940, conducted variously by first Voegelin, Emeneau, and Trager, then in 1940 by teams and procedures described at great length): 62/63, 67/68

Redlands, California (where SC Walter Petersen in 1924 had been teaching Classics since before the First World War, in the University of Redlands, amid orange groves 80 kilometers due East of Los Angeles; he was absent as explained): 8

Reed, Frank Otis (in 1927 Professor of Spanish, University of Arizona; Kent's Obituary Note is in Language 5.49 [1929]): 19a, 21b, 24

Registration Desk of the Organization Meeting that created the LSA 28th December 1924 was manned by Franklin Brunell Krauss and James Roland Ware: 5

Reno, Margarida, was chosen (ca. mid-1942) to 'supply the language content' when José Padín was unable to engage the Portuguese author he wanted in arranging the production of Spoken Portuguese: 126

Report of the First Year's Operation of the Intensive Language Program of the American Council of Learned Societies, 1941-1942, by Mortimer Graves and J M. Cowan, December 20, 1942, facsimile with useless names deleted: 97 — 114

Resignations effective with end of 1937, list of 24, including Joshua Whatmough who was persuaded, by Secretary J M. Cowan, to re-join 1948 and was duly made the LSA President for 1951: 86, 87

Rettger, James Frederick: 45, 46, 73, 76

Reuning. Karl: 19a, 20a, 22b, 23, 25, 26, 27, 133

'Reverse Spanish' and its congeners—600 words, one whole page, here page: 141

Reviewer's Honorarium (began 1925, abolished 1940 by Bernard Bloch): 50

Reynard. Charles Cassil: 45, 46

Richardson. Henry Brush (1929 and thereafter recorded as Assistant Professor of French in Yale University; taught in the L.I. both at Yale and at CCNY): 26, 32, 40

Rise and Development of Standard English [i.e. within England, the defeat of other English by London English from the 11th to the 14th centuries] given 1936—1938 in the Ann Arbor Linguistic Institutes by Fries and Marckwardt: 59, 66

riveret in early modern English displaced by rivulet, John Milton's substitute, and hence (?) William Cullen Bryant's adoption of it, Bernard Bloch wondered: 53

Roberts, Helen H., in 1930 was a Research Associate in Anthropology, Institute of Human Relations, Yale University, and came to the Linguistic Institute at CCNY solely to give one Public Lecture (as far as we know) reported as 'Some Anthropological and Psychological Problems of Language' in the evening of 12 Aug.: 40

Robinson, David M. (1925 LSA Member, is registered in the 1938 List of Members as Johns Hopkins University Professor of Archaeology, Epigraphy, and Greek Literature; 1958 Obituary Note is at Language 34.176/7)

Robinson, Frederick B., was in 1929 President of CCNY and successfully strove to capture the Linguistic Institute for CCNY and valiantly supported LSA and other linguistic/language work at least through 1932: 37, 38, 39, 47

Robinson, Fred Norris (of Harvard, 1926 LSA Member and listed for 1942 as ACLS President and Professor of English at Harvard): 127

Rockefeller Foundation: 94, 95

Rockwell, Leo Lawrence, 1925 LSA Member (then Professor of English Literature, and Director of the School of Languages, Colgate University, Hamilton, N. Y.; in 1958 listed as Director of the Division of Arts and Letters there; in 1936 & 1937 & 1938 taught in the Ann Arbor Linguistic Institutes [and is not counted as one of the visitors!]; in 1960, and later, listed as at Florida Southern College, at Lakeland, Florida): 56 & Plate, 59, 70, 71, 73, 76 [Addenda: FM; no LSA pub.; died, we have been told, 31 March 1967]

Roedder, Edwin Carl Lothar Clemens (8 April 1873—1947): 31, 32, 33, 35, 37, 38, 40, 41, 45, 128

Romance Philology, Phonetic Basis of ([Ralph] Hayward Keniston's 1938 Linguistic Institute course): 64

Rosen, Harold (1928 LSA Member, [interest: Indo-European], named as one leader [mis-typed as 'Rose'] (with Meader, Willey, McQuown) in a Round Table discussion, 12 August 1937, on 'Linguistic Problems Involved in the Proposal for an International Auxiliary Language' and then resigned: 70, 87

Young, William R., Colonel, Field Artillery, was in 1941 the local ROTC Commandant on the Madison campus of the University of Wisconsin when—whether under the influence of the peculiar atmosphere or of the local beer—he wrote a fateful Memorandum, 2nd October, to Washington which we quote here, re USAFI: 117

Zapateco Language: 89

Zollinger, Mrs. Anna R. (1936 LSA Member, then a Student at Ann Arbor; interest: German–Swiss dialects; in 1938 Assistant Professor of German at Brooklyn College; resigned ca. 1966): 73

LINGUISTIC SOCIETY OF AMERICA

OFFICERS FOR 1925

PRESIDENT. HERMANN COLLITZ JOHNS HOPKINS UNIVERSITY
VICE-PRESIDENT. CARL O BUCK. UNIVERSITY OF CHICAGO
SECRETARY AND TREASURER R. G. KENT. UNIV. OF PENNSYLVANIA
EXECUTIVE COMMITTEE. THE PRECEDING AND
    FRANZ BOAS COLUMBIA UNIVERSITY
    O. F. EMERSON WESTERN RESERVE UNIVERSITY
    E. H. STURTEVANT. YALE UNIVERSITY

COMMITTEE ON PUBLICATION

GEORGE M BOLLING. OHIO STATE UNIVERSITY
AURELIO M ESPINOSA. STANFORD UNIVERSITY
EDWARD SAPIR. VICTORIA MEMORIAL MUSEUM. OTTAWA

SECRETARY'S OFFICE.
UNIVERSITY OF PENNSYLVANIA. PHILADELPHIA

January 25, 1925.

TO THE MEMBERS OF THE LINGUISTIC SOCIETY OF AMERICA:

The meeting which was called for December 28th in New York was a great success. It was attended by about 75 persons in the morning and by over 50 in the afternoon. Organization was completed, with the adoption of a constitution and the election of officers, and four scholarly papers were presented. The Society voted to proceed at once with the establishment of a regular publication, though the details were left to the Committee on the subject. It is probable that the first publication will be the proceedings of the organization meeting, with the constitution and the list of members, and the abstracts of the papers presented.

This notice comes to you as one of those who have definitely or provisionally expressed the desire to assume membership in the new Society. If I am not misinformed, will you be so kind as to read carefully all the enclosures and to fill out the blanks? Especially, you are requested to forward your dues to me as Treasurer as soon as may be convenient. The Executive Committee has ruled that all those who received the invitation to join the Society and who pay the dues for 1925 ($5.00) on or before March 31st. shall be considered Foundation Members, and that others must be elected in the usual way by the Executive Committee.

The letters which have been placed in my hands by the Organizing Committee or which have reached me direct, indicate that our initial membership is somewhat over 200. It is important, however, to increase this number as much and as rapidly as possible, in order to extend the influence of the Society and to provide funds for publication. You are therefore asked if you will not, in the very near future, seek to find one or more additional members and send me their names and addresses. At the same time, it is the purpose of the Linguistic Society to work harmoniously with the already existing societies in kindred subjects, and it is not desirable to enlarge our membership by causing persons to withdraw from other societies. Our Society fills a distinct and separate place and should not in any way impair other organizations.

A number of suggestions as to the conduct of the Society were received in the correspondence. These will shortly be extracted and submitted to the members of the Executive Committee. The same procedure will be followed with suggestions which may hereafter be received. In conclusion, the Secretary bespeaks for the Executive Committee the active assistance of all members of the Society in its various activities.

Very truly yours,

ROLAND G. KENT, Secretary.

November 15th, 1924.

Dear Colleague:

The undersigned students of language believe that the time has come to form a society which will enable us to meet each other, give us opportunity for the exchange of ideas, and represent the interests of our studies.

The existing learned societies in related fields have shown hospitality to linguistics; they have patiently listened to our papers and generously printed them. For these and other reasons, students of language will, it is hoped, maintain their allegiance to such societies. Nevertheless, the present state of things has many disadvantages. The most serious, perhaps, is the fact that we do not meet. We attend the gatherings of such societies as the American Philological Association, the American Oriental Society, the Modern Language Association (whose several sections are, in this regard, virtually distinct societies), the American Anthropological Society, and so on. This divides us into groups across whose boundaries there is little acquaintance. No one can tell how much encouragement and inspiration is thereby lost.

Other considerations will suggest themselves. The standing of our science in the academic community leaves much to be desired. A medium of publication devoted entirely to linguistics might, at some future time, be very helpful.

It is planned that the society meet variously with the several societies in related fields.

The undersigned invite you to membership in a linguistic society with some such name as *the Linguistic Society of America*, to be organized at the AMERICAN MUSEUM OF NATURAL HISTORY, NEW YORK CITY, on Sunday morning, DECEMBER 28, 1924, at 10 o'clock. Beside the businses of organization, there will be scientific papers by some of the leading linguistic scholars of our country. Professor Roland G. Kent has consented to act as presiding officer.

If you wish to become a member of this society, please notify one of the organizing committee (L. Bloomfield, G. M. Bolling, E. H. Sturtevant), stating also whether you expect to attend the organization meeting.

LEROY C. BARRETT, *Trinity College.*

HAROLD L. BENDER, *Princeton University.*

LEONARD BLOOMFIELD, *Ohio State University.*

MAURICE BLOOMFIELD, *Johns Hopkins University.*

FRANZ BOAS, *Columbia University.*

GEORGE M. BOLLING, *Ohio State University.*

CARL D. BUCK, *University of Chicago.*

HERMANN COLLITZ, *Johns Hopkins University.*

CARLOS E. CONANT, *Boston.*

FRANKLIN EDGERTON, *University of Pennsylvania.*

AURELIO M. ESPINOSA, *Leland Stanford University.*

GEORGE T. FLOM, *University of Illinois.*

JOHN L. GERIG, *Columbia University.*

PLINY E. GODDARD, *American Museum of Natural History.*

LOUIS H. GRAY, *University of Nebraska.*

HANS C. G. VON JAGEMANN, *Harvard University.*

ROLAND G. KENT, *University of Pennsylvania.*

ALFRED L. KROEBER, *University of California.*

MARK H. LIDDELL, *Purdue University.*

C. M. LOTSPEICH, *University of Cincinnati.*

TRUMAN MICHELSON, *Bureau of American Ethnology.*

WALTER PETERSEN, *Redlands, California.*

EDWARD PROKOSCH, *Bryn Mawr College.*

EDWARD SAPIR, *Victoria Memorial Museum, Ottawa.*

EDGAR H. STURTEVANT, *Yale University.*

JOHN R. SWANTON, *Bureau of American Ethnology.*

BENJAMIN I. WHEELER, *University of California.*

WAR DEPARTMENT EDUCATION MANUAL   EM 526

Справочник
Руководителя

для Spoken Russian, EM 524, 525.

(Guide's Manual and Key to be used with the language manual
Spoken Russian, EM 524, 525)

---

by Leonard Bloomfield

PUBLISHED FOR THE UNITED STATES ARMED FORCES INSTITUTE
BY THE LINGUISTIC SOCIETY OF AMERICA AND THE INTENSIVE
LANGUAGE PROGRAM
OF THE AMERICAN COUNCIL OF LEARNED SOCIETIES